MAN IN SOCIETY

MAN IN SOCIETY
The Old Testament Doctrine

JOHN H. CHAMBERLAYNE
M.A., M.Th., Ph.D.

WIPF & STOCK · Eugene, Oregon

Wipf and Stock Publishers
199 W 8th Ave, Suite 3
Eugene, OR 97401

Man in Society
The Old Testament Doctrine
By Chamberlayne, John Henry
Copyright©1966 Epworth Press
ISBN 13: 978-1-60608-727-5
Publication date 5/1/2009
Previously published by Epworth Press, 1966

Copyright © Epworth Press 1966
First English edition1966 by Epworth Press
This edition published by arrangement with Epworth Press

TO
MARY
Uxor Mea Carissima
In Love and Gratitude

Contents

	Page
Preface	9
1. Introduction	11
2. Hebrew Ideas of Man	19
3. Kinship Relationships among the Early Hebrews	39
4. The Hebrew Family during the Wilderness Period	55
5. Hebrew Society under the Monarchy	83
6. Urban Civilization and its Results	
7. The Value of the Individual	131
8. The Exile and Its Aftermath	159
9. Hebrew Thought and Later Theories of Society	191
10. Epilogue—New Testament Reflections	213
Index of Subjects	241
Index of Authors	246
Index of Biblical and Extra-Biblical References	248

Preface

I AM deeply aware of the honour which came to me when the Fernley-Hartley Trustees invited me to lecture on the subject: *Man in Society*. I wish to express my gratitude to them for this honour. The subject of this study is the Old Testament view of Man and of Society—a theme which is important for its own sake as well as serving as a necessary foundation to New Testament study. For the writer, this subject does in fact fall within a wider field, in which he has been working for some years, namely, the place of the family in the religions of the world. As an unpublished doctoral thesis, he investigated the field of the Chinese family and its cults. Further study needs to be done in regard to the Buddhist faith, the faith of Islam as well as others, so that the relationship between the structure of the family and the faith and value-system of that family may be defined and clarified.

This study is confined to the life of the Israelite in his relationship to his family, his tribe and his nation—in the light of the Hebrew conception of God. The long history of the Hebrew people gave ample scope to developing structures, which can be viewed through the eyes of her prophets and lawgivers. Institutional structures are being widely questioned in our own day—in regard to the permanence of the family, the form of political structures and the ecclesiastical institutions. Light on such institutions may well be given by the Hebrew faith which created a community and faced continual trials generation by generation. Family structures changed their form, political frameworks were built up and then destroyed, ecclesiastical forms and practices changed under the pressures of experience—yet a virile and steadfast faith in God lived on to serve as the base of the Christian faith. Modern political structures are dependent on firm foundations to enable them to endure. Such endurance requires a satisfactory conception of Man as well as of Society. The Old Testament writers sought to find a path to safeguard man's dignity and the solidarity of the community in which a man has to live.

It was a great help to me that I was able to prepare much of the material for this manuscript whilst I was serving as a Visiting Lecturer in Systematic Theology in The Candler School of Theology, Emory University, Atlanta, Georgia, U.S.A. The stimulating atmosphere and the accessibility of books proved most helpful. Chapter 3 has appeared in NUMEN, the International Review for the History of Religions, and I am obliged to the Editor, Prof. C. J. Bleeker, for permission to include it. The scripture quotations in this publication are from the Revised Standard Version, copyrighted 1946 and 1952, for whose use thanks are due to Messrs. Thomas Nelson & Sons, Ltd. The Rev. Dr Frank Cumbers has been most encouraging in this enterprise and appreciation is due to him. It is also fitting that reference should be made to my former Old Testament Tutor, Dr Norman Snaith, whose stimulating thought has been an inspiration over the years.

In the knowledge that the Hebrew faith served as the matrix for our Lord Jesus Christ and the early leaders of the Church, this study may serve as a stimulus to 'search the Scriptures' afresh to equip the man of God 'for teaching, for reproof, for correction and for training in righteousness', in fact, 'for every good work' (2. Tim. 3. 16-17).

Muswell Hill
Lent 1966

JOHN H. CHAMBERLAYNE

CHAPTER ONE

INTRODUCTION

1. The increased interest in early forms of human society. Man's place in Nature and its significance in early culture. Man's experience of 'Thou' in his environment.
2. The Hebrew man's view of his own being. Corporate solidarity in the family and the clan. The place of custom and the rise of Law. Ancient Eastern law-codes.
3. The covenant-law of Israel and the rise of the amphictyony. The place of the king in the sacral community. The king and the administration of justice. Economic pressures and social changes in Israel in their impact on belief and practice.
4. The rise of individualism in the thought of the Hebrews. The influence of the law-codes and the prophets on this conception. Theocracy in the time of the monarchy and during the exile.
5. The Hebrew community and its belief in its mission. Later political philosophers and their conceptions of human society. Individualism and the Collective Doctrine of the State.
6. The influence of Old Testament thought in the growth of the New Testament. The teaching of Jesus on the Kingdom of God and on Man. Pauline anthropology and his view of communal solidarity in Israel and in mankind. The common foundation for man and society in the will of God.

CHAPTER ONE

INTRODUCTION

MODERN communications have created new dilemmas as well as new possibilities for peoples to understand each other. The use of television has provided a means to enable the 'arm-chair traveller' to plunge into the depths of the forest to view wonders previously seen only by the seasoned adventurer. Tribal customs which have been hidden from the white man have now been investigated on visio-tape in the hope that the psychology and myth of such tribes will provide insight into thought and practice of earlier times.

It is not therefore surprising that there has been a re-kindled interest in cultural anthropology, with a wide variety of field studies in those more out-of-the-way places which continue to practice ancient cults. The work of Raymond Firth, E. E. Evans-Pritchard, B. Malinowski and I. Schapera are representative of many workers in this field, whose researches have encouraged younger scholars to spend some period of their lives among 'primitive peoples'.

At the same time, the same spread in communications has helped to break down even faster the links which bound ancient societies together. Tribal loyalties have come into conflict with larger group loyalties, e.g. in new African states, with the result that ancient practices are becoming outmoded with increased 'nationalist' pressures. The ambivalent view regarding polygamy in Ghana is a case in point. So that, at the same time, as an interest is being taken in such studies, the materials for such studies are passing away from before our eyes. The need to secure such materials, before it is too late, is urgent.

These investigations provide insight into the strains and stresses through which tribal units are passing as they enter into a new age of urbanization and technology. But at the same time, such studies also give light on the beliefs and practices of ancient cultures, which were built upon the foundation of tribal life and organization. This can be seen to be profoundly true with regard to the Old Testament. It is a matter for profound regret that suspicion between theological and anthropological disciplines has clouded relationships, preventing workers in one field from giving due recognition to the work of scholars in neighbouring fields. Sociological techniques have their relevance in relation to societies of all kinds, whether the groups are charismatic or secular ones.

This essay is an attempt to recognize fully the sociological, cultural and political factors in the life of the people of Israel, whose world outlook was shaped by their faith and system of values. Man and Society are constantly shaping one another. A man's faith about the world and his fellows shapes his actions and gives rise to myths and rituals. At the same time, every man is born into a society which shapes him (indeed, conditions him) in a variety of ways towards a way of life which is acceptable to his community. His society seeks to make him a 'good tribesman' or a 'good citizen'. The inter-action between the individual as an entity and Society as represented in the particular community in which a person is shaped is a subtle one, having conscious and unconscious factors. It may be possible to unravel some of the conscious factors but it is less easy to lay bare the deeper unconscious factors which form part of the whole racial heritage. Yet these less conscious factors are certainly very creative ones.

Cultural studies of peoples in early as well as in modern primitive societies have brought to light the close kinship which man has believed to exist between himself and his natural environment. The term 'kinship' has been used advisedly. Nature is to primitive man 'neither inanimate nor empty but redundant with life; and life has individuality, in man and beast and plant, and in every phenomenon which confronts man—the thunderclap, the sudden shadow . . . Any phenomenon may at any time face him, not as "It", but as "Thou"." In this confrontation life is related to life in a reciprocal relationship. 'All experience of "Thou" is highly individual' which is viewed in events, which are narrated in creative myths and re-enacted in rituals which are the dramatization of the myths.

The Hebrew man's conception of himself as confronted with

[1] H. Frankfort, *Before Philosophy* (Pelican, 1949), p. 14.

the 'Thou' of his world and his society gives some light on early views of Man in Society (Chap. 2). His community fills a very large place in his world and kinship determines many of his beliefs and practices. His moral and religious life is shaped by his community as he is mainly aware, not of his own existence but, of his place as a tribesman (Chap. 3). Studies in kinship abound but their relevance to Old Testament life have to be treated with caution. However, such studies used in the light of archaeological discoveries, especially of texts, may provide valuable insights into the relationships within the Hebrew family. Custom places a heavy hand upon the pastoral life of the nomad and often lives on undisturbed by urban cultural changes. The community has to be safeguarded from within (by generation and sexual regulations) and from without (by defining relations with the alien).

The unrestricted practice of the blood feud could result in neighbouring groups whose perpetual hostility made social life very unstable. The rise of Law ensued with the development of legal institutions (Chap. 4). Israel's roots in Babylon are seen in the bodies of laws which have come down in the Old Testament. Whereas Egypt had many writers and much litigation, yet there is no collection of laws which has been handed down. The Edict of Horemheb is an administrative document and no Egyptian king has outstanding fame as a law-giver. In Babylonia, there have come to light several collections of laws, which are ascribed to some notable king and some of these codes are very ancient. It appears that in this sphere of social life, Israel drew from a common spring. 'This fundamental unity of Eastern law is of greater importance than the variations to be found between regions and epochs. It is the expression of a common civilization, in which the application of the same juridical principles has produced a similar customary law'.[2] However, in Israel, the law was, above all, religious law, which served to uphold not merely the authority of a human suzerain but the Covenant between Yahweh and his people. Therefore the codes of law served to inform the people of their obligations under the Covenant and also train them in social responsibility. The close connection between their religion and their law resulted in severe penalties against any violation of the Covenant (especially idolatry) but

[2] Roland De Vaux, *Ancient Israel* (trans. John McHugh) (London, 1961), p. 146.

also in a growing humaneness as the conception of Yahweh deepened.

The covenant-law which bound the Hebrew tribes together into a sacral confederation or amphictyony developed during the period of settlement in the Promised Land. The relationship of Israel to Yahweh received a new focus, however, when the house of David secured the sacred Mount Zion and made it a great centre of Yahweh-worship. The place of the king in the religious cultus as well as in the administration of justice followed a pattern which was prominent in Near-Eastern cultures but with significant differences because the sovereignty of Yahweh differed from the over-lordship of other divine kings. The place of the king as the successor to David played an important part in the historical and social mission of Israel (Chap. 5).

However, the growth of the kingship was only one aspect of the rule of Yahweh over his people. Economic changes brought grave political crises in the life of the nation. Cities arose with their commercial magnates and the agriculture of the nation declined. Amid these changes, it was inevitable that the religious life should feel the pressures of the old way versus the new. The old way of the nomadic tradition came to be represented by the prophetic guilds which were opposed to the urban culture, which was closely allied to royal authority. Justice for the common man found a voice of singular power in the Hebrew prophet, who rebuked religion, monarch and city alike in the name of the righteousness of Yahweh. Morality as the demand of Yahweh came to be firmly allied with prophetic faith, as the sign of the true worship of Yahweh. The close connection between the economic, political and social vicissitudes and the moral and religious life of the nation provide an illuminating commentary on the peculiarity of Israel among the nations (Chap. 6).

True morality is more than an acquiescence in the accepted code of the community. Corporate solidarity was an outstanding characteristic of the Israelite as a member of his family, his clan and later his nation. His identification with these groups made his individual role less important. However, with the teaching of the great Hebrew prophets, the loyalty of the individual to Yahweh came to the fore. Whilst the place of the individual had not been overlooked even in the earliest law codes, it came to be more widely significant at a later period. Morality as loyalty to the inner divine law by the individual was re-inforced by the religious devotion of that individual. Herein the value of the individual person came to recognition (Chap. 7).

Individuality had its place in the thought of the Old Testament but the communal responsibility of all individuals was never left far in the background. Even though the prophet had to stand against the State and the nation, yet he did not fail to identify himself with the sin of his people. Therefore, when the nation had been destroyed, her king carried away captive and her capital burnt to the ground, yet the loyalty of Israel to Yahweh continued to sustain her. Blow upon blow might fall upon her, yet she found consolation through her prophets, her sages and her psalmists. The strength of Israel's solidarity in the days of her exile and of the return bears eloquent testimony to her underlying faithfulness to the rule of God and her belief in his power to bring his purposes to pass. The experience of the exile brought to light new facets of Israel's faith both in regard to the place of the individual and of the community in relation to God (Chap. 8).

The devotion to Yahweh which under-girded the Hebrew people during the period previous to the monarchy and endured throughout all the changes of the centuries gave rise to a conception of society which was theocratic and yet gave room for the initiative of the individual. Whilst all the prophets were assured that 'the word of the Lord came' to them (cf. Jer. 1. 2; Hos. 1. 1; Zeph. 1. 1), yet the individuality and personal response of these men are very pronounced. The belief that the sovereign-subject relationship governed the dealings between Yahweh and his people (which included their king) made its demands upon every other aspect of life. In the home, in the market place, in the field of politics and in foreign affairs, the sovereign rule of Yahweh over his people had to be recognized.

Later thinkers have enunciated various theories of society. The thinker whose concern lies in upholding the individuality of man has stressed a theory of government whose function is to safeguard the rights of individuals. As in the case of John Locke, these rights are thought to belong to an *a priori* Law of Nature which a sovereign power is under obligation to uphold. Such rights include a man's right to life, liberty and estate. Yet, such emphasis on individual rights can create an unbalanced society, in so far that the law serves more and more as a protection for the rights of the 'favoured few' (those who have) against those who lack such substance and have not estate. Such lack of capital and estate does, in fact, limit the extent both of a man's life as well as his liberty. His life is greatly affected by his economic status (whether he is in the control of another or others) and his liberty to choose his employment, place of residence, education and scale of values (even his religious beliefs) may well be controlled by the community of which he forms a part. It is therefore not a matter for surprise that Hegel and Rousseau were more concerned to stress the Collective Doctrine of the State, which was in the best position to decide the well-being of the community as a whole. It is the community which has to survive and therefore, despite hardship to individuals, it is the will of the whole which must have priority.

Both these theories need to be considered in the light of the Hebrew conception of God and his relationship to his creation. The worth of man and his individual rights—a concept which finds expression in democracy—has to be held in tension with a view of the community which has goals dependent on its criteria of values and beliefs. Both the individual and the community were safeguarded in the Hebrew conception of society, which placed the goals beyond human measurement in the rule and will of God. It is at this point that the man of religion (particularly the Jew and the Christian) and the humanist part company. This is a shadowed portion of the road, where there is a fork (to which John Baillie refers in his *Invitation to Pilgrimage*)—leading in different directions in accord with the basic assumptions of those on the road. Further exploration of these doctrines of society is long overdue (Chap. 9).

The Old Testament does not stand alone, however, since the person of the Christ accepted the teaching of law-giver, prophet and psalmist as revelation, upon which his own teaching was built. It is therefore necessary to consider the teaching which came from him and his closest followers on the same theme. It has to be recognized that the New Testament could well provide a long volume on its own account in the study of man and society. It is therefore desirable to give particular and brief attention to three aspects of New Testament thought, namely, the influence of Hellenism on the Jewish view of man, the teaching of Jesus on the Kingdom and on man and the Pauline view of human psychology and human solidarity. From such aspects of New Testament teaching, it is possible to see how great a debt the writers owed to their training and upbringing in Judaism. The inter-penetration of New Testament thought by the concepts and beliefs of the Old Testament is clearly evident, though the New Testament makes its own vital contribution to strengthen belief in the value of the individual person as well as to give validity to his debt to his society (Chap. 10).

Any attempt to separate the duties of society to the individual and the responsibilities towards society by the individual makes either party suffer in the process. However, it is not enough to give recognition to the responsibilties that both parties owe to each other. It is clearly necessary to take the responsibility to a deeper level, namely, in the common foundation of man and society in the rule and will of God. By the mutual obligation that both have towards their Creator-Redeemer, it is possible for man to find the fulfillment of every individual talent yet within a society which requires his contribution and offers him a sphere for the service of God and his fellow-men. The social group too finds its own fulfillment in the service of God, who provides the criterion for value and faith beyond the confines of the present. In this service of God, the horizons widen in the further knowledge of his will.

CHAPTER TWO

HEBREW IDEAS OF MAN

1. Primitive psychology. Characteristics of early man. Ancient ways of thought in regard to the world and man's place in it. Psychical bonds between man and the world.
2. Hebrew physiology and the terms used for various parts of the body. The use of chayyim; neshamah; nephesh; ruach; together with the terms for the outward organs of the body and the internal organs.
3. Corporate personality. Man's relationship to his society. The place of the will and Man's freedom. Man and the physical world. Creation.

CHAPTER TWO

HEBREW IDEAS OF MAN

1. *Primitive psychology*

THERE is considerable uncertainty among writers on early societies about the use of the term 'primitive', when it is used in connection with such phrases as 'primitive society' and 'primitive psychology'. However, the term has value to describe those cultures which are less advanced technically—even though it is applied by those cultures which (technically) are more advanced! For example, the technical superiority of Roman soldiers enabled them to gain superiority over and eventually to dominate the peoples whose techniques were more rudimentary. The term is used in this sense by Dr Lucy Mair, in her description of 'Primitive Government'.[1] Anthropologists have used the term 'small-scale' societies whilst sociologists have preferred the term 'pre-literate', which does not bear the odium which (in some quarters) the term 'primitive' has.

Professor E. O. James has pointed out that the same difficulty appears in the use of the term 'early' in connexion with 'society'. The phrase 'early society' may refer either to a mode of life and thought which is (or appears to be) earlier in time or to such a mode which is late in time yet culturally less mature.[2] The term is therefore relative to other states of society which have developed the mastery of techniques, unknown at an earlier day.

Even though man may live in a rudimentary state of culture, it is apparent from the work of anthropologists that they have complex thought-forms. Levy Bruhl claimed that *les sociétés inférieures* lived in a pre-logical state of mentality yet even primitive man distinguished his own existence from that of other beings.[3] Whilst 'the law of participation' was very powerful in his life, yet he was not both man and wolf. His world was filled

[1] Lucy Mair, *Primitive Government* (London, 1962), p. 9.
[2] E. O. James, *The Concept of Diety* (London, 1950), p. 15
[3] Levy Bruhl, *La Mentalité Primitive* (Paris, 1922), p. 19.

with beings which confronted him in terms of life, whether the beings are birds, beasts, plants or men. Therefore, his approach and attitude to his world differed widely from that of modern man. 'Primitive man has only one mode of thought, one mode of expression, one part of speech—the personal.'[4] All the forms of life around him were 'experienced emotionally in a dynamic reciprocal relationship',[5] not as 'It' but as 'Thou'. In such a world, where all things are animate, man had to cope as well as he could by all means possible. Much was inexplicable in terms of the normal, so he assigned the inexplicable to the supernatural. Every object which aroused peculiar or particular attention was similarly attributed to a transcendental source—whether the thunderclap, the dwarf, the neurotic Shaman (or medicine-man) or the strange figured rock rising above his home. As man was less equipped with technical knowledge to meet unexpected and dangerous situations, including the vicissitudes of child-birth and sufficient food-supply, so his dependence on 'supernatural' agencies was greatly increased. His mental powers were limited both by his material surroundings as well as by his lack of technical knowledge.

It is therefore necessary to give some attention to the thought-forms and characteristics of man in early societies, with particular consideration to the thought-forms of the Hebrews. The terms in which they express these thought-forms provide some evidence of their conception of the nature of man, his place in the world and, no doubt, his problems too.

In a world filled with life so kin to his own, close psychical bonds were believed to exist between all living beings. It was no matter for surprise that one's ancestors included the crested dove, a black cockatoo and a particular iguana, as the Papuan regarded them as members of his tribe. To a certain type of primitive mind, as among the Australian aborigines, there was nothing incongruous about thinking of oneself as descended from a honey-ant, a witchetty-grub or a kangaroo. Whilst such totemic ideas were in the far past, when the Hebrew records began to be written down, there may be evidence that in the names of some of the tribes, descended from Jacob, totemic ideas were not absent. However, the belief in the close psychic bond remained

[4] cf. E. Crawley, *The Mystic Rose* (London, 1965), p. 92.
[5] H. Frankfort (ed.), *Before Philosophy* (London, 1949), p. 14.

and also certain animistic conceptions, in regard to a man's own organs, lingered in their minds.

The Israelite, like other primitive peoples, believed that he participated in a totality—a species of which the individual example is simply an expression of the type. Thus Moab is a species or type *(mo'abh)*, of which the individual Moabite (Mo'abhi) is a manifestation. There is a unity about the type which expresses itself in a common will. 'The Hebrew language is full of what we call collectives, because the Hebrew always perceives the general... It is therefore immaterial whether one says *a* lion or *the* lion; it is the species of lion, as manifesting itself in one or perhaps several specimens." The Israelite herds were attacked by *the* lion and *the* bear (1 Sam. 17. 34; Amos 5. 19). Noah sent forth *the* raven and *the* dove (Gen. 8. 7, 8). The abstract idea may in fact express the totality which is seen in the concrete individual instance, such that *tobh* may mean 'goodness' and 'a good person' (its manifestation). It was therefore this totality towards which the Hebrew directed his soul in order to grasp it.

The idea of totality is expressed also in the language of the Hebrew people. Their concepts called forth images, so that *tobh* is 'goodness', the fact of being good and 'a good person' all at the same time, i.e. it is goodness in its various manifestations. So too with *'ish*, 'a man', an image of manliness or maleness. When therefore *'ish tobh* are joined together, there is called up a combined image which makes a new conception. It is often necessary to go to the root-word of a term, so as to determine the use of a particular term in its own context. This use of language to express totality has been examined in some detail by Pedersen,' who has pointed out that, for the Hebrew, the most important use of a verb is to express the occurence of an action, of which the time is of little or no importance. Either the action is completed or it is nascent, it is perfect or imperfect. Yet through all such actions, there runs the central core of a unity, the movement of the soul. 'For the Israelite—as for primitive peoples generally—the mental processes are not successive, but united in one, because the soul is always a unit, acting in one."

---

* J. Pedersen, *Israel: Its Life and Culture*, I-II (London, 1926), p. 110.
' Pedersen, ibid., pp. 110-133.   * Ibid., p. 128.

There is also a close connection between idea and action. This is expressed, for example, in the use of the word 'esa' (counsel). Counsel implies wisdom and understanding in the sense that the good man not merely advises peace but walks in ways of peace, when he counsels peace (Prov. 12. 20). The nation which is 'void of counsel' (Deut. 32. 28) is one that lacks the power to take action. The counsel of a man or of a nation therefore typifies the whole out-working of the soul—the kind of soul that man or nation possesses. When the counsel is wise, there is strength of soul to carry actions to good effect (Isa. 28. 29), an ability which came from the Lord of Hosts. In fact, Yahweh is so strong that he is able to break all counsels which stand against him (Isa. 8. 10).

The unity of the soul makes the body more than a mere machine. What the soul is, the body is and this is true of all the parts of the body. With the close connection of idea and action, so as the soul perceives, so outward action followed as part of the perception. Moreover, perceptions are not mere images which flit across the consciousness but contain part of the content of that which is perceived. In the perceptions, there are appropriated qualities of that which is perceived. When animals, which are conceiving, see some streaked objects, then they appropriate a measure of 'streakedness', with the result that the young which they produce are streaked (Gen. 30. 37-42). There is in fact a continuum between the soul, the idea, the environment and the event, so that whilst outward connexion may not be visible to the eye, there is an inner connexion through the pervasion of soul.

Such pervasion is not confined to sense-organs but through a far wider area of phenomena, including dreams, witchcraft, totemism, demonology and angelology, rising to the activity of the Spirit of God. Such phenomena are deemed to involve man in his fullness, that is, as a member of a group, since, for primitive man, the group is more apparent to a man than his own individuality. The consciousness of a common life within a group, whether it is that of the clan, the family or tribe, is seen as part of a wider extension to his own personality. If he sins, his whole group suffers the penalty. In the light of such conceptions, we need to examine the psychology of the Hebrews. This throws light on the nature of a man of Israel and how he acts. It will then be clearer to observe this man in the developing modes of his society, to see the Hebrew man in the course of the historical vicissitudes of his nation. He and his people were closely bound together in a common destiny. This destiny was expressed through the thought-form of the language.

2. Hebrew Physiology

In the light of what has been written above, it is not surprising that Hebrew psychology has to be investigated through their physiology. Therefore, as among early peoples, man is regarded as a unit of psychic power, viz., 'soul-stuff' (Zielestof),* so this 'soul-stuff' is perceived as pervading the members of the body as well as things in contact with the body, e.g. blood, shadow, footprints, weapons, etc. It has moreover to be borne in mind that there is always in Israelite thought a close link between psychical functions and physical associations.

Man who is a psycho-physical organism (a unit of vital power) has various members but these have their psychical properties as well. A number of Hebrew terms are used to describe man. Some terms are used to express the life of a man in general, namely, *chayyim, neshamah, nephesh* and *ruach*, whilst other terms are used to describe the parts of the body. The whole and the part are closely related so that Dr Wheeler Robinson has suggested the phrase, 'diffused consciousness', to the Hebrew practice of ascribing a given activity, sometimes to the body as a whole and sometimes to one part of the body (that part acting as though it were on behalf of the whole). The independent terms for the organs of the body will therefore be described.

(a) *The life of man.* It is evident to most people in most ages that there is a distinction between the animate and the inanimate. The term '*chayyim*', which occurs about a hundred and fifty times in the Old Testament, appears to convey this distinction. It appears first with reference to 'living creatures' (i.e. animals) (Gen. 1. 20, 24) but it is not used of plants (1. 11). It is found with reference to springing water (26. 19). The term '*chayyim*' expresses the meaning of 'a living being', in the case of animal (1. 20, 24) and man (2. 7), though it is recognized that man is more than the animals, since he is given authority over them by naming them (2. 19). Man has a body like the rest of the animal kingdom and can move about but he is able to do

* cf. A. R. Johnson, *The Vitality of the Individual in the Thought of Ancient Israel*, p. 2, note 3.

much more than others. Most evident in this 'living being' is the distinction between a body with breath and one without one. Man learned that when breath left the body, the flesh became dust ('when thou takest away their breath, they die and return to their dust' Ps. 104. 29).

Therefore, the term 'the breath *(neshamah) of life'* is used as a synonym for the physical side of life. This term is used twenty-three times in all, normally conveying the idea that it belongs to God and is given to man. Thus, in Gen. 2. 7, 'God formed man of dust... and breathed into his nostrils the breath of life'. On six occasions, the word is used of God, as in Isa. 30. 33, and occasionally for other 'breathing things' (Deut. 20. 16), but normally it is used of men (1 Kgs. 17. 17).

In the Israelite conception of man, the term which is given pride of place is the 'somewhat elusive term',[10] *nephesh*, which has a wide range of meaning. It may well be that the original concept in this term had to do with 'breath' but the evidence of its early meaning is scanty. In the Authorized Version, the term is found translated in forty-two different ways, so it is evident that it is not easy to find an English term to fit the Hebrew term. Most frequently the translators, in the Authorized Version, used the term 'life' (on 117 occasions) and 'soul' (428 times). In the text, Gen. 2. 7, we have the sentence: 'man became a living being' (nephesh), in which *nephesh* is used in a sense which is also used of animals, 'to live'. In the use of the term 'nephesh', it is apparent that the Hebrew physiology is not far distant from her psychology, in that the cognate terms in Accadian and in Ugaritic mean 'throat' or 'neck'. Physical aspects of the body are regarded as having a psychical function as well. Dr Ryder Smith has maintained that *nephesh* has three chief uses: (i) 'life' as opposed to 'death'; (ii) as a synonym for a personal pronoun and (iii) as that aspect of our being which experiences feeling or willing.[11] (Dr H. Wheeler Robinson makes a similar distinction in his classification; as (A) Principle of Life (282); (B) Psychical (249) and (C) Personal (223), with (iii) and B and (ii) and C corresponding respectively).[12]

[10] A. R. Johnson, ibid., p. 9; cf. H. W. Robinson, *Christian Doctrine of Man,* 3rd edit. (1926), pp. 11-27.
[11] C. Ryder Smith, *The Bible Doctrine of Man* (1951), p. 7.
[12] H. Wheeler Robinson, ibid., p. 16.

'Life' as opposed to 'death' is frequently expressed by the use of this term, as may be seen in such examples as 'All the men who were seeking your life are dead' (Ex. 4. 19 J); 'it shall be life for life' (Deut. 19. 21); in Elijah's plea, 'they seek my life to take it away' (1 Kgs. 19. 10), and in the phrase in Jeremiah, 'Your lovers despise you; they seek your life' (4. 31).

The second usage (which Robinson describes as 'personal') may be seen in the use of the term as a personal pronoun, as in 'behold, I have never defiled myself' (lit. 'my *nephesh*') (Ezek. 4. 14) and 'you shall not defile yourselves' (lit. 'your *nephesh*') (Lev. 11. 43) (with any swarming thing). This mode of using the term is found frequently in the Psalms, as in such verses as—'Turn, O Lord, save my life' *(nephesh)* (6. 4); 'thou dost not give me *(nephesh)* to Sheol' (16. 19) and 'deliver my life *(nephesh)* from the wicked' (17. 13). In this last instance, the passage is well rendered by the use of the personal pronoun 'me' in place of 'my life'. Similarly, 'O Lord, thou hast brought up my *nephesh* from Sheol, restored me to life from among those gone down to the pit' (30. 3). Related to this 'personal' use is the plural form to denote 'people', as in Gen. 46. 27 (P). ('All the persons of the house of Jacob, that came into Egypt, were seventy').

The use of the term *nephesh* to describe 'the conscious vital principle' is seen even more clearly in the third usage, namely, to express that aspect (particularly the affective one) of the personality, which experiences oscillations in mood, so that the 'nephesh' may be said to be sad ('Was not my soul grieved for the poor' (Job. 30. 25) as well as to rejoice ('Then my soul shall rejoice in the Lord') (Ps. 35. 9); to sink into despair ('My soul is cast down within me') (Ps. 42. 6) as well as to hope (in the same verse); to be impatient ('the people *(nephashim)* became impatient on the way' (Num. 21. 4. JE) as well as to be patient ('And what is my end, that I should be patient') (Job 6. 11). In particular, the term is used to express attraction and repulsion—to love and to hate, with emphasis in regard to the last on loathing. Therefore we find in the Song of Solomon, the phrase 'him whom my soul loves' (3. 1, 2, 3, 4), whilst there is reference elsewhere to those 'who are hated by David's soul' (2 Sam. 5. 8). This use is also found of the Lord ('the Lord tests the righteous . . . and his soul hates him who loves violence') (Ps. 11. 5). There are a number of examples of the more emphatic use, namely, to loathe, in such

Hebrew Ideas of Man

instances as ('they shall make amends for their iniquity, because their soul abhorred my statutes') (Lev. 26. 43) and ('Does thy soul loathe Zion?') (Jer. 14. 19). It has been pointed out, by Audrey R. Johnson, that the 'nephesh' is subject to various forms of attraction 'which move it to activity in one direction or another through the excitation of desire'.[13]

This use may be seen, in regard to physical desire, in the case of Shechem the son of Hamor the Hivite, who found that 'his *nephesh* was drawn to Dinah the daughter of Jacob' (Gen. 34. 3) or as with 'a man given to appetite' *(ba'al nephesh)* (Prov. 23. 2), although the term may also be used with a volitional shade of meaning, as in the case of the captive woman whom the master has made his wife but now has lost interest in her, he then 'shall let her go where she will' *(lonaphshah)*. In this aspect, there is sometimes found that unity of psychic aim, the unity of the group, which is found in Jehu's words of warning to his friends, 'If this is your *nephesh* (mind), then let no one slip out of the city to go and tell the news in Jezreel' (2 Kgs. 9. 15).

Thus, 'life' in many of its manifestations came to be expressed by this term, in fact, 'loss of vitality, in any degree, from simple despondency to death itself, is idiomatically expressed as the breathing out of the *nephesh*',[14] as in the plight of Jerusalem, whose mothers are now bereft of their children and have now 'given up the *ghost*' (AV) (Jer. 15. 9). The same living link is expressed more clearly in that 'blood' and *life* are closely connected, so 'the blood is the *nephesh*' (Deut. 12. 23), 'the *nephesh* of every creature is the blood of it' (Lev. 17. 14) and 'the life *(nephesh)* of the flesh is in the blood' (Lev. 17. 11). Yet, there is also a strange polarization which is prominent in Semitic languages, whereby the term *nephesh* is also used to denote the 'dead' (Lev. 19. 28) or 'a dead body' (the *nephesh* of one of the dead) (Num. 6. 6).[15] The three usages of the term *nephesh* are closely connected and at the same time *neshamah* and *nephesh* are closely connected. Nevertheless, whilst these terms are expressive of 'life', yet they lack ethical content. This content is denoted by further terms, with particular reference to the term '*ruach*',

---

[13] A. R. Johnson, *The Vitality of the Individual in the Thought of Ancient Israel* (1964), p. 13. Further references to examples of such 'oscillation in mood' are given in the notes on page 12 in this work.
[14] A. R. Johnson, ibid., p. 11.   [15] Ibid., p. 22.

The fourth term *ruach* is connected with the breath as indicative of life. It is connected etymologically with a root common to most Semitic languages which indicates air in motion, particularly 'wind'. The term is common in the purely physical sense, varying from a gentle refreshing breeze ('whiff of air': Jer. 2. 24), which may be found in the evening as a contrast to the hot noontide ('cool *(ruach)* of the day': Gen. 3. 8), to the vigorous scorching east wind which strikes the vineyards (Ezek. 17. 10) and tears down houses (Job. 1. 19), whilst at sea it lashes the waves into a tempest (Ps. 107. 25; Jonah 1. 4), shattering great ships (Ps. 48. 7). This variableness in the wind's intensity, with its changeable ways, may well have suggested that the term would serve as a description of the changeable moods of human beings, under the term 'spirit'. In the 378 occasions, where the Hebrew term is found in the Old Testament, the AV renders it by the term 'spirit' (232) and 'wind' (91), with the term 'breath' (29).

The physical energy and verve of a man like Elijah marked him as one richly endowed with 'spirit' which others wanted (2 Kgs. 2. 9). The rise and fall of the wind reflected the ebb and flow of spirit in the life of man, so vitality came to be regarded as due to the presence or absence of *ruach*. Jacob's *spirit* revived when he knew that Joseph was alive (Gen. 45. 27). Samson's conflict with the Philistines left him thirsty but after drinking from the spring at Lehi, his *ruach* returned (Judg. 15. 19). When the Queen of Sheba saw the grandeur of the court of Solomon and his wisdom, 'there was no longer any *ruach* in her' (she was not her usual 'breezy' self[26]) (1 Kgs. 10. 5). Similarly, when Gideon soothed the angry feeling of the Gideonites, their '*ruach* against him abated' (Judg. 8. 3), as the wind sinks after a storm.

The ebb and flow of life were regarded as due to the absence and presence of *ruach*. This term came, in fact, to be developed strongly on the psychical side as well as on the physical plane. The term thus had emotional content, so that despondency was expressed by saying that a man's *ruach* grows dim (Isa. 61. 3), becomes faint (Ps. 143. 4) or vanishes (Ps. 143. 7). The term came to denote almost any mood, disposition or frame of mind, whether in man's emotional, intellectual or volitional life.

However, in exilic times and after, the term came to take a

[26] A. R. Johnson, *ibid.*, p. 26.

Hebrew Ideas of Man

particular direction in its use, namely, the *ruach* came to refer not to a man's spirit but a particular type of *ruach*, defined by an adjective—a kind of extraneous influence whose origin is ascribed to Yahweh or is left unindicated. Even at an earlier date, Isaiah saw the citizens overcome by a state of coma, as Yahweh poured out upon them 'a *ruach* of deep sleep' (Isa. 29. 10) and Hosea regarded Israel's proneness to apostacy as due to a '*ruach* of whoredom' (Hos. 4. 12). Isaiah also mocked the land of Egypt, where civil strife was imminent, by stating that 'Egypt's *ruach* will be emptied out' (Isa. 9. 3), due in part to Yahweh's introduction of a 'spirit of confusion' (Isa. 19. 14) into their national life. Similarly, when the new era begins (that Day of Yahweh), Yahweh will ensure that 'a spirit of judgement is (given) to him who sits in judgement' (Isa. 28. 6), just as the able administrator is filled with 'a spirit of wisdom' (Deut. 34. 9) and Yahweh endows the skilled craftsman with 'an able mind' *(ruach)* (Exod. 28. 3 (P)).

It is not therefore a matter for surprise that psychical powers should be attributed directly to the '*ruach* of Yahweh', since He is '*ruach* and not flesh' (Isa. 31. 3), as He sustains 'the *ruach* of all flesh' (Num. 16. 22)—'moving' over the cosmic waters at the creation of the world (Gen. 1. 2) and making himself felt in the affairs of men (Ps. 139. 7; 143. 10). When the *ruach* 'falls' upon an individual (Ezek. 11. 5), it may 'enter in' (Ezek. 2. 2) or a man may feel that he is in the grip (lit. 'the hand': Ezek. 3. 14; 8. 3) of it. He may, at other times, be 'carried away' in ecstasy (Ezek. 3. 12; 8.3). On the other hand, possession by the *ruach* of Yahweh may issue in temperate qualities, such as those which will characterize the ideal servant of Yahweh—'there shall rest upon him the *ruach* of Yahweh, the *ruach* of wisdom and discernment, the *ruach* of counsel and might, a *ruach* of knowledge and the fear of Yahweh' (Isa. 11. 2). The intelligence of the ordinary person is, moreover, ascribed to the same source—'it is the ruach in a man, the breath of the Almighty, that makes him understand' (Job. 32. 8). Both men of standing and those of humble station are dependent upon the *ruach* of Yahweh—a dependence which involves not only their physical survival but also their psychical potentialities.

Man's response to the divine activity lies in his responsibility to rouse his own *ruach* to act to please Yahweh, for example, by offerings to be used for the tent of meeting from those 'whose ruach moved him' (Exod. 35. 21 (P)), i.e. his essential self. Above all, the devout Israelite desired to tune his own *ruach* with that of Yahweh's. 'Create in me a clean heart, O God, and put a new and right *ruach* within me. Cast me not away from they presence, and take not thy holy *ruach* from me. Restore to me the joy of thy salvation, and uphold me with a willing *spirit (ruach)*.' (Ps. 51. 10, 12). By receiving 'a *ruach* of grace and supplication' (Zech. 12. 10), the Israelite might come before Yahweh with a 'broken *ruach*' (i.e. not self-willed). Yahweh dwells on high 'with the contrite and lowly in *ruach*', 'reviving the *ruach* of the lowly' (Isa. 57. 15). It is the gift of life in its fullness that Yahweh gives to those whose spirits respond to Him.

(b) *Part for the whole.* Whilst some terms are used to express life in its various aspects, yet independent terms are used for various organs of the body which appear to feel and act—as though such organs acted on their own behalf. Therefore, the outward organs are regarded in this way—as in the case of the hand ('Your hand will find out all your enemies': Ps. 21. 8; 45. 4; Job 26. 13); the arm ('Awake, awake, put on strength, O arm of the Lord': Isa. 51. 9); the foot ('Let not the foot of arrogance come upon me': Ps. 36. 11); the eye ('A king who sits on the throne of judgement winnows all evil with his eyes': Pr. 20. 8); the ear ('Does not the ear try words as the palate tastes food?' Job. 12. 41); the mouth ('I will pay thee my vows, that which my lips uttered and my mouth promised': Ps. 66. 14) and the tongue ('my tongue shall tell of thy righteousness': Ps. 35. 28). Whilst these terms are regarded as feeling and acting, yet the Hebrews recognized that there is a centre of activity, a unity which lies behind these several actions. Thus, we find that, in the prophet Amos, there is the sentence: 'I will set my eyes upon them' (9. 4). It is probable that the Hebrew conceived that the psychic energy of the soul was concentrated, for the action required, in a single organ, e.g. in the Temple, Isaiah said, 'I saw the Lord' or 'My eyes have seen the King' (Isa. 6. 1, 5).

In similar fashion, the inward organs may be used to express feeling. In particular, 'the heart is the entirety of the soul as a power'[17] and may be used of any experience, whether intellective, conative or affective. The term used *(leb or lebab)* is used in close

---

[17] Pedersen, I, ibid., p. 150.

association with the term *nephesh*, though *leb* tends to refer to intellectual content whilst *nephesh* is more closely linked with feeling. When the terms are used together, they refer to the whole man—as 'my heart and flesh sing for joy to the living God' (Ps. 84. 2). From an earlier meaning, *leb* connotes the 'inner man' (the literal heart), as in such expressions as 'my heart is like wax' (Ps. 22. 14) and 'I will give you a heart of flesh' (Ezek. 36. 25), where the term *(leb)* conveys the idea of the physical organ but with a strong current of feeling attached to it. The terms—*leb* and *lebab*—are also used to express the idea of 'mind', as found in such texts as 'make the heart of this people fat . . . lest they understand with their heart' (Isa. 6. 10) and 'the wise in heart will receive commandment' (Pro. 10. 8). Moreover, there are other instances in which the same Hebrew terms are used to convey the idea of the action of the will, as the fulfillment of thought, in such cases as 'They said in their heart, We will utterly subdue them' (Ph. 74. 8), 'his mind plots iniquity' (Isa. 32. 6) and 'A man's mind plans his way' (Pro. 16. 9). The same terms are elsewhere used to describe men's characters, whether to express their courage ('the valiant man whose heart is like the heart of a lion': 2 Sam. 17. 10) or their pangs of conscience ('David's heart smote him': 1 Sam. 24. 5), for which the term *lebab* is most frequently used. Good men are characterized as having 'uprightness of heart' (Deut. 9. 5), 'integrity of heart' (1 Kgs. 9. 4), 'a pure heart' (Ps. 24. 4) and 'a true heart' (1 Kgs. 8. 61), whilst evil men are seen by their 'hard hearts' (Deut. 15. 7), 'loftiness of heart' (Deut. 8. 14; Ps. 24. 4) and their 'perverseness of heart' (Ps. 101. 4). The wide use of these two Hebrew terms in the Old Testament is evident from the fact that they are used more than eight hundred and fifty times in various meanings in different contexts.

The terms which denote the lower parts of the trunk of the body were used by the Hebrew to express intense emotions of pleasure and of pain. In the first place, there were those portions of the body which were used in the sacrificial system, namely, 'the entrails, and the appendage of the liver and the two kidneys with their fat' (Lev. 8. 16). In the case of a 'peace offering', these portions were offered to the Lord (Lev. 3. 9-11). In the second place, there were the group of terms which describe such organs in the lower part of the body as the 'bowels', the 'belly' and the 'womb'.

The term 'bowels' *(me'im)* is used in a physical sense for the internal organs generally ('my heart . . . is melted in my breast': Ps. 22. 14) and a child is said to come forth from the mother's bowels (RSV. 'womb': Ps. 71. 6). But from this inner depth, there issues forth a compassion which feels anguish or pity for those who are distressed. In his distressed compassion for his doomed people, Jeremiah cries out, 'My anguish! my anguish!' (RV. 'My bowels! my bowels!': Jer. 4. 19), whilst Isaiah feels sorrow for Moab ('My soul (bowels) moans like a lyre for Moab': Isa. 16. 11). This feeling is attributed also to the Lord, by Deutero-Isaiah, who declares that 'the yearning of thy heart (bowels) and thy compassion *(rachamim*—womb) are withheld from me' (Isa. 63. 15). The term 'belly' is most frequently used of the physical organ, so that 'delicious morsels . . . go down into the inner parts of the body (belly)' (Pro. 18. 8) but the term *(beten*—belly) is used with some reference to emotion, as in the text, 'It will be pleasant if you keep (the words of the wise) within you (in thy belly)' (Pro. 22. 18). As this term is sometimes used for a woman's womb (Ps. 139. 13), so the plural term for 'womb' *(rachamim)* is used to express the 'mercies' which were deemed to issue from the womb. The use of *rachamim* for 'mercies' or 'compassion' is applied to men as well as to the Lord. Thus, '(The Medes) will have no mercy *(rachamim)* on the fruit of the womb *(rechem)*' (Isa. 13. 18) and 'the mercy *(rachamim)* of the wicked is cruel' (Pro. 12. 10) refers to men, whilst there are many uses of this term for the Lord as in ('that the Lord may turn . . . and show you mercy': Deut. 13. 17) and 'Have mercy on me, O God . . . according to thy abundant mercy' (Ps. 51. 1).

When the Hebrew wanted to speak of 'body', he used 'flesh' *(basar)* rather than the more precise Hebrew term *(geviyyah)* which is seldom used. 'Flesh' is used over against other parts of the body, to include the rest of the body, as, for example, over against *nephesh* (Ps. 63. 1). But whilst the term is used in a physical sense for a man's body (Lev. 14. 9), yet it has other meanings, namely, to signify man's weakness in contrast to the Lord's strength ('Cursed is the man who . . . makes flesh his arm': Jer. 17. 5). 'He remembered that they were but flesh, a wind that passes and comes not again': Ps. 79. 39) as well as designate psychical qualities, generally of an affective nature. Thus, the

Hebrew Ideas of Man

flesh can 'sing for joy to the living God' (Ps. 84. 2); it may faint for God (Ps. 63. 1) and may dwell secure through trust (Ps. 16. 9). The use of the phrase, by Jeremiah, 'no flesh has peace', appears to signify more than physical discomfort or even physical distress and indicates that Israel is in spiritual and mental confusion as well. The terms 'all flesh' in such texts as 'all flesh shall see it together' (Isa. 40. 5) and 'let all flesh bless his holy name for ever and ever' (Ps. 145. 21) express the ability of mankind to know and bless the Lord which is more than a physical pursuit.

The survey of such terms makes clear that 'in the Hebrew concept of a living man there is *nothing* that is merely physical'.[18] Man is seen as a totality but that totality may be expressed through the several organs or parts of the body. It is the working of the soul—'an entirety with a definite stamp, and this stamp is transmuted into a definite will'.[19] There is no evidence of a dichotomy, such as is found in Greek thought, between body and soul but rather a totality which thinks, wills and does. This 'psychic whole' does not merely embrace the personality of the individual man because that man is part of a larger totality. It is therefore inadequate to take such terms and regard them in isolation from each other or from the larger social unit to which man belongs. The inner and outer organs are channels for the activities of the soul *(nephesh)* but this soul is part of an extended or larger 'self', the larger social unit to which a man belonged. The nature of this larger 'self' needs further exploration.

3 *The wider self*. Much attention has been given in studies of primitive peoples to the strong corporate sense which pervades the lives of men in such societies. Raymond Firth expressed this solidarity, in describing the lives of the Tikopian people, by useing one of their own phrases in the title of his book, namely, 'We, the Tikopia'. So, too, in Israel, the individual was vividly aware of his solidarity with his people, to such an extent that Dr Wheeler Robinson described the concept of solidarity as a 'corporate personality' (a situation in which the individual is most aware of himself in terms of the group of which he forms a part). The extent of this larger unit to which an individual belongs is difficult to define. 'The individual is regarded as a centre of power which extends far beyond the contour of the body and mingles

---

[18] C. R. Smith, *The Bible Doctrine of Man*, p. 25.
[19] Pedersen, I-II, *ibid.*, p. 103.

with that of the family and the family property, the tribe and the tribal possessions or the nation and the national inheritance, to form a psychical whole—with extension in time as well as space'.[20] The individual was, in fact, caught up in a mystic bond which united the whole of his society and embraced within it both the ancestors and future generations. His society consisted in a number of units, each of which were part of the larger unit and each of which had a focus. The smallest unit was the family which had its focus in the father of the household. The largest unit was the nation which had its focus in the worship of Yahweh and more particularly, in the Judaen kingdom, in the royal house, which had its own focus in the reigning King, the present 'Son of David', who acted as the focus of the nation as a physical whole.[21]

This conception of the 'wider self' resulted in a number of significant features in the life of Israel. If the father of a household committed an act against the sanctions of the wider society, then his group bore the cost—lest the offence should spread as a festering sore through the whole social body. The household bore with the father the cost of his sin, as in the case of Achan, who had taken the 'devoted things' from among the spoil. His whole family were burned with him and then stoned with stones (Josh. 8. 24-25). This had its corollary in regard to the nation that if the king failed, then the nation failed. If there was a violent disturbance of the national life, such as a prolonged drought or an outbreak of plague, then it was attributed to some action of the king, who involved the whole people in his activities. When famine came in the days of David, it was attributed to the covenant-breaking acts of his predecessor, Saul, so seven of Saul's sons were handed over to the Gibeonites to die. 'They were put to death in the first days of harvest, at the beginning of barley harvest' (2 Sam. 21. 9). Similarly, when David sinned by numbering the people, the prophet Gad warned him that serious trouble would come on the people, so pestilence followed (2 Sam. 24. 10-25). Further instances of the importance of the king in relation to the well-being of the nation will be given in Chapter 5.

The 'wider self' of an individual extended also beyond the mere contour of his body (by an 'extension' of his personality) to those things which were associated with him. His psychic force

[20] A. R. Johnson, *Sacral Kingship in Ancient Israel* (1955), p. 2.
[21] J. Pedersen, *Israel*, III-IV, p. 84.

entered into his words, his name, his household, his servants and his property. He and his formed a totality which 'belonged together'. Most prominent in this regard is the power of a man's soul which goes out for good (the blessing: *salah*) in contrast to the power which goes out for evil (the curse: *ala*). This power is often embodied in the word: 'the word is the form of vesture of the contents of the soul, its bodily expression. Behind the word stands the whole of the soul which created it'.[22] But the word in blessing which goes forth is not merely the word of that individual soul. 'Behind the blessing of the individual stands the fathers; from them he has derived it, and its strength depends on their power. When all is said and done, it rests in powers which lie behind all human capability.'[23] The power of this word of blessing has been emphasized by Dr. Dorothy Emmet, in her book, 'Function, Purpose and Powers'. The word had a charismatic influence, which was the expression of the powerful individual who pronounced it. Such was the influence of the divine behind the individual that sometimes the individual was unable to control the blessing, which was more powerful than the speaker. This is seen in the case of Balaam, whom Balak desired to curse Israel but instead the word that came from Balaam's lips served to bless Israel (Num. 23. 11-12). Similarly, when Isaac had blessed Jacob, he could not retract his words (Gen. 27. 35). If this is true with man, it is even more so, in the case of the Lord. The term 'word' *(dabhar)* also implies an action (Gen. 15. 1; 22. 20), so the word was dynamic and expressed the event which followed the word. When Abraham's servant returned from his mission, to find a wife for Isaac, he told Isaac 'all the *debharim* he had made' (Gen. 24. 66), i.e. he narrated all he had said, done and experienced. The word is not therefore an abstract concept, not a mere 'lip-word' but an idea, its verbal clothing and the matter itself, a perfectly concrete effect. When such a word emanates from the Lord, then its power and action is correspondingly great. The close connection between word and event is also brought out in the actions of the prophets, who thus expressed the action of their souls. Isaiah went about barefoot and naked for three years, to proclaim the fact that the Assyrians would thus be dragged away naked and barefoot (Isa. 20. 2-3). The

---

[22] Pedersen, ibid., I-II, p. 167.
[23] Ibid., p. 194.

Assyrian defeat lay already deep in the soul of the prophet and forces were under way to bring such an event to pass. The prophet acted to reveal what was *essentially* happening, at the heart of things, because of his particular insight. Underlying the event, whether it is the rainbow, the circumcision or the sabbath, there lay the covenant within them. The sign had power because of the dynamic force of soul which lay behind it. If Pharoah refused to recognize the power of the first sign, then another would be given to endorse the first (Exod. 4. 8-9). All these signs are *tokens* of soul.

A man's psychic force might dwell in his name. Therefore to know his name enabled an opponent to have power over him. Jacob strove with his opponent by the ford of the Jabbok, seeking the name of his adversary (Gen. 32. 29). In like manner, when a man died without issue, it was his brother's duty to raise up an heir, by levirate marriage, so 'that his name may not be blotted out of Israel' (Deut. 25. 6). Absalom raised up a pillar to keep his name in remembrance (2 Sam. 18. 18). Bildad speaks of the wicked man 'who has no name in the street' (Job 18. 17). Thus a man's name was deemed to be an expression of his soul.

It has been seen that Achan was not destroyed alone for his disobedience to the ban but the whole household was destroyed with him. A man's household and his possessions were an extension of himself, that totality of soul that pervaded everything that was his. So the cup that belonged to Joseph had a portion of his soul (Gen. 44. 5). Thus to steal it merited slavery for those who were involved (Gen. 44. 16). The warrior Jephthah the Gileadite equates himself and his land ('What have you against me, that you have come to me to fight against my land?'), when he sent messengers to the king of the Ammonites (Judg. 11, 12). The prophet Elijah gave his strength into his staff and gave it to Gehazi, his servant, who was to take it to heal by its use the Shunammite boy (2 Kgs. 4. 29). A similar power lay in the staff of Moses (Exod. 17. 9).

The strong sense of corporate solidarity, which Wheeler Robinson described as 'the idea of corporate personality', gave the Israelite an awareness of his place in Israel which was far more vivid than his sense of individual awareness. It is on this account that the place of the family and the household loom so large in the Old Testament. Similarly, as the tribal unit lost its force with the rise of the kingdoms, so the place of the king, especially in the Southern kingdom, became very significant. This will be seen in the family and kinship arrangements as early as the period of the partriarchs, as may be seen in the next chapter. It was the family, in particular, as the extension of the soul of the head of the household, that continued to hold an important place as the primary unit in society.

Nevertheless, it must not be overlooked, as Aubrey Johnson and Walther Eichrodt have pointed out, that the individual had significance also in the thought of ancient Israel. As early as the time of entry into the promised land, when the Book of the Covenant (Ex. 20-23) was promulgated, there is evidence that the individual wrongdoer is to be punished, for his misdeeds, to protect the community.[24] At the same time, it is assumed throughout the Old Testament that man has freedom, within certain limits set by the sovereignty of God. This limited freedom permits him to choose whether to do good or to do ill to his neighbour; to choose whether he will move to this place or another. This freedom is exercised too in the conception of man's 'dominion' over nature, though this is not clearly apparent until the period of the Priestly documents (post-exilic) (Gen. 1. 26; 9. 2). Creation and man are linked by this conception from an early date (Ps. 8. 6). A further important factor is the sense of responsibility that man has towards his Creator which is evident from an early period. Responsibility is an important attribute of being a man and this becomes clearer as time goes on.

[24] W. Eichrodt, *Man in the Old Testament* (1951), p. 10.

CHAPTER THREE

KINSHIP RELATIONSHIPS AMONG THE EARLY HEBREWS

1. The Patriarchs and their place in the 2nd millenium. Their manner of life and social practice. The possibility of an earlier matriarchal pattern. Evidence from the Nuzi texts.
2. The domestic arrangements of Abraham and the Hurrian texts. The respective positions of the son and the slave. The presumptuous slave-mother and her mistress. Feudal obligation linked to the possession of real property.
3. Marital customs reflected in the tradition of Isaac. The importance of mother's brother's family. The Jacob saga and the Nuzi texts. The significance of the blessing. Preferential marriage and permitted marriage relationships, with Jacob and Esau.
4. Jacob's dealings with Laban. His marriage and sororal polygyny. The place of legal adoption in ancient culture. Jacob's departure from Laban and evidence of nomadic wanderings in early texts. Ancient sites of the Middle Bronze Age.
5. The clan-family and the father's house in the pastoral tradition. Religious ties within the household. The bond between the God and the clan. Ethical relationships within the pastoral clan. Group loyalty and solidarity with wider implications.

CHAPTER THREE

KINSHIP RELATIONSHIPS AMONG THE EARLY HEBREWS

THE patriarchal narratives were held by Jewish tradition to have been penned by Moses, who lived centuries after the events recorded. The development of Biblical criticism and methods of modern historiography did not uphold the older Jewish traditional view but replaced it by the hypothesis that the Hexateuch was composed of four major (together with other minor) documents (J, E, D and P), the earliest of which (J) was dated in the ninth century and the latest (P) after the exile.

This hypothesis led Biblical critics to view the early traditions of Israel with considerable scepticism as it would seem that none of them were remotely contemporaneous with the events narrated. Whilst it was recognized that historical reminiscences might be embedded in the traditions, yet one hesitated to give too much weight to any particular part of them. In fact, the patriarchal narratives might well provide light on the customs and practices of the period in which they were written down but they were unlikely to give more than a minimal amount of information about Israel's pre-history as a nation. Abraham, Isaac and Jacob were explained as eponymous ancestors of later clans. They were regarded as aetiological myths, whose existence as living persons were not infrequently denied. Their religion was held to be the projection back into earlier days of later beliefs, which priests and others desired to root in ancient times.

The judgement of earlier scholars has undergone considerable revision since J. Wellhausen set forth the views described above. The documentary hypothesis still finds general acceptance, though some Scandinavian scholars, particularly the Uppsala school, stress oral tradition in preference to methods of literary criticism.[1] A revaluation of the patriarchal traditions has in fact

[1] cf. C. R. North, *The Old Testament and Modern Study*, (H. H. Rowley, ed.), Oxford, 1951, p. 48f.

become the more necessary because of the new light cast by archaeological research upon Israel's origins. Even a century ago, there was little objective light upon the ancient civilizations and the various cultures of the Middle and Far East. Without an objective frame of reference, it was difficult, to put it mildly, to assess and evaluate the customs and practices, which appeared to be so far removed from the times when the records were written down. Their historical worth seemed greatly to be open to doubt, if not worthless.

There has been a radical change in this situation. Dozens of sites have been excavated with the result that thousands of texts and inscriptions have come to light. 'We now have texts by the literal tens of thousands contemporaneous with the period of Israel's origins."[2] These texts bear witness to the fact that Israel's traditions faithfully reflect the period of the early second millenium, the age to which they claim to belong. The traditions of Israel testify to their ancient lineage, apart altogether from their historical veracity. It is in the light of these documents that the material in the Old Testament has to be reviewed afresh to assess the value of tradition in it.

It must inevitably be recognized that the whole task of evaluation is a highly complex one. Not only is there the long process of oral transmission to be taken into account but also the events themselves, e.g. of the patriarchs, have to be seen at times as complex group movements concealed beneath the ostensibly personal activities of individuals. Thus, the destruction of Shechem by Simeon and Levi (Gen. 34) was hardly the work of two lone individuals but of two clans (cf. Gen. 49. 5-7).

Nevertheless, whilst much must remain obscure, it is possible to examine the patriarchal material in the light of the world of their time and discover the extent to which the traditions bear testimony to the life of their own age.

It would appear that the stories of the patriarchs fit authentically into the period of the second millenium rather than into that of any later period, so far as the evidence can inform us.[3] More particularly the narratives in Genesis 12 to 50 reflect a period

---

[2] J. Bright, A History of Israel, p. 63.
[3] H. H. Rowley, 'Recent Discovery and the Patriarchal Age', Bulletin of John Rylands Library, 32 (1949), pp. 44-79.

between the twentieth and the sixteenth centuries, though some scholars would place the patriarchal age considerably later.[4] Important as evidence in this matter are two factors, namely the early Hebrew names and the customs of the patriarchs, together with their general mode of life. The early Hebrew names fit well into a class known to be current in Mesopotamia and Palestine, especially among the Amorite element in the population.[5] It is more particularly in regard to the patriarchal customs that we have concern and therefore we must now turn to consider these in greater detail.

In the earliest known historical times, the Hebrews, like other Semitic peoples, had a firmly established patriarchal society. There are some traces, however, that this patriarchal system was superimposed upon an earlier social arrangement, whereby descent took place through the female line. The mother named the child and it is only in the 8th century, that there are stated the first certain cases of the choice of names by the father (Hos. 1. 4, 6, 9.: Isa. 8. 3).

This older type of society in which the woman lives with her parents after marriage and has her husband to visit her or stay in her home is prominent in many early societies. Robertson Smith in his 'Kingship and Marriage in Early Arabia' called this form of marriage 'sadiqa marriage', in which the tent or the home belongs to the wife. This appears to be the case in the Jahwist account of human marriage in Gen. 2. 24: 'Therefore a man leaves his father and his mother and cleaves to his wife, and they become one flesh'. Therefore, a union between children of the same father was permissible and was not regarded as incestuous, whereas the union between children of the same mother was abhorrent. Sarah was the daughter of Abraham's father and by her marriage to Abraham, became the mother of the son of promise but Sarah and Abraham did not have the same mother (Gen. 20. 12). Even as late as the time of David, Amnon (David's son) sought to ravish his half-sister Tamar, who replied: 'Now therefore, I pray you, speak to the king; for he will not withhold me from you' (2 Sam. 13. 13). There is no indication that mar-

[4] C. H. Gordon, *Introduction to Old Testament Times* (1953), pp. 75, 102ff.
[5] W. F. Albright, 'Northwest-Semitic Names in a List of Egyptian Slaves from the Eighteenth Century B.C.' (JAOS, 74 (1954), pp. 222-223).

riage between them would be unlawful or dishonourable, though Tamar resents being his victim in a passing fit of lust.

If the tent belonged to the woman, then it was the husband who 'went in to his wife', as Jacob did to Leah (Gen. 29. 23) and to Rachel (Gen. 29. 30), as well as to their maids, Zilpah and Bilhah respectively (Gen. 30. 4). Similarly, Abraham went in to Hagar, his wife's maid (Gen. 16. 4). This created a strong bond between the children of the same mother. When Abraham's servant sought to gain Rebekah's hand for Isaac, it is not only Bethuel (her father) who is consulted but her brother Laban as well (Gen. 24. 50). Similarly, when Dinah, Jacob's daughter, was ravished by Shechem the son of Hamor the Hivite, her brothers (Simeon and Levi) take revenge. (This incident, whether personal or tribal, indicates the sense of responsibility felt by close kin ties.) It is probable that this conception of 'sadiqa marriage' continued to hold its place in Israelite practice. Moses married a Midianite woman, who stayed in her own country with her two sons (Exod. 18. 3-6), until his later return to her territory. Gideon had his wife at Shechem, though Gideon lived at Ophrah. When Gideon's son, Abimelech, wanted support for his cause, he went to his mother's kinsmen for support (Judg. 9. 1-3). To them he was able to say, 'Remember also that I am your bone and your flesh', though there does not appear any such link with Abimelech's father's clan. Samson appears to have taken as wife a Timnite woman, whom he visited from time to time, presenting her with a gift, when he did so (Judg. 15. 1). Marriage with father's relations, even father's sister, did not rouse disapproval, as in the case of the parents of Aaron and Moses (Ex. 6. 20). Therefore, in the relationships with the father's family, the link appears to be weak but with the mother's family, there is a strong and enduring bond at all times.[6] Later law forbade also union between the children of the same father as well as those of the same mother (Lev. 18. 9). Some scholars have held that the term 'mishpāhā' (normally translated as 'family') points to the matriarchate, as the term may originally mean 'concubine' or 'matriarchal wife', with the family as a unit based on a uterine relationship.[7]

[6] A. Lods, *Israel* (1930), (Eng. trans. by S. Hooke (1932), pp. 192-4.
[7] cf. H. H. Rowley, *Record and Revelation* (ed. H. W. Robinson) (1938), pp. 161-2.

However, in historical times and, in particular, by the time of the conquest, the tribal organization of Israel had been established on a patriarchal basis. This is apparent even in the narratives of the patriarchs, concerning whom much light has been given by the discovery of the Nuzi texts of the fifteenth century. These texts inform us about the customs of a predominantly Hurrian (Biblican 'Horites') population in Northern Mesopotamia, where the Hurrians secured control of an area of an older Amorite culture. Elements of the customs of the older Amorite population were probably taken over into the legal arrangements of the Hurrians.

By means of these texts, several incidents in the life of Abraham are clarified. The need for an heir is prominent in the story of Abraham as well as in Hurrian society. But provision was made, as these texts indicate, whereby a favoured slave or adopted child might be legally entitled to become the heir, if there was no natural issue, which Abraham anticipated that he might have to do in the case of his home-born slave, Eliezer of Damascus (Gen. 15. 1-4). If a natural son was born to Abraham, then the adopted son would have to give precedence to the natural son. Another text gives a marriage contract, which has a clause whereby if the wife is unable to provide an heir, she shall provide a concubine for her husband who may give him an heir on her behalf. In one contract, it is specified that the concubine provided is not to be any cheap slave but an Egyptian. Thus, Sarah gave her slave Hagar the Egyptian to Abraham, saying, 'Go in to my maid; it may be that I shall obtain children by her' (Gen. 16. 1-4). This gave a privileged position to Hagar but did not displace Sarah from her place as chief wife. When Sarah appealed against the contempt of Hagar, Abraham reaffirmed Sarah's status and reduced Hagar to her ordinary status as a slave (Gen. 16. 6). This punishment for a slave-mother who has a child by her master and then presumes on her position is found in the Code of Hammurabi (paragraph 146), which states that 'if later that female slave has claimed equality with her mistress because she bore children, her mistress may not sell her; she may mark her with the slave-mark and count her among the slaves'.[*] Other legal wives in Israel, no doubt, had trouble in this matter (Prov. 30. 23). But a child of such a union with a slave

[*] J. B. Pritchard, ANET (Ancient Near Eastern Texts), p. 172.

Kinship Relationships among the Early Hebrews 45

could not be expelled from the home with his mother, according to Nuzi law, which may well explain Abraham's reluctance to send Hagar and Ishmael away (Gen. 21. 10f).

When Isaac was born, he became the heir and took due precedence over Ishmael, the slave's son. As a Nuzi text points out, 'to the sons (of the main wife) shall be given the lands and buildings of every sort'.⁹ Although he was the son of promise, Isaac has no great part in the narrative. The Priestly narrative refers to his circumcision (Gen. 21. 4) and the Elohist writer gives great prominence to the testing of Abraham, who, in obedience, is willing to offer up his chosen son in sacrifice. This narrative indicates the break with human sacrifice which took place in Israel, presumably far earlier that in the surrounding nations. Abraham's place as the father of the faithful is also emphasized in the same account (Gen. 22. 16-18). Abraham is depicted as the father of all who later believe (Rom. 4. 11). This is seen also when Sarah dies and needs burial.

Although Abraham is promised the land, yet he remained a 'sojourner', dwelling in tents. Yet, it is pointed out, the patriarchs were not entirely 'strangers' because they did come to own a plot of earth, namely, the burial place of the Cave of Machpelah, which Abraham purchased from Ephron the Hittite (Gen. 23). This was an 'earnest' of the later fuller possession, which Abraham's heirs were to receive. This narrative is commonly assigned to P and therefore to a late date but it may well reflect much older material, as it is paralleled in Hittite law, which is found in the Boghazköy texts (14th cent. B.C.). Under this law, feudal obligation was linked to real property ownership rather than to the person.¹⁰

This plot of land, which is usually identified with the cave under the mosque at Hebron, was used not only for the burial of Sarah but also for Abraham (25. 9), Isaac (35. 29), Rebekah and Leah (49. 31) and also Jacob (50. 13). Apart from this possession and possibly, a few cultivated areas (Gen. 26. 12), the patriarchs were ass-nomads, for whom even the camel may have been a later adoption, an anachronism introduced at a later date for contemporary readers (cf. Gen. 12. 16, 24).

But in regard to marital custom, Isaac has to have a bride

⁹ J. B. Pritchard, ANET, p. 220.
¹⁰ Ibid., pp. 188-197 (especially paragraphs 46-47).

from within the kin (Gen. 24. 4, 38). As among many Hamite peoples today, the bride chosen is from his father's brother's family. This bride, Rebekah, is the daughter of the youngest son (Bethuel) of Nahor, Abraham's brother. This preference for the younger or youngest son is a noticeable feature, in the Old Testament, of the doctrine of Election. Here it is the daughter of the younger son. Jacob is the younger brother (Gen. 25. 26). Joseph was the elder son of Rachel but a younger son of the family (Gen. 37. 3). David was similarly the youngest son (1. Sam. 16. 11). Rebekah is chosen from Bethuel's family to be the bride of Isaac, where she dwells in the tent of his mother (Gen. 24. 67).

The importance of the kinship ties is seen most clearly in the Jacob saga, upon which the Nuzi tablets have thrown much light. The story of the sale of the birthright by Esau (Gen. 25. 29-34) may be compared with the Nuzi account, in which one brother sells a grove, which he has inherited, for three sheep. With an eye on the later inheritance, Jacob offers food to his famished brother, Esau, but Jacob says, 'Swear to me first'. So Esau swore to him and sold his birth-right to Jacob (Gen. 25. 33). This was a presage of further trouble between them.

The crisis between the brothers came over the gift of the 'blessing', which was deemed to be a communicable power handed down from father to son. This is a power of the soul which lives on in the psychic community of the family.[11] As the 'blessing' was with Abraham (Gen. 22. 17), so it passed to Isaac (Gen. 26. 3, 24), who was able to pass it on to his sons. This 'blessing' was deemed to be an active power, so that if the rights of its holder were violated, then punishment fell on the violater. Thus, when Abimelech attempted to take Sarah, he was threatened with disaster (Gen. 20. 3), just as in a parallel experience attributed to Isaac, Abimelech recognized that Isaac's success is a power to be treated with care, as he is the 'blessed of the Lord' (Gen. 26. 29). This inheritable asset has already received attention in the previous chapter and will arise from time to time in the further development of the Hebrew family.

Jacob, although he was the younger brother, greatly desired to receive this gift. His mother, whose favourite he was, also wanted him to receive it. As the gift was a double-edged one,

[11] J. Pedersen, *Israel*, p. 190

bringing disaster on the unworthy, Jacob was fearful lest it might bring him under a curse instead of a blessing (Gen. 27. 12). His mother put his fears to rest. She told him that any ill-result would fall upon her. After this incident, she did in fact never see her son again. Jacob carried out her orders and received the 'blessing' from his father, who when he learned what had happened realized that the gift could not be recalled (Gen. 27. 35). This brought bitter conflict between the brothers, so that Jacob had to find some place of safety elsewhere.

One of the basic patterns which is found in primitive society is the 'custom of privileged familiarity of a sister's son towards his mother's brother which is found in some peoples of Africa, Oceania and North America'.[12] Therefore, it was fitting that Rebekah should advise her son to go to stay with her brother. Moreover, marriage with a mother's brother's daughter in such society is a widespread form of preferred marriage. This involves two important sociological principles. Firstly, such marriage was preferred as contrasexually (i.e. from a son through his mother (a woman) through her brother (a man) to the mother's brother's daughter (a woman), who becomes the son's bride). Secondly, such a marriage serves as a satisfactory form of compensation, almost on the basis of exchange. A man who marries exogamously (out of his group) thereby deprives her group of her services. But his daughter returns to the maternal group when she weds her maternal uncle's son. Thus a proper balance is kept between the two groups.[13] Rebekah and Isaac therefore bid Jacob their son seek a wife from among the daughters of Rebekah's brother, Laban (Gen. 27. 46 and 28. 2). Similarly among the clans, who live in the Chinese countryside, one of the most favoured forms of marriage is the one with mother's brother's daughter.[14] Therefore, Jacob had adequate cause in family custom to leave his home to go to Paddan-aram, where Laban lived and where a preferred bride might await him (Gen. 28. 5-7).

Esau sought to satisfy his parents by a cross-cousin marriage

[12] A. R. Radcliffe-Brown and Daryll Forde (edd.), *African Systems of Kinship and Marriage* (1950), p. 83. (cf. A. R. Radcliffe-Brown, *Structure and Function in Primitive Society* (1952), Chap. I, 'The Mother's Brother in South Africa'.).
[13] J. Lazard, *Institutions of Primitive Society*, pp. 57ff.
[14] F. L. K. Hsu, *Under the Ancestors' Shadow* (1949), p. 82.

with his father's half-brother's daughter (Gen. 28. 8-9). Such a marriage was permitted but was not a preferential marriage in a patrilineal society. Such marital rules had as their function the need to preserve, maintain or continue an existing kinship structure which might be endangered if those too closely related were allowed to marry one another. It was on this account that incest was universally condemned as creating havoc in the family, although the evidence has still to be collected for a scientific judgement.[15] Nevertheless, it is probable that among the Hebrews, there was a dislike of incest from an early period as evidenced from the story of Lot's connection with his daughters (Gen. 19. 30-38). At a later date, rules were established to clarify the issue (Lev. 18. 6-18).

Jacob's stay with his uncle enabled him to combine business with pleasure. It was needful for him to find an acceptable bride, particularly in the light of the blessing of Abraham, which was to become his and 'to his seed after him' (Gen. 28. 4). Jacob's meeting with Rachel at the well is idyllic in its setting, even though Jacob kissed Rachel before he had introduced himself— a practice of which Calvin disapproved.[16] As a kinsman in the household, Jacob had a privileged place but his desire for Rachel could not be without some compensatory service, in lieu of dowry, to obtain her as a bride. Therefore, Jacob works for Laban for a statutory period to secure his bride. Laban deceives Jacob by giving Leah as a bride to Jacob instead. Jacob stays on in the home to work to gain Rachel as well.

Thus, Jacob marries the two sisters, a type of marriage which is known as 'sororal polygyny', which is a very widespread institution. 'Among the Australian aborigines this is held to be the ideal form of marriage.'[17] This did not preclude Jacob from a romantic preference for Rachel (ch. 29. 30), because the seven years for Rachel 'seemed unto him but a few days because of the love that he had for her' (verse 20). When Rachel did not conceive children, she gave her servant (Bilhah) to Jacob so that she might have children by her servant. Leah acted similarly in giving her servant (Zilpah) to Jacob, to provide Jacob and her mistress

[15] J. R. Fox, 'Sibling Incest', *British Journal of Sociology*, XIII, 2 (June 1962), pp. 128-150.
[16] G. von Rad, *Genesis*, p. 284 (note).
[17] *African Systems of Kinship and Marriage*, p. 64.

with further children. This practive has been noted above as common from the Nuzi texts.

Other aspects of the relationship between Jacob and Laban also will merit consideration. In the Nuzi texts, there is evidence of a legal device whereby a man might adopt his daughter's husband who thereby became the man's heir. Thus a man named Nashwi adopted Wullu, the son of Puhi-shenni. If Nashwi had no son of his own, then Wullu was to take the gods (teraphim) of Nashwi. Nashwi gave his daughter Nuhuya in marriage to Wullu but on the condition that if Wullu takes another wife, he shall forfeit the lands and buildings of Nashwi.[18] Such a method of adoption may well have taken place in the case of Jacob. There is no mention at first that Laban had any sons. When Jacob's marriage with the daughters of Laban takes place, he might have been deemed to be the heir. But when Laban has sons, then Jacob is displaced and is no longer the heir, as his wives point out: 'Is there any portion or inheritance left to us in our father's house? Are we not regarded by him as foreigners?' (Gen. 31. 14). Therefore Jacob made plans to leave the household of Laban and managed to outwit Laban, by leaving stealthily. But Laban still regarded all Jacob's goods, wives and children as his own. 'The daughters are my daughters, the children are my children, the flocks are my flocks and all that you see is mine', says Laban to Jacob, when he has caught up with him. But a most important factor appears to be the possession of the household gods, which marked the person as the legitimate heir as in the case of Wullu above. Laban is then very anxious to recover the household gods (Gen. 31. 30-35), which Rachel is equally desirous to keep for her husband (Gen. 31. 19 and 34). When Jacob and Laban agree to part company, it is noteworthy that in their agreement Laban binds Jacob (Gen. 31. 50) to marry no other wives, just as Wullu is bound in the Nuzi text above.

Jacob then travels on with his flocks and herds to the lands, where his father and grandfather had roamed. Evidence from the Mari texts shows that there was freedom of movement possible over all parts of the Fertile Crescent. The Execration Texts of the Egyptian Middle Kingdom (20th-18th centuries) indicate that the land of Palestine, which was held but loosely (if at all) at that time by Egypt, was receiving a new population which

[18] J. B. Pritchard, ANET, pp. 219-220.

accords well with the arrival of such pastoral nomads. In particular, the patriarchs are depicted as roving in the central mountain area of Palestine from the area of Shechem south to the Negeb, in the Negeb and east of the Jordan. They do not appear to have roamed in northern Palestine, the Jordan Valley, the Plain of Esdraelon nor (apart from the far north) in the coastal plain. It is evident that the towns mentioned, such as Shechem, Dothan, Bethel and even Jerusalem, were in existence in the Middle Bronze Age, so that some contact with such places was at least possible. The picture of tribal chieftains who have not yet settled down as feudal lords fits well into the period between the twentieth and sixteenth centuries. The shepherd clans appear to move about in a land of peace and conduct their affairs without undue outside interruption. Their period of wandering long remained as a cultic confession, even at a much later date: 'A wandering Aramean was my father' (Deut. 26. 5).

The importance of this tradition of pastoral families cannot be over-estimated in the life of later Israel, in which the clan (mishpāhā) is the connecting link between the tribe and the household or father's house (Num. 2. 34). Further consideration to the clan or family (mishpāhā) will be given in the next chapter but it is noteworthy that the nucleus of the *mishpāhā* is bēth ābh, the father's house. This latter is connected with the term *bayith*, which is a common Semitic word, denoting the dwelling, house or tent but also all of those who live in and around the building, i.e. the household. The tribe and the city both had a place of importance in the lives of the Israelites but 'the household everywhere preserved its importance as the centre of life, because it represents kinship in its most intimate sense. The laws and manner of thinking of the Israelites are throughout stamped with it'.[19]

The unity within the household was re-inforced by religious ties. A number of terms indicate a close personal tie between the father of the family or clan and his God. These are: the God of Abraham (Gen. 28. 13; 31. 42, 53); the Kinsman of Isaac (*pahad yishaq*: Gen. 31. 42, 53)[20] and the Champion (Mighty One) of

---

[19] J. Pedersen, *Israel*, p. 51.
[20] W. F. Albright, *From the Stone Age to Christiantity* (1957), p. 248. He suggests 'kinsman' in place of the older rendering 'Fear of Isaac', which is found in all English versions.

Jacob (Gen. 49. 24). Each has his God as the patron diety of the clan, so that whilst Jacob swears by the Kinsman of Isaac (Gen. 31. 42) in making his covenant with Laban, the latter swears by the God of Nahor, his father (verse 53). It is probable that the cult of the ancestral deity was a simple one, though the cult was not without images, as the teraphim of Laban indicate. Whatever place the worship of the moon-God Sin had in earlier Semitic worship in Ur and Haran, it appears clear that the great official polytheisms of Mesopotamia have no place in the patriarchal record. Similarly, there is no trace of the orgies of the fertility cults of Canaan. Even human sacrifice is ruled out of the cult of the patriarchs. The clan-father (or housefather) performed the rites, which included the blood sacrifices of animals. The various clan cults were no doubt subsumed under that of Yahweh when the clans became united 'into the blood stream of Israel'.

Important factors in this simple cult-relationship were the personal bond between the God and the clan, which was upheld by divine promise, and the contractual arrangements between the worshipper and his God. The promise was of land and progeny if the clan was faithful, as seen in Genesis chapter 15. The relationship was deemed to be a covenant (contract) which depended on the worshipper's trust (Gen. 15. 6). This early contractual element came to have greater importance later, especially in the Sinaitic covenant, attributed to Moses. The early covenant with the patriarchs seems to be of much simpler mould but had larger potentialities for future relationships, which caused A. Alt. to style the god(s) of the patriarchs as *paidagogoi* (tutors) to Yahweh, the God of Israel.[21]

Nevertheless, this early nomadic and pastoral tradition had important consequences also on the ethical side of later Israel's life. Leadership depended on the personal sagacity and courage of great individual personalities, not upon the superior authority of certain hereditary individuals or an aristocracy. The common interests of the community served to limit the powers of the nomad, who bowed to this authority but no other. Moreover, it was possible to move on from the overbearing influence of an undesirable neighbour. Therefore, freedom of the person and a sense of equality marked the relationship between shepherd clans.

[21] A. Alt, *Kleine Schriften zur Geschichte des Volkes Israel*, I, p. 63.

Both these factors had their repercussions in the conflicts between prophets and kings in later times.

Furthermore, the nomad's life is a hard one. 'By day the heat consumed me, and the cold by night, and my sleep fled from my eyes', says Jacob to Laban (Gen. 31. 40). The constant danger from the elements, and from human and animal perils made constant vigilance imperative. There was no place for an enervating luxury, which the townman could enjoy. Therefore, the nomad has normally a high standard in his moral code, especially in sexual matters. Thus, similarly among the Masai as herdsmen, there is an ethical standard considerably higher than among their agricultural neighbours in Africa.

The existence of a pastoral clan depends upon the loyalty of its members to one another and upon regulations against murder. The loyalty of its members is expressed in the laws regulating marriage, which are designed to keep the blood pure. Therefore the fear of incest and the agreement about preferential marriages served to knit the clan together and avoid conflict from contrary instincts. The belief in the power of 'the blood' is such that it is deemed to have a personality of its own and in any case was too sacred to be touched (Lev. 17. 14).

The group must also ensure that its members have security against unlimited blood-feud and murder. In the case of Abel, Cain is told: 'The voice of your brother's blood is crying to me from the ground' (Gen. 4. 10). The cry for vengeance is an ancient one. The call to requite the honour of the group may take the form to 'go one better', which Lamech appears to have done. 'I have slain a man to my wounding and a young man to my hurt': Gen. 4. 23). Blood unrevenged was deemed to bring disaster on the community, so more stringent laws were needed to be laid down to prevent unhindered bloodshed by conflicting groups.

As relationships between the sexes needed regulation, so too did the relationships between the age-groups. Respect for tradition and for the authority and experience of the elders of the clan is set forth in the fifth commandment: 'Honour thy father and thy mother', which undoubtedly dates from a very early period. Jeremiah looked back to the early days of Israel's history with wistfulness (Jer. 2. 2, 3), as days when Israel was closest to the Lord's intention. There is ample reason to believe that the ethical standard of the pastoral period was a high one and this came to have a peculiar and particular importance for later Israelite history, because the tradition and outlook of the primitive days remained strong in at least some part of the community. This does not appear to have been so among other ancient peoples and so provides a pointer towards the fusion of faith and morality, which was an inheritance which Israel was to give to the world.

CHAPTER FOUR

THE HEBREW FAMILY DURING THE WILDERNESS PERIOD

1. *The development of the patriarchal family. The significance of the father. Types of slaves—attempts to improve their treatment. Other social groups—the hired workmen and the sojourners.*
   Family custom as the basis of later legislation. The regulation of relationships between the sexes. The protection of wives and daughters. The need for male heirs. The use of the levirate form of marriage in Israel. The responsibility of the next-of-kin. Prohibited degrees of inter-marriage.

2. *The significance of covenant-law. The rise of legal norms to define relationships between groups. A Covenant society based upon law—issuing in a sacral league. The leadership of the Judges. The 'honour' of the chieftain. Maintenance of justice—by personal strength and kin-vengeance.*
   Wider solidarity demands restriction of blood-feud. The law of retaliation. Need for a criterion for justice. Yahweh's demands as the criterion. Common law shaped by His demands. Manslaughter differentiated from murder. Blood belongs to Yahweh alone. Cities of refuge. The use of the oath.

CHAPTER FOUR

THE HEBREW FAMILY DURING THE WILDERNESS PERIOD

1. *The development of the patriarchal family*

THE patriarchal records make it clear that the family as a unit was well established by the time that the Israelites (or some of them) went down to Egypt and became settled there. The reverence for the family bond became firmer, even though the records which have come down to us have a large admixture of wide tribal material above and beyond any particular domestic records which may have survived in the process.

During the period which preceded the settlement in Canaan and the organization of the monarchy, it is probable that legal and customary practices freely intermingled. As among nomads today, the family as an extended unit is often strong and has a high code of sexual morality. Therefore, it is probable that during this period the Hebrew family came to adopt and develop codes of family morality which became legalized in the period of codification later. The care of the women, the treatment of daughters and their place in the family economy, the treatment of slaves and arrangements between families were governed by customary practices before any definite legislation was promulgated. These practices will be outlined in this chapter, together with the conception of law which came to be the foundation of the life of Israel. The usages customary among the family formed a pattern for wider relationships, whether within the circle of the kin, the tribe or later the nation. The details of the code in protecting the family served to protect Israel, when in due time the families were scattered. Her law proved to be her strength. It has to be made clear that the family usages developed slowly and gradually. It is unlikely that we will ever know for sure the age of some of the customary usages which became law but there is reason to believe that many of them date back to the period previous to the entry into the promised land.

The Hebrew Family during the Wilderness Period 57

During the period in the wilderness, the patriarchal system must have been tested and tried. It is clear that it is the man who dominates in that it is the father's house after whom the man is called. Yet marriage as the union of man and woman is given great prominence in the lives of the Israelites. In the Priestly record, man and woman together make '*adham*' (man) (Gen. 1. 27), whereas in the older Yahwist record, it is related that Yahweh first created man. Yet the man thus created needed to be wholly man by the help-meet, woman, who is taken out of him (Gen. 2. 18, 21-23). It may well be that the priestly writer who is so often concerned with genealogies is concerned with man as a genus in God's creation, whereas the Yahwist writer is more concerned with man's place as most prominent in creation, the ruler, to whom authority has been given. Woman is dependent upon him but she is part of him, bearing him children, yet his indispensable helpmeet in the care of the family.

The man's relation to his family is expressed in the term, *ba'al*, the possessor and the master. He is the ruling will within the psychic community. Kinship and authority both found a focus in the term 'father'. Thus, Naaman was called father by his servants (2 Kgs. 5. 13); the priest leads the cultic community and so is called father (Judg. 18. 19) and Elijah is called father by his disciple. From the man as father, the family emanates as a psychic community, embracing the wives, the slaves, children and property. Among the slaves, it is true that some were bought but most prominence is given to the 'son of the house' (the houseborn slave) (Gen. 14. 14; 15. 2f.; 17. 12, 27; Jer. 2. 14). The slave who has been in the home for a long time may be regarded with respect as the 'elder of the house', performing important tasks for the house-father (Gen. 24) and (as already mentioned) may even inherit (Gen. 15. 4). The slave had to be circumcised (Gen. 17) and was admitted to the family worship. The closeness of this link with the household is seen in that the slave of the priest may eat of the holy thing—which is forbidden to the strange guest or the paid labourer and even to the priest's daughter who has married a stranger (Lev. 22. 10-12). The position of the slave came to be an embarrassment, though it is probable that these unfree servants were generally of foreign birth and acquired in war or purchase. But as some Israelites prospered so other Israelites fell on hard times, apparent from the legislation which made provision for the Israelite who had to sell his daughter. She had to be sold to a fellow-Israelite and not to a foreign people (Exod. 21. 7-8). If a thief is penniless, he might be sold as a slave (Exod. 22. 2). An Israelite's family might be taken by a creditor to repay a debt (2 Kgs. 4. 1). Debts may well have caused such social decline in many families.

Nevertheless, efforts were made to remove the burden of serfdom from Israelites. According to the Book of the Covenant, an Israelite slave had to be released after six years of slavery, if he desired to be free (Exod. 21. 2ff.). If he is married when he becomes a slave, then on his release his wife shall be released with him. But if the master has given him a wife, then the wife and the children belong to the master and, on the day of release, only the man is to be set free. The Deuteronomic law required the master to set the man free in the seventh year and also to provide the former slave with gifts, so that the freed man could maintain himself. Provision was to be made from the flock, the threshing floor and the winepress (Deut. 15. 12-18). This more humanitarian attitude which is no doubt due to the prophetic perception in the later Deuteronomic law developed further, so that, at a later period, in the 'Law of Holiness', it is forbidden to an Israelite to accept a fellow-Israelite ('your brother') as a slave. He may only accept his 'brother' as a hired-servant or a sojourner *(gēr)*, until the year of Jubilee, when he must be permitted to return to his own home. This arrangement was made to enable the hired man to pay off his debts and make adequate provision to live as a free man. On the other hand, it was permitted to the Israelite to buy male and female slaves but only among foreigners and strangers *(gērīm)*. If an Israelite has to sell himself to a wealthy stranger, it is his family's duty to redeem him (Lev. 25. 39ff.).

Whilst the slave was in the household of his master, he was entirely at the master's mercy. If the master struck the slave, so that the slave was badly injured that he only lived for a day or two, then the master was free. He was only dealing with his own. However, if the master struck the slave in the eye, so that the eye was destroyed, then the slave was to be set free. The same was true if the slave lost a tooth. If the master struck his slave with a rod, so that the slave dies under his hand, then the master had to be punished (Exod. 21. 20-21; 26-27). Although these regulations are found in the Book of the Covenant, which presuppose a more settled agricultural community, yet it seems probable that this Code has affinity with earlier Sumerian law as well as some Canaanite code of a contemporaneous period. When the slave had received his freedom, it is probable that he joined the ranks of the hired men, possibly continuing to serve his former master.

Also attached to the household, there were other groups (to which reference has been made), namely, the hired workmen *(lāmas)* and the 'sojourners' *(gērīm)*. Whilst it may well have been that many people of Canaan were killed as the Israelites advanced into the land and that some towns were conquered, yet it is unlikely that there was wholesale extermination. It is then a matter for conjecture to investigate what happened to those Canaanites which survived. It would appear that these remaining Canaanites became hired-workers (Josh. 16. 10; 17. 13), as the various tribes became strong enough to overcome them (Judg. 1. 28, 30, 33, 35). It is claimed that these people of earlier days (the Amorites, the Hittites, the Perizzites, the Hivites and the Jebusites) were used by Solomon for forced labour as he did not employ Israelites for forced labour (1 Kgs. 9. 21). However, it is reported elsewhere that Jeroboam was ruler over 'all the burden of the house of Joseph' (1 Kgs. 11. 28), a 'forced labour' of which the whole community complained. These *lāmas* were essentially corvée-workers, as a form of serfdom, yet they were distinct from the unfree slaves.

The 'sojourners' *(gērīm)* were those who were living in the midst of a community which was not their own. Such a stranger was in an insecure position vis-à-vis the community, as he lacked the support of his own kindred or township to uphold him in any dispute. In Greece, such persons were the 'perioikoi' who had personal freedom and right of property but were excluded from the privileged circle of citizens. Their specially vulnerable position was recognized by placing them under the direct protection of Zeus Xenos, the father of the gods. The 'gēr' in Israel might be an Israelite, away from home (Judg. 17. 7-9; 19. 16) but probably was more frequently a stranger or foreigner—whether a traveller on a journey (Job 31. 32) or one who had attached himself to the Israelite community, by living in its midst. Their presence was sufficiently numerous for the legislation to make ample reference to them. In many cases, they were no doubt to be identified with conquered but only partly assimilated populations.

It appears that these *gērīm* were often poor, as they are mentioned among the less fortunate who are to have the 'left-overs' in the fields and vineyards (Deut. 24. 19), together with the widow and the fatherless, with whom they are to enjoy the tithe of the Levite (Deut. 14. 29). They are identified with the poor (Lev. 19. 10; 23. 22). These 'strangers' were employed as hired labourers (Exod. 20. 10; Deut. 24. 14) and were generally identified with this social group (Lev. 22. 10; 25. 6, 40). It was not difficult to use such a person as a social scapegoat in a time of crisis, so the law emphasized that Israelite and alien *(gēr)* must be judged by the same principles (Deut. 1. 16). The Israelite was bidden in the law to love the stranger and not to oppress him, being mindful that of old Israel itself had been '*gērīm*' in Egypt (Exod. 22. 21; 23. 9; Lev. 19. 33-4; Deut. 10. 19; 24. 17-18).

Within the circle of the kin, there are to be found the seeds of the law of later days. Family custom and practices served as a preparatory ground for the growth of ideas. As the moral code of nomads is often high, the code of Israel owed much to its earlier origins. This included the regulation of relations between the sexes, especially as wives and of daughters are regarded as valuable family possessions. The violation of a daughter would mean that the bride-price would be lower than if she were a virgin, therefore it was in the family interest to preserve the females against violation. As an economic asset, as a form of labour supply, she was part of her father's property. If she had retained her virginity and passed from the hand of her father to that of the son of another family, of whom she became the bride, then her family had to receive (from the bridegroom's family) a bridal sum *(mohar)*, 'not merely as a compensation but as a mental balancing of what is given by the family of the bride'.[1] From the viewpoint of the family she enters as a bride, this woman is important to ensure posterity. When the doctrine of the life beyond was shadowy, then one mode of survival on earth lay in one's progeny. Her barrenness was not merely a source of frustration but (next to adultery) her greatest shame. This sense of shame is seen clearly in Rachel's lament to Jacob: 'Give me children or I shall die!' to which Jacob naturally and hotly

[1] J. Pedersen, *Israel*, I-II, p. 68.

replied: 'Am I in the place of God, who has withheld from you the fruit of the womb?' (Gen. 30. 1-2). Similarly, Hannah was provoked by her husband's rival wife, Peninnah, who had children whereas she had none. 'Her rival used to provoke her sorely, to irritate her, because the Lord had closed her womb . . . Therefore, Hannah wept and would not eat' (1 Sam. 1. 6-7). When she received Samuel, she believed that her rebuke had been taken away. Among other patriarchal peoples, there is the same passionate desire for sons.[2]

Therefore, the daughters of the clan (or later, of the village) were strictly protected by stern laws—to ensure premarital chastity. This protection was to safeguard them from their own ardent desires as well as from the attention of marauding males. This is made clear in the instructions laid down in Deuteronomy 22. 23-27. If the betrothed maiden (a virgin) is approached by a man and lies down with him, when she is within the city and could call for help, i.e. if she consents with the man by refraining from securing help, then she and the man must be stoned. But if the betrothed virgin is in the country and is unable to call anyone to assist her, then only the man is to be put to death. It is clear from this passage that betrothal was regarded as the equivalent of marriage, in that the betrothed virgin is to suffer death with the man 'because he violated his neighbour's wife'. In fact, 'the marriage ceremony was a legal formality rather than a religious rite (its main feature involved fetching the bride from her father's house); but betrothal was far more important. Unfaithfulness during the period of betrothal was adultery, punishable by stoning'.[3]

Various measures were adopted to ensure that the family's position with regard to the unmarried daughters was safeguarded. If she became damaged goods then her value to her family (or to any other family) was thereby decreased. Therefore, if a virgin was seduced (before any *mōhar* had been paid), then the man responsible had to marry her—with the payment of fifty shekels of silver to her father—and she became his wife (Deut. 22. 28-29). If, on the other hand, the father was opposed to this man who had seduced his daughter and refused to permit them to

---
[2] cf. 'Three things are unfilial and having no sons is the worst', Mencius, Bk. iv., Pt. I., ch. xxvi (trans. Giles, L.).
[3] 'Marriage', K. Grayston, *Theological Word-Book of the Bible*, p. 139.

marry, then the father could keep her at home but collect from her seducer 'money equivalent to the marriage present for virgins' (Exod. 22. 16-17). Neither the daughters (Lev. 19. 29) nor the sons of Israel were permitted to become cult prostitutes, nor was the hire of a harlot or of a Sodomite to be brought into Yahweh's house, in payment for a vow (Deut. 23. 17-18). If the daughter of a priest played the harlot, then she profaned her father and had to be burned with fire (Lev. 21. 9). When such a high value was placed upon virginity, it might have been easy to claim that the young woman was not a virgin at the time of marriage, so that the husband had been cheated by receiving damaged goods. To meet this situation, the parents of the young women were required to bring the tokens of her virginity (i.e. the sheet or under-garment stained with the blood of the broken hymen) to the elders of the community. If the girl's husband was spurning her without excuse and had lied about her, then he had to be whipped and fined one hundred shekels of silver. This sum was to be given to the father of the young woman as he had safeguarded the good name of Israel. The punishment on the girl's husband was meted out because he had soiled the good reputation of a virgin of Israel. But if the husband's claim was true and it was established that she was not a virgin at the time of the marriage, then her harlotry (whilst still in her father's home) must be punished by the men of her city stoning her to death (Deut. 22. 17-21).

Such care safeguarded the purity of the family stock. The family needed to be assured that a true son of the family inherited the property and heirlooms of the family. If a man died childless, then his brothers had the responsibility to ensure that he had at least a putative heir provided for him by means of levirate marriage. It is not easy to establish the age of this practice in Israel but there is no question that it came to have immense importance in the life of the people. It is probable that the law of the levirate in Deuteronomy (25. 5-10) made more precise the accepted customs of a much earlier day, respecting the obligations of male kin towards dead kinsmen. The duty of the next of kin was extended to others in degrees of nearness in other matters, like blood-revenge, and it appears probable that it was true in this respect also.[*]

[*] H. H. Rowley, 'The Marriage of Ruth' in *The Servant of the Lord*, p. 171.

In Genesis 38, there is the story of Tamar, who is denied her proper right in Judah's third son (Shelah), therefore she secures (by trickery) the next 'near relative' *(goēl)*, namely, the father of the sons, Judah himself. In Hittite law, there was a provision that in cases where there was no brother-in-law to perform the duty, then it devolved upon the father-in-law.[5] This early story attributed to J may well indicate that in ancient times the duty of raising children to bear the name of a dead kinsman extended beyond the strict limit of a brother-in-law. (Though the story itself may well have been introduced into the narrative as a compliment to Tamar's astuteness in teaching her father-in-law his duty!) In any case, it seems almost certain that the custom of levirate marriage had its roots in pre-Israelite practice.[6]

The law, as it came to be defined and restricted, may be most clearly expressed by the biblical passage itself: 'If brothers dwell together, and one of them dies and has no son, the wife of the dead shall not be married outside the family to a stranger; her husband's brother shall go in to her, and take her as his wife, and perform the duty of a husband's brother to her. And the first son whom she bears shall succeed to the name of his brother who is dead, that his name may not be blotted out of Israel' (Deut. 25. 5-6). The reference to 'brothers who dwell together' may have specific reference to their joint responsibility for the administration and continuance of the family estate but perhaps the phrase should not be unduly pressed. However, it is clear that the point at issue is the importance of offspring rather than the idea that the next brother inherited his brother's wife as one among other responsibilities of the inheritance. 'In Israel levirate marriage was limited to the one purpose of raising an heir for the dead. Hence the emphasis is not on the childlessness of the widow, but of the deceased."[7]

This passage may further indicate ancient practice in other details. It is 'the first son' whom she bears who shall succeed to the inheritance of the deceased brother, though in later times a daughter (i.e. a child of either sex) might inherit, thereby making levirate marriage unnecessary in such a case.[8] Moreover, the

---

[5] H. H. Rowley, ibid., p. 167 (. 3).
[6] *Ibid.*, p. 178 (n. 1).
[7] *Ibid.*, p. 170 (n. 2).
[8] L. M. Epstein, *Marriage Laws in the Bible and the Talmus*, 1942, p. 96f.

question arises whether the son born would fall heir to his father by paternity as well as the deceased brother by a legal fiction. This complication may well have arisen and given rise to the verses of the law which follow: 'And if the man does not wish to take his brother's wife, then his brother's wife shall go up to the gate to the elders, and say, "My husband's brother refuses to perpetuate his brother's name in Israel; he will not perform the duty of a husband's brother to me".' (This could well arise when friction existed in a household between brothers as in the case of Er and Onan in Gen. 38 or more simply, when the younger brother was already married and had a wife.) 'Then the elders of his city shall call him and speak to him: and if he persists, saying, "I do not wish to take her", then his brother's wife shall go up to him in the presence of the elders, and pull his sandal off his foot and spit in his face; and she shall answer and say, "So shall it be done to the man who does not build up his brother's house". And the name of his house shall be called in Israel, The house of him that had his sandal pulled off' (Deut. 25. 7-10).,

The passage presumes that the younger brother was available for marriage and also indicates a powerful solidarity in loyalty to the family. The closing sentence is obviously a term of abuse for one who had neglected his plain duty. The childless wife is prevented from fulfilling her duty to her husband's family and therefore she is given the task of imposing the punishment, by drawing off the shoe and spitting in his face. This whole passage may be compared with the narrative in Ruth 4. 1-8. The next of kin is unable to fulfil his obligation to marry Ruth, the widow of the dead, 'to restore the name of the dead to his inheritance'. The reason given by the next of kin is, 'lest I impair my own inheritance' (verse 6), so he drew off his sandal and gave it to Boaz, who was thus able to marry Ruth, since Boaz was next in line as kinsman. The 'drawing off of the shoe here signified the abandonment of the obligation resting on the kinsman in respect of the property and in respect of Ruth, and it clearly opened the way for Boaz to do what he could not else have done'.* The account in *Ruth* emphasizes the kinsman's release from obligation in contrast to the view in *Deuteronomy*, where the purpose of drawing off the shoe was to symbolize the woman's freedom from the

* H. H. Rowley, ibid., p. 174.

control of her brother-in-law.[10] It was the duty of the next-of-kin to safeguard the inheritance and this could best be done by raising up male heirs (even though only by a fiction) for the dead man. If a man had no male heirs, his daughters might inherit in Israel (Num. 27. 1-11). It is not clear, in the claim that Boaz makes that he has bought 'from the hand of Naomi' all that belonged to her husband and her sons (Ruth. 4. 9), by what right Naomi as widow of Elimelech possessed her deceased husband's inheritance. Presumably, in the normal case, the inheritance would pass, on the death of Naomi's husband and of her children, to the next-of-kin. On the other hand, it may well have been that Boaz, in taking over all the effects of Naomi's family (including Ruth), was making use of a formula which covered all such effects, whether they were many or few. The whole practice of levirate marriage may well have been handed down from a pre-monogamous state of society, which would not have raised any problem of bigamy. Moreover, it may well be that such a levirate marriage was fulfilled when a single son had been born. The brother-in-law had completed his duty and obligation when he had provided the dead with an heir. This appears probable from similar practice elsewhere, as in India, where in the Laws of Manu, a brother may be authorized to beget a son for one who has no issue, but only a single son is permitted.[11]

Although levirate marriage continued as a practice in Israel, in so far that it is presupposed in New Testament times (Mark 12. 18ff.), yet it conflicted in later times with the prohibited degrees within which a man may not marry. Marriage with a brother's wife came to be viewed as a form of incest. The later practice is seen in the book of Leviticus: 'You shall not uncover the nakedness of your brother's wife; she is your brother's nakedness' (18. 16). Such action is 'impurity' and results in childlessness (20. 21). It is probable that whilst levirate marriage was permitted for the sole purpose of providing an heir, yet, as a general rule, the practice of marriage with a brother's wife was excluded. (In the verses in Leviticus, mentioned above, there is no indication whether the brother, whose wife is taken, is alive

---

[10] J. Morganstern, *Hebrew Union College Annual*, vii, 1930, p. 169 (cf. pp. 170f.).
[11] *Sacred Books of the East*, xxv (*The laws of Manu*, tr. by E. Buhler), 1886, ix. 59f.; pp. 337f. cf. ix. 69f.

or dead. If the brother is alive, then sexual relations would be excluded as a form of adultery—to which these verses may well refer.) Later Judaism interpreted levirate marriage as a device by which a man could get rid of his brother's childless wife when he inherited the brother's property. Levirate marriage may not always have required full marriage. It was not required in the case of Judah and Tamar, whereas, in the case of Boaz and Ruth, full marriage took place. As the monogamous rule became firmer in Israel, so full marriage with the brother-in-law or next-of-kin would become more generally accepted.

When a man married, he and his wife formed, not merely a physical unit but a psychic unity. This unity would be disturbed if a man entered into further physical relationships of an intimate nature, which could not be reconciled with it. This would happen when a man took his own wife and also his son's wife. The latter was forbidden as incest (Lev. 20. 12). Similarly, a man was forbidden to take a woman and her mother (Lev. 20. 14). Two different intimate relations by a man to the same woman created social chaos. Similarly, a woman could not stand in two different intimate relations with the same man. The family as a unit had to be safeguarded and perpetuated.

The term 'intimate' in this context refers to kinship relationship rather than physical intercourse as such. If physical intercourse between a man and two women (who were themselves closely related) took place, then an emotional situation was liable to take place within the family circle, which would be faced with continual conflict. To prevent such situations arising, certain degrees of proximity of kinship were prohibited from marriage with each other. These prohibitions no doubt also helped to keep apart and ensure respect between age-groups. A man was not permitted to marry his father's wife nor the wife of his father's brother nor the wife of his mother's brother. These women already stood in an intimate relationship with the man within the family circle and to introduce such a new relationship would create difficult psychic disturbances for all concerned. Similarly, a man was forbidden to enter into physical intercourse with his own sister (the daughter of his own father and mother). The penalties enjoined depend upon the proximity of the relationship. If a man marries his mother or daughter-in-law, they shall be put to death. But if a man marries the wife of his brother or his father's brother, then the marriage will prove childless (Lev. 20. 11-21). Certain relationships are not mentioned in the record in Leviticus. Marriage with the wife of one's mother's brother is permitted in a patriarchal society, in which the relationship through the mother has become weaker. Also, there is no mention of the marriage of a man with his daughter. This may be due to an accidental omission or to the fact that such endogamous marriage within the kinship group would strongly militate against the well-being of the group, so that it was not even considered worthy of mention. These arrangements for the family belong to the Priestly source, which probably may be dated in the late 5th century B.C. However, it is probable that the material in these marriage laws dates from a much earlier period, since the necessity to establish the stability of the family must have been felt from a very early period.

2. *The significance of covenant-law*

Every community has its norms by which it can survive. In due time, the practice of kinship-revenge for bloodshed can cause chaos unless some limitation is placed on continual reciprocal revenge. The family's instinct of self-preservation could not permit the death of a kinsman by the violence of a member of another group without compensation. The extent of the compensation was determined by a person or group which was acceptable, as a court of appeal, by both parties. Whilst each kinship-group was independent this was difficult but as groups became knit together, it became possible within the larger community to establish norms of wider acceptance. Thus law came into being. 'A social norm is legal if its neglect or infraction is regularly met, in threat or in fact, by the application of physical force by an individual or group possessing the socially recognized privilege of so doing.'[12] Malinowski, in *Crime and Custom in Savage Society*, pp. 20-21, has insisted that law, at least in terms of the 'sum of duties, privileges and mutualities that bind the joint owners to the object (or enterprise) and to each other' existed in primitive societies, like that of the Trobriand Islanders. He would in fact differentiate between 'civil law' and 'criminal law'—between rules of religion, ceremony and etiquette (on the one hand) and those more fundamental ones concerned with life, property and kinship structure (on the other).

[12] E. A. Hoebel, *The Law of Primitive Man* (Oxford, 1954), p. 28.

Whilst early custom, no doubt, lay behind the later legislation of Israel, it is apparent that law served as a foundation from the earliest-known records of the Hebrew people. The faith and organization of the clans of the Hebrews rested on the covenant law which was a central factor in Israel's life. The confederation of twelve clans, all of whom claimed descent from the ancestor Jacob, formed neither a racial nor a national unit but a sacral league, such as the Greeks called an 'amphictyony'. It was a sacral league formed in covenant with Yahweh in the wilderness period. 'The very nature of covenant society requires some concept of law.'[13] The stipulations of the covenant served to regulate the relationships between the people and their God and with one another. Therefore however indefinitely expressed, such stipulations served the purpose of law, to be enforced by those who were regarded as entitled to do so—on the divine or human plane. It has been claimed that 'the Book of the Covenant (Exod. 20-23) . . . goes back at least to the time of entry into the Promised Land and presumably codifies still earlier customs'.[14] Eichrodt further claims that even in such an early period, the Covenant Law not merely gave protection to the community in cases of individual deviation but also indicates the claim made by the Law on the individual. As an attempt was made to apply the stipulations to the day-to-day disputes and grievances, it was inevitable that a legal tradition would develop.

It is not easy to establish how much legislation developed during the pre-monarchic period, though aspects of Pentateuchal law have similarities to second-millenium Mesopotamian law (e.g. the Law of Hammurabi). Alt has pointed out the two major categories of the form of law in the Pentateuch, namely, the casuistic ('if a man . . . then . . .') and the apodictic ('thou shalt/shalt not'[15]). The former is paralleled in many ancient codes whilst the latter is not entirely unique to Israel's code, yet it is particularly characteristic of her code. As the covenant-code, in its apodictic form left many areas of life unregulated, it became necessary to legislate (perhaps to begin a form of case law!) for such areas. In its present form, the Book of the Covenant pre-

---

[13] J. Bright, *A History of Israel*, p. 149.
[14] W. Eichrodt, *Man in the Old Testament*, p. 10.
[15] cf. A. Alt, *Die Ursprunge des israelitischen Rechts* (1934), reprinted in *Kleine Schriften* I, pp. 278-332.

The Hebrew Family during the Wilderness Period 69

supposes the conditions of a settled agricultural community, though it may describe 'normative judicial procedure in the days of the Judges'.[16]

The sacral league, which was bound together by the covenant law, which helped to create as well as to sustain the relationship, operated under conditions that may be seen from the Book of Judges. When danger was imminent from a marauding people, seeking to enter Canaan, as Israel had done, then there arose a judge *(shophet)*, a chieftain upon whom the 'Spirit of the Lord came', like Othniel and Samson (Judg. 3. 10; 14. 6). These war-leaders were chieftains upon whom authority rested because of their strength of soul. These men, like Jephthah and Gideon, acted as counsellors of their fellow-tribesmen and called out the wider federation of clans, when occasion demanded, to repel the foe. Because this leader was deemed to have a charismatic quality, so his people were the receiver of his benefit and any honour given to him was regarded as the confirmation of his call. This is apparent in the case of Saul, who stood in this succession. By his defeat of the Ammonites, he displayed his power of soul and revealed that he was set apart to be the greatest among his people. Whilst he is regarded as the bestower of favours he is to be held in honour but if his honour is not renewed, then he ceases to be chief. The significance of his chieftainship lay in the fact that whilst there were a number of heroes in any particular group of clans, yet the honour belonged to the chief alone for the deeds which they performed. When Joab was about to take the capital of the Ammonites, he sent a messenger to David, saying: 'Now, then, gather the rest of the people together, and encamp against the city and take it; lest I take the city and it be called by my name' (2 Sam. 12. 28). The honour for such a capture should belong to the leader alone and Joab knew that trouble would ensue if he exalted himself at the expense of his chief. His exploits were to redound to the glory of his leader. This was particularly the case, as will be seen, when the leader was Yahweh's Anointed. Such honour belonged as part of the blessing which Yahweh gave. It belonged not merely to the charismatic individual but to his circle. The whole of his community looked to him to maintain his honour for the benefit of all.

When Gideon defeated the Midianites, the Ephraimites who

[16] J. Bright, *ibid.*, p. 151.

were held to be the chief group felt that they had been out-faced by his victory. They felt that the glory which would accrue to his family would exalt them, in wider circles, over themselves. Gideon treated the situation with great tact. Although he had won the major victory, he called out the Ephraimites who captured and killed two princes of the Midianites, namely, Oreb and Zeeb. But the Ephraimites were still angry that they had not been called in to fight in the major battle. Gideon sought to soothe their vehemence by a soft answer. 'What have I done now in comparison with you? Is not the gleaning of the grapes of Ephraim better than the vintage of Abiezer? God has given into your hands the princes of Midian, Oreb and Zeeb; what have I been able to do in comparison with you?' So their anger towards him was abated (Judg. 7. 24; 8. 3).

This episode describes a situation which could be paralleled in a Bedouin encampment. A certain family claims the headship and is held in high honour. If any other family exalts itself by brave exploits, there may arise a conflict of honour between the two families. Gideon was not prepared to challenge the honour of the Ephraimites, for the sake of his clan, the Abiezerites, so he gave the glory and honour to Ephraim. When Jephthah went to fight the Ammonites without the support of Ephraim, he was similarly rebuked and they threatened to burn down his house (Judg. 12. 1). Jephthah responded by attacking Ephraim, of which many were slain. This incident similarly shows their sensitiveness in the matter of honour.

These judges did not necessarily call all the tribes into action but normally looked to their own tribes and neighbouring ones for support against an invader. However, in retrospect, they were regarded as the leaders of the sacral league for the time being and were bound by the law of Yahweh, who gave success to their arms. This loyalty to Yahweh was the result of the covenant which involved stipulations that the Divine Overlord laid upon his subjects. These stipulations were not merely in large and general terms but had to be applied to daily situations. It was inevitable, therefore, that a legal tradition should develop. It is possible that even in the desert, case law developed as necessity arose—as tradition claims in the appointment of the elders (Exod. 18. 13-27), who administered justice and no doubt had other responsibilities. If the Decalogue can be regarded as of early date, i.e. of the wilderness period, it is evident that most of the commandments are stated, with the provision of sanctions, which in most cases involves death (Exod. 21. 15, 17; 22. 20). Theft requires only restitution (Exod. 22. 1-4). Manslaughter is distinguished from murder (Exod. 21. 12-14). These instances taken from the Book of the Covenant, together with many other provisions, may be paralleled in other codes. But the legal tradition, as a whole, grew in the light of customary and traditional law which existed among the various peoples who were absorbed into the structure of Israel—peoples whose legal and social traditions (like those of the patriarchs) were ultimately of Mesopotamian origin. Such justice would be administered by the clan or village elders in accordance with tradition.

The maintenance of justice in old Israel depended on the strength of one's own right arm. If a life was taken by violence, then the soul of the family-unit which had suffered loss must be set at peace by blood-vengeance. A clear instance of such vengeance is seen in the account of Gideon in his treatment of the two Midianite chiefs, Zebah and Zalmunna (Judg. 8. 4-21). Gideon had defeated the Midianite forces and driven them back across the Jordan. He continues to pursue them, however, and succeeds in capturing the two chiefs, Zebah and Zalmunna. When they are brought to him, Gideon asks them the question: 'Where are the men whom you slew at Tabor?' They answered, 'As you are, so were they, every one of them; they resembled the sons of a king.' Then Gideon said, 'They were my brothers, the sons of my mother; as the Lord lives, if you had saved them alive, I would not slay you.' Gideon then turns to his eldest son Jether and says, 'Rise and slay them.' But the youth did not draw his sword; for he was afraid, because he was still a youth. Then Zebah and Zalmunna said, 'Rise yourself and fall upon us, for as the man is, so is his strength.' And Gideon arose and slew Zebah and Zalmunna; and he took the crescents that were on the necks of their camels.

This vivid narrative shows the lack of doubt in the mind of either party concerning what needs to be done. A life or lives have been taken from the blood-kin of Gideon ('the sons of my mother'), therefore the soul of the group has to have vengeance. Double honour would accrue if a mere youth were to strike down these chiefs—a youth would gain a man's honour thereby, so

Gideon offers the duty to his eldest son. But the task makes the youth quail, so his father has to fulfill the duty, taking not only their lives but their valuables as well. Gideon's task was seen to be the positive one of healing the breach made among his kin by these Midianite chieftains. How long this process could continue is not clear, because indefinite blood-feud tends in time to wipe out both groups. The most violent example is Lamech, who kills seventy-seven for one (Gen. 4. 23-4). Such a wrecking of vengeance on one's opponents reveals the extreme importance of ensuring that one's honour is duly avenged. The events in the life of Samson which has so much violence and is reminiscent of the endeavours of Hercules have a bearing on this matter. His attitude to the Philistines is on a tit-for-tat basis. When Samson learns that his Philistine bride had been given to another, by her father, then he replies: 'Now I am quits with the Philistines, when I do unto them mischief!' (Judg. 15. 3).[27] So he caught three hundred foxes and chased them into the standing grain of the Philistines, who duly avenged the deed by burning down the home of his bride and her father. Samson then acts again, smiting them 'hip and thigh with great slaughter'. The Philistines then come to his home to capture him and he is taken prisoner, only to break loose and lay about him with the jawbone of an ass. At length, by the wiles of Delilah, he is overcome by the Philistines who gouge out his eyes. However, he reasserts himself in the end by pleading to Yahweh to give him strength to avenge upon the Philistines just one of his two eyes. This strength is given and he pulls down the pillars of the house where all the lords of the Philistines were feasting, killing them as well as himself. But he has requited his honour and his soul is satisfied. Vengeance is complete and the family is at peace.

Another illustrative example of the importance of honour is seen in the relationship between David and Shimei. When David had to flee before the supporters of Absalom, he was met on the road by a kinsman of Saul, named Shimei, who cursed David as a man of blood and threw stones at him (2 Sam. 16. 5-8). David's misfortune was attributed by Shimei to his treatment of the house of Saul. Despite his followers' desire to cut the man down, David let Shimei continue to treat him so. Later, David returned in triumph and Shimei begged for mercy. In such a day of joy,

[27] Pedersen, ibid., p. 381.

The Hebrew Family during the Wilderness Period 73

David did not wish to mar the occasion by violence, so he forgave Shimei and confirmed it by an oath (2 Sam. 19. 23). However, the insult to David's honour remained. His soul retained a sense of shame through the curse of Shimei which rested upon him. It would have been possible for David to have nullified the curse by avenging himself upon Shimei but this was not possible because he had given his oath not to take his life. To be cursed as a 'man of blood', moreover, was a breach not merely on David himself but also on David's kin. As David could not act, it fell to his son to take action for him. David's charge to Solomon included the clearing-up of debts of honour left by David (1 Kgs. 2. 5-9).

Among these debts, there was the settlement with Shimei, about whom David said to Solomon, 'You are a wise man; you will know what you ought to do with him.' Solomon called Shimei to him and forbade him to leave the precincts of Jerusalem, adding that if Shimei did so, the punishment would be death. To take responsibility away from himself, Solomon then calls on Shimei to confirm by oath that if Shimei leaves the city, his blood will be on his own head. (Presumably Solomon knew that some occasion would arise when Shimei would wish to leave the city and then Shimei would be in his power.) Three years passed and then, one day, Shimei learned that two of his slaves had run away to Achish of Gath. Shimei went to Gath to find his slaves and duly brought them back to the city. However, King Solomon had learned of his absence from the city and summoned Shimei to appear before him. Solomon rebuked Shimei for breaking his own oath and then reminded him how he had spoken evil of David. 'You know in your own heart all the evil that you did to David my father; so the Lord will bring back your evil upon your own head. But King Solomon shall be blessed, and the throne of David shall be established before the Lord for ever.' Then the king instructed Benaiah who went out and struck down Shimei and he died (1 Kgs. 2. 39-46). It was a triumph for Solomon's wisdom to clear the family's escutcheon in this way. Solomon had not incurred guilt because the man was bound by his own oath but in his destruction, peace had been restored to David's soul. As the responsibility is shared by the family as a unit and the unit is regarded as the extension of the man's own personality, so the man's children can restore a loss to his personality.

The demand for justice is one with the demand for vengeance, since fertility and blessing depend upon justice. When honour has been violated or an oath broken, blessing cannot return to the family or the group until the person violated receives satisfaction and is willing to restore blessing to the offender. Justice unrequited can only bring disaster and misfortune.

Instances of such vengeance occur from time to time in the Old Testament so it is not possible to give a detailed account of all. Some narratives in the life of David belong to the early years of the kingdom yet they bear on them the stamp of old Israel—the practices of an earlier age, from a nomadic and pastoral age into an urban-agricultural one. There is little doubt that such accounts from the family-life of David reflect practices which long existed among the clans of the tribes of Israel and Judah and so throw light on the earlier period.

During the reign of David, there was once a famine for three successive years. After consulting the Lord, David learned that his predecessor, Saul, had incurred blood-guiltiness by killing some of the Gibeonites. These Gibeonites formed part of a remnant of the Amorites, whom the Israelites had sworn to spare from destruction. So David said to the Gibeonites, 'What shall I do for you? And how shall I make expiation (atonement), that you may bless the heritage of the Lord?' The Gibeonites answered that they did not want silver or gold, nor did they want to claim any man of Israel. So David asked again, 'What do you want me to do for you?' They replied: 'The man who consumed us and planned to destroy us, so that we should have no place in all the territory of Israel, let seven of his sons be given to us, so that we may hang them up before the Lord at Gibeon on the mountain of the Lord.' The king agreed to do this and handed over the two sons (Armoni and Meribbaal), which Rizpah bare to Saul, together with five sons of Merab, the daughter of Saul. In the normal state of affairs, Jonathan's son (as the eldest) would have been offered to the Gibeonites but David had a Yahweh-oath between Jonathan and himself, so he spared Mephibosheth, Jonathan's son. Therefore to make up the demand of the Gibeonites, David had to consider other possibilities. Saul's sons had died in battle on Mount Gilboa with their father and in opposition to David. Therefore, it was necessary to find sons from a daughter of Saul, since they would serve to wipe out the breach caused

The Hebrew Family during the Wilderness Period 75

by Saul. There has been some controversy over the significance of the time of their death—'they were put to death in the first days of harvest, at the beginning of barley harvest' (2 Sam. 21. 9). Did their death coincide with some ancient fertility rite connected with the first days of harvest?

This incident is followed by another fragment which appears to be a strange contrast. After having permitted the sons of the house of Saul to be hanged by the Gibeonites, David then hears that Rizpah, the concubine of Saul, had sought to show respect to the bones of her sons by Saul, David therefore sends to Jabesh-Gilead, whose men had stolen the bones of Saul and Jonathan and has the bones buried in the family tomb of the house of Kish, in Zela, in the land of Benjamin. Thus honour will rest upon David and his house for such respect and Yahweh will give his blessing. There is only one reference of vengeance being taken on a tribe (Judg. 19-21) when Benjamin supported the town of Gibeah against the rest of Israel and was defeated. Normally, vengeance was a matter for the family as a unity.

However, there is evidence that vengeance could take place within the family, as in the case of Absalom, who avenged the seduction of his blood sister Tamar, by killing his half-brother, Amnon, who had seduced her. Yet such behaviour dispelled peace from the family and Absalom had to flee to his mother's family (2 Sam. 13) until at length his father was persuaded to let him return. The wise woman who persuaded the king had, however, to take upon herself the peril of receiving a slayer of a brother into the family circle. 'On me be the guilt, my lord the king, and on my father's house; let the king and his throne be guiltless' (2 Sam. 14. 9).

Such instances throw light on the nature of early conceptions of justice. Vengeance is considered to be the right of the party offended, the party being understood to be the family group. On such a group basis, there is need for a go-between, who is known in the Old Testament as the *go'el*, the next-of-kin who has to uphold the family name. He is the one who, by levirate marriage, has to continue the family name and uphold his brother's honour, marrying the widow of the deceased brother to raise up children for him. This man is the restorer of the family's fortunes and the Law laid down the order of sucession, namely, 'If a man dies, and has no son, then you shall cause his inheritance to pass to his daughter. And if he has no daughter, then you shall give his inheritance to his brothers. And if he has no brothers, then you shall give his inheritance to his father's brothers. And if his father has no brothers, then you shall give his inheritance to his kinsman that is next to him of his family, and he shall possess it' (Num. 27. 8-11). It is therefore understandable why Zimri, who seized the throne of Israel, took the violent step of wiping out every male kinsman of the house of his predecessor (1 Kgs. 16. 11). No *go'el* remained to take vengeance on him for his action. However, other families might see fit to hold the same ambition as he did to his detriment. Each family had its honour to uphold and if any damage is done, then restoration must take place. This served as a mode of its survival.

Together with the law of restoration, there was another principle operative in early law, namely, the law of retaliation *(lex talionis)*. This also is set forth in the Book of the Covenant and emphasizes that individual retribution for misdeeds was recognized from the wilderness days. 'When men strive together . . . if any harm follows, then you shall give life for life, eye for eye, tooth for tooth, hand for hand, foot for foot, burn for burn, wound for wound, stripe for stripe' (Exod. 21. 22-25). This law is later reiterated in Deuteronomy 19. 21 and in Leviticus 24. 20, where it is expressly stated: 'When a man causes a disfigurement in his neighbour, as he has done it shall be done to him, fracture for fracture, eye for eye, tooth for tooth; as he has disfigured a man, he shall be disfigured.' This principle goes beyond that of restoration. It rests on a balance of right or justice for its own sake. On this basis, it is important that the unjust one should be punished as much as the offended one should be repaid. Beside any psychic adjustment, it is the qualitative measure of an action that is taken into account.

Such a conception indicates that a legal state exists between parties and that the unlimited right to take what you can is now restricted in the interest of the wider community. It is probable that this development was due to older codes of law, in particular, those of Babylonia, which were spread through the cities of the Fertile Crescent. The Assyrian Code acts on a similar principle and the Israelite wording is practically verbatim with parts of the Code of Hammurabi of Babylon (c. 1680), an Amorite document which reflected other older legal traditions and which had provisions shared by the other Amorite kingdoms of Mesopotamia. In contrast, the Hittite law was based on social status, so when a freeman was injured, four men had to be handed over for bondage, whilst even for the death of a slave two men had to be given.

The claim that justice should be done was to have important repercussions upon the thought of Israel. If vengeance is seen as a claim for justice, then there arises the problem of the criterion for justice. Thus, the covenant-law (together with the wider conception of law itself) came to be regarded as the province of God, on which it was beyond the wit of man to trespass. Justice as the preserve of the gods is also prominent in Greek thought. In the thought of Israel, justice belonged to Yahweh and he was above both parties. If an offender had over-reached himself by his act, then a complement was needed to restore the balance, to bring back wholeness or totality to the situation. The retaliation becomes a part of the restoration, in a negative way. Whereas in the past, the restoration is seen as a rooting out of violation (by killing the offender), now in the retribution, a limb or an organ is taken from the offender in return. The offender in place of wholeness receives weakness.

Thus, the wilderness days saw the beginnings of the social arrangements, which were to take firmer shape in the course of Israel's history. The older forms of law came to be replaced by new codes, as a more humanitarian climate of thought arose and as Israel's faith moulded the older codes. One of the most important factors in the moulding of her law was the relationship between Yahweh and Israel. Covenant-law served to shape the growth of legal codes. Social chaos was avoided by the ordered arrangement between groups within the community, especially the family groups. The date of some of these codes is not always clear but their place and importance within the community is beyond doubt. Some of them were of later development but a reference to certain principles within them is in place within this context. Significant in this respect is the law of manslaughter, which is differentiated from murder. Justice is to be upheld because this belongs to Yahweh and must be acceptable to him. In later times, vengeance must be left to him alone as he knew best.

There is reference to the distinction between manslaughter and deliberate murder as early as the Book of the Covenant. 'Whoever strikes a man so that he dies shall be put to death. But if he did not lie in wait for him, but God let him fall into his hand, then I shall appoint for you a place to which he may flee. But if a man wilfully attacks another to kill him treacherously, you shall take him from my altar, that he may die' (Exod. 21. 12-14). The place of refuge was the local altar to which a man fled for protection, taking hold of the two horns of the altar, as Adonijah did, when he feared the vengeance of Solomon (1 Kgs. 1. 50). It was the responsibility of the *go'el*, the avenger, to drag the murderer away from the altar to despatch him in vengeance for his crime. But if the man died inadvertently, 'as when a man goes into the forest with his neighbour to cut wood, and his hand swings the axe to cut down a tree, and the head slips from the handle and strikes his neighbour so that he dies' (Deut. 19. 5), then the man responsible is not worthy of death but can flee for protection, in earlier times, to the local altar but later, to a city of refuge, of which three were named in the land of Israel (Deut. 4. 41-43).

The distinction made in Israelite law between murder and manslaughter is attributed by Pedersen to 'the peculiar mixture of Arabian and Babylonian types which Israel represents'.[18] In his view, the primitive law of restoration, with unlimited blood-vengeance, belongs to the Arab-Bedouin heritage, whilst the law of retaliation comes from the Babylonian-Amorite heritage. The distinction existed in Hittite law and in Assyria, so it may well be claimed that Israel adopted the law of retaliation both as a strand in her earlier Semitic history as well as part of the Canaanite codes in the land in which she settled. There is little doubt that the establishment of the cities of refuge became necessary, when the drive towards centralization of worship caused the destruction of the high-places of local fame.

The Deuteronomic Code which appointed the three cities of refuge is widely attributed to the 7th century, possibly with a close connection to the reform in religion under Josiah, King of Judah, in 621 B.C. This view advanced by de Wette, Graf and Wellhausen, has been contested by other scholars, R. H. Kennett, A. C. Welch and E. Robertson, but most other views present

[18] J. Pedersen, *ibid.*, I-II, p. 395

The Hebrew Family during the Wilderness Period 79

greater difficulties than the Graf-Wellhausen one.[19] Certainly the removal of the sanctuaries laid down in the Deuteronomic Code made necessary an alternative place for the fugitive to seek protection. This protection was further widened in the later period, if we may trust the record of the Priestly Code, which refers to six cities of refuge, three on each side of Jordan (Josh. 20; Num. 35. 9-29). These passages give further details, namely, that the fugitive must be examined and his case decided through witnesses, of which there must be at least two; if he is not guilty, he may live in the city of refuge, beyond which he is ever open to the hand of the avenger. On the death of the high priest of that time, he is permitted to return to his own home town without fear of further vengeance. Whilst this Priestly record in its present collected form dates from a post-Exilic period, there is little doubt that much within it (including the material mentioned above) dates from a much earlier period and was incorporated by the Priestly writers when they brought together the narratives of the history of their people.

Within this law of retaliation, another principle is also operative however. This is the principle that, in the case of man, life must be given for life but not simply on the ground of blood-vengeance or retaliation but on the ground that to take a man's life was to deface the Lord's image. In the Priestly record, this principle is assigned as early as the Flood. In the blessing of Noah, there is the warning: 'Whoever sheds the blood of man, by man shall his blood be shed; for God made man in his own image' (Gen. 9. 6). In this same passage, men are warned against the life of creatures, i.e. the consumption of the blood. 'Only you shall not eat flesh with its life, that is, its blood' (verse 4). This warning against the blood, which belongs to Yahweh-Elohim alone (Elohim in the above passage), it reiterated in the legal codes (Lev. 17. 10-13). Because the blood of a man is so precious, no ransom is acceptable for a murderer but he must be put to death (Num. 35. 31f.). The blood, which is the life, belongs to God and so can only be atoned for by life. A very much later passage, in the Book of Jubilees, brings out this fact clearly. 'Take no gift for the blood of man, that it is not to be shed unexpiated, without punishment; for the blood which is shed maketh the

[19] G. W. Anderson, A Critical Introduction to the Old Testament (1959), pp. 40-4.

earth sin, and the earth cannot be cleansed of the blood of man except by his blood who shed it. And take no gift and no satisfaction for the blood of man. Blood for blood, that thou mayest be acceptable to the Lord, the supreme God' (21. 19f., cf. 7. 33). In this passage the act of retaliation has become righteous, as the shedding of man's blood is clearly seen as sin and therefore has to be expiated before God.

Whilst a gift may not be accepted in satisfaction for blood, as the Gibeonites refused to accept silver or gold (2 Sam. 21. 4), yet gifts could expiate other offences. When Abimelech returned Sarah unscathed to Abraham, he also sent a gift of slaves and cattle to cover his offence (Gen. 20. 16). This quit him of any further claim, which Abraham or Sarah might make upon him ('and before everyone you are righted'). Such a gift may also be seen as part of himself, so that if an owner has a bull who kills a man, the owner pays a ransom for his own soul in compensation (Exod. 21. 30). The psychical basis is present in early law in the Book of the Covenant.

There is unfortunately too little evidence as to the judicial proceedings in early Israel. It is clear that such procedure as there was had a close connection with the local sanctuary. Therefore, when a crime was committed and the criminal was not known, then a curse was pronounced on him before the altar (1 Kgs. 8. 15) but such a curse might also be pronounced elsewhere (Judg. 17. 2). It was no doubt the common practice for the two parties to appear before the priest and plead their case. He would then have to determine justice between the accuser and the accused. However, in the decision, it was recognized that psychic factors were operative—an inner law which found expression in the oath. If a man told the truth, then his soul received strength but if he lied, then his soul became disordered and he would be struck down by misfortune.

The swearing of the oath was not merely the concern of the individual as his family would (often literally) stand behind the individual to support him. In some cases, the people of the township would be called on to swear an oath to purge them of the charge of shedding innocent blood (Deut. 21. 7). The force of such an oath is illustrated in the case of a woman, who is accused of adultery. She is made to drink water, which is charged with a curse, then she herself takes the oath of the curse, to the effect that if she lies, her body may swell and her thigh fall away (Num. 5. 11-31). There is little doubt that, apart from any other factor, psychological factors were operative to bring such issues to pass in these cases, as missionaries among primitive peoples, e.g. the Bantus, have observed. When the oath had been taken, then the judge's task was completed. Moreover if the guilt was established, then the judge had to determine what the restitution or restoration should be. Sometimes, the priests acted as judges, as has been mentioned, in which case their decision was regarded as the decision of God (Exod. 18. 16; 1 Sam. 2. 25). Out of a common respect for justice and the efforts of the violated to have their rights accepted, there arose in a free manner the Israelite judicial system of later times.

CHAPTER FIVE

HEBREW SOCIETY UNDER THE MONARCHY

1. *Yahweh's overlordship in the sacral league of clans. The place of the judges as charismatic leaders to unite the league against invaders. The rise to power of the Philistines and their threat to Israel.*
2. *The rise of the human kingship in Hebrew society. Evidence of resistance to the conception of a human king. Grounds for resistance—from prophetic and priestly quarters. The human king as the representative of Yahweh, as seen in charismatic gifts. Saul, son of Kish, as a bridge between the old and the new.*
3. *The rise of David. His relationship with Saul. The gift of the blessing. David's devotion to Yahweh—with resultant success. The rise of the close relationship between the heir of the Davidic line and Yahweh. The Spirit's action in David's work. The righteousness demanded of the Davidic king, as seen in the 'royal psalms'.*
4. *The significance of Mount Zion. The close link between this sanctuary and the royal house of David. The king's place in the religious cultus. The two priesthoods of the Ark and of Mount Zion. Their conflict and the triumph of the Zadokite priesthood of Zion.*
5. *The vital place of the king's role in social affairs as well as in the natural order. The royal concern with justice—in Near Eastern Kingdoms and in Israel. Justice as dispensed by the elders and the priests. The king's place as the focus of the life of the nation.*

CHAPTER FIVE

HEBREW SOCIETY UNDER THE MONARCHY

FROM the beginning of her history as a nation, Israel's God was Yahweh. When Israel left Egypt, her faith was communicated or mediated to her by an outstanding religious genius, the leader Moses, whose personality had its impact on the whole of Israel's later development. From the experience of the sacred mount, this people came forth with certain firm convictions, viz., that they were the chosen people of Yahweh and were bound to him in solemn covenant. Henceforward, Yahweh was their supreme ruler who acted through charismatic leaders in each generation. The solemn covenant which bound them to him was similar to those which other nations accepted—treaties of suzereignty which imposed conditions on the vassal-nation. To express Yahweh's overlordship, certain symbols had significance from an early period—the Ark was deemed to be his throne, the rod of Moses was his sceptre and the sacred Umim and Thummim were his tablets of destiny. This conception of Yahweh's sovereignty over his people which came to her in her early days as a nation remained as a permanent element in her faith—she was an elect people, living under covenant, which made demands as well as offered promises.

Israel in Palestine is seen first of all as a confederation of clans, united in Covenant with Yahweh, who is acknowledged as King. This confederation had its focal point in the sacred shrine where the Ark of the Covenant was housed. This shrine, for much of the early period, was located in Shiloh. There the sacral league (or amphictyony) has its centre, where, in monthly turn, the tribes carried out duties. When particular danger threatened, then a judge *(shophet)* arose, to call out the clans and repel the foe. These leaders were provided by Yahweh to fight his holy war. They were not kings but were his Spirit-filled representatives. The judges were not permanent nor were they able to establish any hereditary rule. They were men 'on whom the Spirit of

Yahweh rushed' (Judg. 3. 10) and had peculiar charismatic gifts (highly enriched personal qualities) which marked them as Yahweh's men or women. The élan of the desert and the wind of the Lord's Spirit marked Israel and her leaders in these days. The confederation may be seen to have consisted in a large number of family units at Sinai. These units formed the nucleus of a community which grew gradually by the addition or accretion of other units, possibly united by earlier blood or kinship ties, which became attached to them. The picture revealed in part in the Book of Judges depicts the life of Israel for the two centuries which preceded the rise of the monarchy. 'The impression one gains—of continual if intermittent fighting, with peaceful interludes alternating with times of crisis both external and internal—is a thoroughly authentic one. It tallies perfectly with archaeological evidence, which shows that the twelfth and eleventh centuries were as disturbed as any in the history of Palestine."¹ Many towns were destroyed and some of them, like Bethel, repeatedly suffered during this period.

The climax came when the Philistines, who had arrived in Palestine within a generation of Israel, embarked on a succession of attacks, which sought to conquer all Canaan. The amphictyony was too loose in organization to meet these attacks and collapsed before the Philistine advance. The Egyptian Empire in Canaan had fallen to pieces, so the way was wide open for a new power to seize the control of Palestine. The Philistines as a ruling aristocracy over a predominantly Canaanite population were eager to seize their opportunity to gain the hegemony formerly held by Egypt. Israel was ill-trained and ill-equipped to meet the onslaught, especially as the Philistines had the monopoly of iron (1 Sam. 13. 19-22).

There is evidence that there was resistance to the conception of a king in Israel. This is clear from the narrative relating to Gideon, who was invited to rule over Israel. He was invited to make his house a royal house but his answer was clear: 'I will not rule over you, and my son will not rule over you; the Lord will rule over you' (Judg. 8. 23). His son, Abimelech, did in fact try to establish kingship for himself by ingratiating himself with his mother's kinsmen in Shechem. He slaughtered his half-brothers, seventy in number, except for Jotham, who escaped.

¹ J. Bright, A History of Israel, p. 154.

Jotham, from the top of Mount Gerizim, narrated the fable about the trees who sought to choose a king from among themselves. The valuable trees—the olive, the fig and the vine—were too occupied with the task of producing fruit and so refused to be rulers because they did not wish to sacrifice their fruitfulness to grow tall to sway over the other trees. Only the small prickly bramble was willing, with the consequence that the good trees had to bend under it and were stunted in growth to avoid various disasters (Judg. 9. 7-15).

With this view of kingship, Jotham caricatures the known local kingships, where the rulers were not men who were exalted by prestige and ability above their fellows but were mere 'demanders', who did not bring blessing by their quality of soul but rather made others stoop to their lowness. This may reflect the type of tyrant who ruled in many a Canaanite city but it can hardly be a true reflection of the leaders in early Israel. In any case, Abimelech was killed in his attempt to rule by violence, so his kingship did not last.

It is probable that the priesthood of Yahweh did not approve of the kingship as they regarded Yahweh as the true king and they were his representatives, together with the prophets who bore a peculiarly close relationship to him. The attitude of the prophets hardened against the kingship in later times but the priesthood became closely identified with the house of David. With the monarchy, a new era of authority opened.

The dislike for the kingship which is evident in the story of Gideon emerges clearly also in the series of narratives which relate to the choice of Saul as king. There is no doubt that a conflation of stories is present in narratives about Saul, as well as in the case of Samuel and of David. The young man, Saul, has the fine qualities of physique and spirit, which Israel desired in their king. Yahweh informed Samuel beforehand that Saul would come to him for help and Yahweh instructed Samuel to anoint Saul as chief over Israel to resist the Philistines. Samuel and Saul shared a sacrificial meal and then, before they parted, Samuel anointed Saul, who received the promise also that 'the spirit of Yahweh shall descend upon thee'. On his journey home, 'God gave him another heart' and he met the prophets and prophesied with them (1 Sam. 9. 1-10, 16).

It is in such accounts that we see the marks of the leadership of the Lord for which Israel looked. The prophets bore their share as they were the 'extension of the Lord's personality' by which Yahweh made his will known but the chief himself had to have charismatic gifts which were outstanding. These were evident in Saul's place among the company of prophets. But even more, it was evident when Saul showed his strength in rousing the tribes of Israel to assist the city of Jabesh-gilead against Nahash, the king of the Ammonites. As in the earlier case of Gideon, so when Saul heard that Nahash had made outrageous demands on Jabesh, then 'the spirit of the Lord came mightily upon Saul', who cut in pieces his oxen and threatened that whosoever did not come out to follow him would be treated in a similar way (1 Sam. 11. 1-7). The awe of the Lord came upon the Israelites who 'came out as one man' to support him and after he had defeated Nahash and the Ammonites, the Israelites went to Gilgal to make Saul king before Yahweh. After this event, Saul proved himself further by opposing the Philistines, who were closely pressing his frontiers and holding back the energies of Israel.

The description of Saul's leadership is more closely allied to the accounts of the 'judges' than to the kingship which came after him, of which David was the true architect. As in the case of Gideon and Jephthah, though possibly over a wider area, yet Saul's authority rested largely on the support of his kinsmen. His right-hand man was Abner, a near relative. He is depicted in the narrative as sitting under the tamarisk, in his own town of Gibeah, surrounded by Benjaminites (1 Sam. 22. 6f.). His success as a war leader drew Israelites over a wide area to look to him for protection. How wide was the extent of his control is not known. His responsibility, under the Spirit of Yahweh, was to preserve the holiness of the Lord's people intact and to this end, Saul placed a vow of abstinence upon the soldiers until victory was secured (1 Sam. 14. 24). In similar fashion, Jephthah made his vow which resulted in the sacrifice of his daughter (Judg. 11. 30-31) at a time when he sought to preserve the Lord's help by sacrifice.

However, whereas the older chief was concerned about preserving the blessing for his family, Saul was concerned about retaining the blessing over Israel. The struggle for the blessing which appeared earlier in the account of Jacob and Esau appears again in the struggle between David and Saul. The blessing of the Lord's favour was deemed to rest upon his chosen-one. One of the most mysterious events in the whole account of Saul's reign is his swift rejection as the Lord's chosen. Within a matter of days, Saul is cast aside by the Lord's prophet (1 Sam. 13. 13-14). The story of his rejection is told in two offences which were ritual ones and offended the Lord's holiness. The first was Saul's disobedience in failing to wait until Samuel came to sacrifice. Saul went ahead and sacrificed on his own (1 Sam. 13. 11f.). The second story gives the description of Saul's victory over the Amalekites. Saul had been instructed by Samuel to destroy the Amalekites. Saul gained the victory but held back part of the spoil, including the king Agag. This spoil had been devoted to Yahweh. For a like offence, Achan was stoned to death under Joshua (Josh. 7. 15, 25). So Saul was rebuked by Samuel who told him, 'to obey is better than sacrifice and to hearken than the fat of rams'. Saul acknowledged his failure and pleaded with Samuel to return with him to sacrifice and to worship the Lord. But Samuel's refusal is final. 'The Lord has torn the kingdom of Israel from you this day, and has given it to a neighbour of yours, who is better than you. And also the Glory of Israel will not lie or repent; for he is not a man that he should repent' (1 Sam. 15. 22-28).

This second narrative has a number of important elements in it. There is little doubt that the story reflects the bias of later ecclesiastical writers who wished to exalt the priest at the expence of the king. The fact that failure came to Saul is attributed to the failure on his part to fulfil the command of Samuel. There was no prohibition on a chief offering sacrifice before battle in the early period, so Samuel's prohibition shows that the writers are more likely to have in mind the sacrificial practice (under a recognized priesthood) of their own post-exilic time. However, there are early elements in the story, in that the king's unwillingness to accept the absoluteness of the *hērem* (ban), by holding back part of the spoil, resulted in placing the king himself under the ban, in the same way as had happened to Achan in the previous period. Whilst there is some doubt about the use of the phrase 'the Glory of Israel', it is probable that it refers to the blessing which rested on the chosen of Yahweh, as an extension of Yahweh Himself. Once the blessing had been removed and the Lord's choice had been given to another, then the lot was cast and

Hebrew Society under the Monarchy

that was that. Saul might regret that events had taken the course which they had but he could do nothing to reverse the decision. In any case, the narrative proceeds with the account of Samuel's obedience. Samuel did go down to Gilgal with Saul and hewed Agag in pieces. Then Samuel parted from Saul for good.

The record of Saul and of his elder son, Jonathan, serve as a prelude and introduction to the king who, above all, was devoted to Yahweh and showed by his achievements that the blessing of Yahweh rested upon him. This is introduced, in particular, by the visit which Samuel makes to Bethlehem. Samuel goes there, on Yahweh's command, to anoint a successor to Saul. He takes with him a heifer for a sacrificial meal and there he invites Jesse and his sons to attend the feast. After meeting the sons of Jesse, one by one, Samuel asks at last for the youngest who is still in the fields where he is looking after the flocks. The youngest son, David, is then anointed in the midst of his brothers and 'the Spirit of the Lord came mightily upon David from that day forward' (1 Sam. 16. 1-13).

Later generations looked back nostalgically to their greatest king, David, in the simple rural background of his youth. Yet this event had special significance in the life of Israel. Previously, in the case of Abraham (with his faithfulness), of Gideon and of Samson (with their exploits), there was a certain measure of recognition by Yahweh for their faithfulness. But in the case of David, there is emphasized his lowest place in the family and the divine choice of him. Yahweh looked on the heart and so David was chosen to lead the people of Yahweh.

There are two accounts of the first meeting between Saul and David—in one account, his bravery against Goliath brought him to the notice of the king (1 Sam. 17) and in the other account, his skill as a musician brought him into king Saul's presence. From the time of their meeting, their relationships fluctuated although Saul's son, Jonathan, never wavered in his loyalty. Eventually, jealousy drove Saul to try to rid himself of David, who became a wandering soldier, accompanied by bands of discontented men, who were willing to throw in their lot with him. Nevertheless, David never took advantage to take Saul's place or Saul's life, even though he had opportunity to do so. This respect for the Lord's anointed remained with him. When Saul sought to capture David among the Wildgoats' Rocks David had his opportunity to get rid of Saul. But his reply to his men is unequivocal, 'The Lord forbid that I should do this thing to my lord, the Lord's anointed, to put forth my hand against him, seeing he is the Lord's anointed' (1 Sam. 24. 6. cf. also 26. 10-11). The blessing which rested on David, he did not have to wrest from Saul. It came from Yahweh and so it became the possession of David without violence on his part. On the other hand, it is probable that Saul was aware that the promise (the blessing) had left him. On the return from the defeat of Goliath, the women came out of the cities, singing and playing their instruments. But their songs make Saul angry, because they sang, 'Saul has slain his thousands, and David his ten thousands'. Saul realized that David's greater victory caused the people to ascribe more to David, so Saul asked himself the question: 'And what more can he have but the kingdom?' (1 Sam. 18. 8). Therefore, henceforth, despite Saul's attempts to place David in danger, David's escape unscathed revealed his possession of the blessing. David explains his view of the matter to Saul when he again had Saul in his hand in the wilderness of Ziph. David offers back to Saul the spear which he had taken from the ground by the head of the king. 'Here is the spear, O king . . . The Lord rewards every man for his righteousness and his faithfulness; for the Lord gave you into my hand today, and I would not put forth my hand against the Lord's anointed. Behold, as your life was precious this day in my sight, so may my life be precious in the sight of the Lord and may he deliver me out of all tribulation' (1 Sam. 26. 22f.). David is aware that as Yahweh had anointed Saul, then it is for the Lord to dispose of him ('As the Lord lives, the Lord will smite him') (1 Sam. 26. 10). If David were to act prematurely, then he might well find himself exposed to Yahweh's wrath and so become open to destruction also. The holiness would be contagious and he would be subject to a like ban. When at length, Saul died on Mount Gilboa, he did so at the hand of an Amalekite upon whom he called to kill him. But David shrank from such action and rather than be held as an accessory in such a deed, he had the Amalekite destroyed (2 Sam. 1. 15).

In their descriptions of the activities of David, the writer or writers reveal the powerful element of devotion to Yahweh, which David showed in his early youth and then later in days of privation and pursuit. This devotion was rewarded by the

Hebrew Society under the Monarchy

kingship and despite his sins, he remained, in the eyes of Israel, the ideal king. Although he was successful, yet he did not depart from his loyalty as was the case with other kings, both in the northern and southern kingdoms. Throughout his days, he remained a devoted servant of Yahweh, so the writer (himself presumably a devoted Yahwist) found no detail of this hero's life lacked interest. With the death of Saul, there was an interlude whilst Ishbosheth, Saul's son, reigned for two years over Israel (2 Sam. 2. 10). But the men of Judah anointed David as their king, until with the death of Ishbosheth all the tribes of Israel came to Hebron to acknowledge David as king (2 Sam. 5. 3). The occasion was made a particularly solemn one, because 'King David made a covenant with them at Hebron before the Lord' and they anointed David king over Israel. David's devotion is seen in the covenant which other kings do not appear to have made. This act of David committed him to act righteously. If he acted otherwise, he could expect disaster as he had committed sin by breaking the covenant with Yahweh.

The significance of this covenant with Yahweh and with the people may in part explain the intense loyalty of the southern tribes to the house of David. In terms of national solidarity, this relationship came to identify the well-being of Israel with loyalty to this particular royal house. This will be made clear in the course of this chapter. But the immediate result for Israel is apparent. With renewed national loyalty to Yahweh and unity under an able king, Israel defeats the Philistines and brings back the ark of God. In the rejoicings which took place with the return of the ark it is made clear that David took his full share. 'David and all the house of Israel were making merry before the Lord with all their might, with songs and lyres and harps and tambourines and castanets and cymbals' (2 Sam. 6. 5). 'And David danced before the Lord with all his might; and David was girded with a linen ephod' (verse 14), so that his wife Michal, the daughter of Saul, 'saw King David leaping and dancing before the Lord; and she despised him in her heart' (verse 16). David then proceeded to offer burnt offerings and peace offerings before the Lord and, having done so, he blessed the people in the name of the Lord of hosts. When he came in to bless his own household, Michal did not hesitate to rebuke him for his lively, if not vulgar, demonstration of his devotion to Yahweh. David's reply is simply that it is fitting that he should show such joy and that he was prepared to lower himself yet further to honour Yahweh. 'And David said to Michal, "It was before the Lord, who chose me above your father, and above all his house, to appoint me as prince over Israel, the people of the Lord—and I will make merry before the Lord. I will make myself yet more contemptible than this"' (2 Sam. 6. 21). Such signal self-offering by David did not go unrewarded. In a negative direction, the Lord of fertility was deemed to have withheld conception from Michal who had no child. In a positive way, 'the Lord gave victory to David wherever he went' (2 Sam. 8. 6), which included the capture of the stronghold of Zion, the fortress of the Jebusites, who had managed to hold off previous Israelite attacks. David captured this stronghold which henceforth was called the city of David. To this place he brought the ark of the Lord and he hoped to build a suitable permanent dwelling-place for the ark. But the loyalty of David is recognized most clearly in the speech of Nathan, the prophet, who promises, from the Lord, that 'your house and your kingdom shall be made sure for ever before me; your throne shall be established for ever' (2 Sam. 7. 16). The whole of this chapter is the prophetic recognition which is given to such a loyal servant of Yahweh whose blessing so obviously rests upon him. This whole incident has important repercussions for later times as the king's part in priestly and sacred ceremonies is deemed to be the fulfilment of the promises made to David. The people came to regard the royal house of David as necessary for their survival.

Two matters call for special consideration. The first of these is the relationship between the king and Yahweh. It is clear that the relationship is very intimate because it is the king who leads his people in worship by offering sacrifice and prayer on the solemn important occasions in the national life and also it is the king, who during the four hundred years of the Davidic dynasty himself superintends the organization of the cultus in all its aspects, whether it is David who brings the Ark into the newly captured city of David or Josiah undertaking a thorough-going reform.[2] The second matter is the significance of Mount Zion. From the evidence of the Egyptian Execration Texts of the XII dynasty (2000-1780 B.C.), in which the name of Jerusalem occurs, the city had a thousand years of history before it was captured by

[2] A. R. Johnson, *Sacral Kingship in Ancient Israel* (1955), p. 12.

Hebrew Society under the Monarchy 93

David. Whilst the capture of the city had significance as an example of David's prowess and political foresight, there is reason to believe that the city had its own Jebusite cultic traditions, which made their own contribution to the importance of Jerusalem as the city of David and the earthly abode of the heavenly king.[3]

The king's appointment by Yahweh was expressed by the use of the familiar rite of anointing the king, which David received on three occasions (1 Sam. 16. 13; 2 Sam. 2. 4; and 5. 3). Solomon also was anointed (2 Kgs. 1. 39). The sacred commission came from Yahweh Himself and was communicated by the word of both prophet and priest who acted as Yahweh's messengers.[4] This rite was no doubt regarded as a channel whereby the king was endowed with the Spirit *(Ruach)* of Yahweh—a symbolic action which reminded the people of Israel that Yahweh had imbued the king with power and so it would be manifest in the king's character. 'The special endowment of the Spirit is clearly associated with the rite in question, when it is said of the founder of the Davidic dynasty that, on his being chosen for this high office: 'Samuel took the horn of oil and anointed him in the midst of his brethren; and the Spirit of Yahweh burst upon David from that day forward' (1 Sam. 16. 13).[5] Aubrey Johnson has shown clearly that from the first the activity of the Spirit was regarded as an extension of the Personality of Yahweh. Therefore, such activity was not considered to be an impersonal force nor was restricted to exhibitions of personal prowess, whether by Joseph, Gideon or Samson. When the spirit came upon David, the result was that David became like the divine 'Angel' or 'Messenger' *(malak)*, with whom he is compared for his foresight (2 Sam. 14. 17, 20), and 'must himself have been regarded as a potent extension of the divine Personality'.[6] The sacrosanct nature of the king's person would no doubt arise out of this intimate connection. David's unwillingness to act against the life of Saul has already been noted and the cursing of a king could be treated as though it were the cursing of God (1 Kgs. 21. 10, 13).

[3] Ibid., p. 29.
[4] A. R. Johnson, *The One and the Many in the Israelite Conception of God* (1942), pp. 36f.
[5] A. R. Johnson, *Sacral Kingship*, p. 13.
[6] cf. A. R. Johnson, ibid., 14. cf. *The One and the Many*, pp. 32ff.

A further expression of the close bond between the Davidic king and Yahweh is found in the short poem, known as 'The Last Words of David' (2 Sam. 23. 1-7). This poem is similar to the so-called royal psalms, which point up the highly important place of the king in the social order as well as in the cultic order. Like Psalm 72, this poem shows the high ideal of righteousness which came to be associated as necessary for the House of David for survival. It also reveals that this ideal of righteousness was not man-made but rooted in a covenant, which was clearly 'ordered in all things and secure', between David (the founder of the dynasty) and Yahweh (the nation's God). The oracular nature of the Words form the natural outpouring of the anointed leader of Israel, who was inspired and upheld by the Spirit of Yahweh. The righteousness which is expected of the Davidic king is clearly set forth in Psalm 72 as this king has 'to defend the cause of the poor of the people, give deliverance to the needy, and crush the oppressor' (verse 4).

Another Psalm which comes within the category of Royal Psalms is Psalm 132, in which the first ten verses are a hymn beseeching Yahweh to continue His favour towards the house of David. The rest of the psalm (vv. 11-18) is an oracular utterance in which there is a reiteration of Yahweh's promise that He will keep His covenant with David and will bless His chosen Zion. This psalm may be associated with a dramatic commemoration or liturgical re-enactment of the occasion when the Ark was brought to Zion and so of the foundation of the Jerusalem cultus in close association with the establishment of the Davidic dynasty.

The covenant between Yahweh and David is treated at greater length in Psalm 89. This Psalm repeats the promises given elsewhere—with the everlasting covenant between Yahweh and the descendants of David, with 'righteousness and justice as the foundation of his throne', but with the further promises that Yahweh's chosen Messiah (Anointed One) shall not merely be the servant of Yahweh but also Yahweh's son and also be Yahweh's 'first-born, the highest of the kings of the earth' (verses 26-7). These are promises that are found elsewhere in the Psalter and came to take an important place among the hopes of Israel.

Despite these promises, there is ample evidence that the Davidic kings were reminded that they needed to be humble for

Hebrew Society under the Monarchy

they were human, compassed about with the cords of death (Ps. 18. 4) and subject to humiliation (Ps. 22. 14f). As vice-regents of the divine King, they could not depend on their own strength but looked to Yahweh for strength in time of need. Whilst it was necessary for the earthly king to rule in righteousness, this duty rested on the obligation to exalt the divine King, whose praise was sung in so many of the Psalms (96, 103, 110). There has been much discussion whether the Hebrews employed the conception of such a divine King as early as the settlement in Canaan. This is uncertain because of the lack of definite evidence regarding the date and historical value of certain important passages, namely, Exod. 15. 18; 19. 6 (JE); Num. 23. 21 (JE); Deut. 33. 5; 1 Sam. 8. 7; 12. 12 and Judges 8. 23. It appears, however, that whether or not the use of the term 'King' *(melek)* was used for Yahweh in the pre-monarchic period, it was used in the days of the early monarchy, reminding the royal house that they were not lords unto themselves but were subject to the heavenly King, to whom Israel truly belonged by choice and election.

This connection between Yahweh and the royal house of David was strengthened by the cultic traditions which were associated with Mount Zion, which came to be viewed as the earthly abode of the divine King. Whilst David had a great victory in gaining this fortress, he does not appear to have destroyed the Jebusites, who dwelt there. He paid a fair price to Araunah the Jebusite for his threshing floor, in order that he might erect an altar to Yahweh (2 Sam. 24. 16ff.). As his capital, this city stood, like Washington, D.C., between the north and the south, on neutral ground, identified neither with his own southern tribes of Judah nor with the northern tribes of Joseph, who had supported Saul. This city had its own traditions and no doubt brought them into the on-going stream of the life of Israel. It is not clear how old is the story of the meeting of Abram and Melchizedek, king of Salem (Gen. 14. 18-20), which bears the marks of an early priestly attempt to justify payment of tithes by Israel to the Jebusite priesthood. Joshua had opposition from Adoni-zedek, the king of Jerusalem, which resulted in the defeat of this king who was put to death (Jos. 10. 1-27). At a later date, Ezekiel made a scathing reference to the origins of this city, which had been so exalted in the annals of Israel. 'Your origin and your birth are of the land of the Canaanites, your father was an Amorite and your mother a Hittite' (Ezek. 16. 3). Yet the names Melchizedek and Adoni-zedek were used as divine appellatives and the term used for the God of Melchizedek, namely, 'God most High' (Elyon) may well be the appellation of the high God who had been worshipped in the ancient Jebusite stronghold, among the Canaanites, prior to the city's capture by David. The tutelary god of Jerusalem may well have been the god Salem.

David was faced with certain cultic problems when he brought the Ark into the former Jebusite city. The Ark had its priests, who had cared for the ancient sanctuary in Shiloh (1 Sam. 14. 3; 22. 9). With the Philistine destruction of the sanctuary at Shiloh, the priestly families connected with that sanctuary continued to serve as priests at Nob. When Saul as king discovered that the priests at Nob had helped David a rebel, Saul then instructed Doeg the Edomite to destroy the priests. The entire city of Nob, called the city of priests, was put to the sword. One of the sons of the priest Ahimelech, a man named Abiathar escaped to David, who promised to safeguard him against further violence (1 Sam. 22 9-23). Henceforward the lives of David and Abiathar were linked in peril and in success.

When David entered the Jebusite city, there was presumably a priesthood connected with the local shrine—a Jebusite cultus with its worship of the 'most High' and its high-priestly order of Melchizedek, which had its own ritual and mythology. Whereas the older priesthood of Shiloh and Nob were represented by the priest Abiathar, so the original priesthood in Jerusalem appears to have been represented by Zadok, the priest. In the various lists of royal officials, the names of these two men are found together as 'Zadok and Abiathar were priests' (2 Sam. 20. 25; 19. 11).

However, there is reason to believe that conflict naturally arose between such ancient priestly families. The old family which had cared for the Ark since wilderness days would resent the services of those who claimed long service in the ancient sanctuary in Mount Zion. Under David, the two priestly families appeared to have continued to work under royal patronage, as both were joined to the king by personal bonds of devotion. But David appears to have leaned more heavily on Zadok for support, especially when both Zadok and Abiathar fled with him before the advance of Absalom (2 Sam. 25. 24-29). However,

Hebrew Society under the Monarchy

David instructed the two priests and their respective sons to return to Jerusalem with the Ark.

When it became clear that David's life at last was drawing to a close, open conflict between the priests took place. Abiathar, who had supported David in the early days and had been with him in Hebron, supported as David's successor, Adonijah, a son who was born in the early period (2 Sam. 3. 4; 1 Kgs. 1. 7). Whilst it cannot be proved that Zadok did in fact belong to the Jerusalemite priesthood of an earlier period, yet it is clear that when Adonijah's revolt took place, Zadok took the part of Bathsheba, who belonged to Jerusalem and whose son Solomon had been born to her during the period when David ruled in the city. It was in fact an open breach between those who belonged to the Davidic period of old Israel and those who belonged to the new era, the day inaugurated by the capture of Jerusalem and setting the Ark there.

David clearly showed his hand by calling upon Nathan the prophet and Zadok the priest to anoint Solomon king over Israel (1 Kgs. 1. 34). Solomon was duly established on the throne and did nothing straightway against those who had sought the throne. However, as on other occasions, Solomon bided his time until another opportunity presented itself. He also waited until David had died and he was no longer held by the oaths that David had given. It was not long, however, before Adonijah, who still claimed that the kingdom was his (1 Kgs. 2. 15), sought to secure the wife of his late father. This provided Solomon with a ground to claim that Adonijah really sought the throne and so Adonijah was put to death. At the same time, Solomon got rid of Joab, the captain of the host, who had supported Adonijah, and replaced him by Benaiah, the son of Jehoiada. But Abiathar the priest also came under suspicion because of his earlier connections with Adonijah. Therefore, Solomon 'thrust out Abiathar from being priest unto the Lord' (1 Kgs. 2. 27), sending him back to his family fields at Anathoth. Abiathar's life was spared because he had carried the Ark of the Lord God before David and because he had shared all the afflictions which came upon David. However, the sequel is clear, 'Zadok the priest did the king put in the room of Abiathar' (1 Kgs. 2. 35) and among the princes of Solomon was 'Azariah, the son of Zadok, the priest' (1 Kgs. 4. 2).

The conflict between Zadok and Abiathar may serve to highlight a change which was taking place in the social and religious life of Israel, namely, that after the capture of Jerusalem, David found in the Jebusite cultus a ritual and mythology which would prove most fitting to carry out Yahweh's purpose for Israel and to bind Israel more closely to his own royal house. It appears to have been David's intention to build a fitting shrine for the Ark in Mount Zion but the actual fulfillment of this intention fell to the hand of Solomon, whose Temple became the focus of the worship of Yahweh. From henceforth, it appears that the house of Zadok remained the leading priestly family in Jerusalem but this family also sought to associate or apply to itself the ancient pre-Jebusite titles. Whereas in earlier days, it was deemed desirable in Israel to have a priest of the Levites, such as the Levite who was invited to establish the priesthood of Dan (Judg. 18. 30), so in the days of the monarchy in the various towns there were 'the priests, the sons of Levi' who carried out their ministrations. In particular, the priests in Jerusalem are referred to as 'fellow-Levites who stand to minister there before the Lord' (Deut. 18. 7). All priests at this time appear to come within this category, as 'Levitical priests' (Deut. 17. 9, 18). However, by the time of the close of the monarchy and no doubt before, as indicated in Deut. 18. 7., the Zadokite priesthood was regarded as Levitical, whatever may have been its original locus. Thus, we find in the vision of the restored temple of Ezekiel, that there are 'the priests . . . the sons of Zadok, who alone among the sons of Levi may come near to the Lord to minister to him' (Ezek. 40. 46). Later, there is reference to 'the Levitical priests of the family of Zadok' (Ezek. 43. 19) and to 'the Levitical priests, the sons of Zadok' (44. 15), though there is also reference to those 'Levites who went far from me' (44. 10), straying after idols. It might well be part of the policy of David that he brought in some of the older Levitic priests to serve in the new priesthood of the royal cult. The old was grafted on to the new to serve the new age, which dawned with the advent of this favoured son of Yahweh (1 Kgs. 3. 6).

The Temple which Solomon built served the purpose of binding the people together in loyalty, not only to their national deity (Yahweh) (as the amphictyony had done), but also to the sacred royal house, who had gained this ancient sacred site on the Mount Zion for the sanctuary. The dedication of this Temple took place at the celebration of a great autumn festival,[7] namely, the Feast of Tabernacles, when the gift of rain was sought for fertility,[8] but above all, an occasion when Yahweh was worshipped as King, perhaps as universal King (Zech. 14. 16. Verse 9 refers to Yahweh as universal King). On the occasion of this festival, the people dwelt in booths. These booths were interpreted, in later Israel, as a reminder of the wilderness days when Israel dwelt in tents in the desert. It is highly probable however that the agricultural festivals of Canaan came to be adopted by the Israelites and then were re-interpreted by them in the light of their historic traditions. The Feast of Tabernacles may well have been one such festival. A number of Psalms have been associated with this great autumnal celebration, which was celebrated in the Jerusalem Temple during the period of the monarchy. Such Psalms serve as 'enthronement Psalms' to magnify the Kingship of Yahweh, of which Psalms 29 and 95 may be taken as examples.

The first of these two Psalms (No. 29) may have been a hymn of the early Jebusite cultus of Jerusalem which was adapted for use to celebrate the triumph of Yahweh after the capture of the city.[9] The vision of Isaiah may well have been associated with such a celebration (cf. Isa. 6. 1 and Ps. 29. 3-9). Certainly the glory of the Lord filled the Temple for the celebration. The other Psalm (No. 95) exalts the strength of the Lord in His creation and emphasizes Israel's obligations towards Him. The first part of the Psalm takes the form of a call to worship so mighty a Lord (verses 1-7), but in the second part of the Psalm the leader becomes the representative of Yahweh Himself and addresses the people with a warning against apostasy. It has been suggested that the leader may have been a cultic prophet, who served as 'an extension of the divine Personality'. Whether this is the case or not, the first part of the Psalm celebrates that aspect of Yahweh's power which is manifest in creation, which represents the Canaanite tradition and mythology, whilst the second half of the Psalm recalls the experience of the desert wanderings of the Hebrews. In this way, the strands in this Psalm represent two

[7] N. H. Snaith, *Jewish New Year Festival* (1947), p. 47ff.
[8] M. Patai, *Man and Temple* (1947), pp. 24ff.
[9] A. R. Johnson, *Sacral Kingship*, p. 55.

traditions that 'both together formed an important element in Jerusalem during the period of the monarchy'.[10]

If this interpretation of the material does indeed throw light on the actual events in Jerusalem, then this celebration served to remind the king and the people, year by year, of their obligations to the conditions of the covenant. Although we do not know the actual details of the Davidic covenant, yet it is clear that the king became a trustee of the Lord's people. On the one hand, he had intimate approach to Yahweh and came under the influence of his Spirit, yet he remained a man, who, in relationship with his people, remained *primus inter pares*. He ruled over his brethren (Deut. 17. 15, 20). Therefore, whilst the tribal memories of the Sinaitic covenant remained strong, pledging the people to walk in ways of righteousness and truth, a new factor was introduced into this loyalty. If there was to be national prosperity and peace, then the righteousness of the nation must be expressed in the righteousness of the king, who was bound more particularly by his fidelity to Yahweh under the terms of the Davidic covenant. It was the king who had to protect his people. He had to administer justice, namely, he had to make clear for the people the righteousness in Yahweh's laws and to ensure obedience to the laws. As the guardian of the Lord's peace, he had to ensure that right relationships existed between brethren within the borders of his territory. Therefore, consideration needs to be given, in particular, to the royal concern with justice.

The place of the king in the social order was believed to have its repercussions in the natural order. Only by devotion to Yahweh could the king expect to bring prosperity and survival to his people. The 'vitality' of the nation depended on his fidelity. Abundant life for the nation depended on the removal of obstacles both within and without the nation and it lay in the duty of the king to provide such liberty and freedom for his subjects. Thus, in the 'Last Words of David' (to which reference has been made above p. 94), the king claims: 'Will Yahweh not cause to prosper all my help and my desire?' (2 Sam. 23. 5), in which the term 'help' or 'salvation' refers to or represents freedom from whatever interferes with fullness of life.[11]

This responsibility meant that the king was not entirely free

---

[10] A. R. Johnson, *Sacral Kingship*, p. 61.
[11] *Ibid.*, p. 17 (note 5).

Hebrew Society under the Monarchy

to live just as he chose or to enjoy wealth at the expense of his fellows, since he had been raised up under covenant to act as the servant of Yahweh and to promote the well-being of the Lord's people. This responsibility was accepted under the terms by which he became king, namely, under the conditions of the Davidic covenant. Moreover, as the leader of the royal and national cultus, he was called to lead his people to celebrate not only the freedom which Yahweh provided over human foes but also the wider triumph over cosmic forces, namely, Death and Darkness, which enabled Yahweh to create the habitable universe. Out of his success over the cosmic chaos of a primaeval time, Yahweh became enthroned as king among the gods. It was this triumph which was celebrated in the great festival in Solomon's temple, from the 10th until the 6th century, B.C. As the Lord began in overcoming the forces of darkness, so his ultimate will to set men free from all that hinders fullness of life was set forth in ritual drama and mythology.

The ancient cosmogony which looked forward to a 'realized eschatology' was directed in particular towards the ruling member of the house of David. It was upon him that the hopes of Israel rested. He was the focus of the life of the nation as a corporate whole, among whom he must above all be just.

The functions of the king were many as he acted as a vital link between his community and the deity, whose vice-regent he was. Most prominent among these functions was the administration of justice, which required the endorsement of the deity. The king as the representative of his god had to dispense justice and if any other person sought to do so, it was a challenge to the royal authority. The royal duty to dispense justice is evident from the Code of Hammurabi (c. 1700 B.C.):

> 'At that time Anu and Enlil called me by name
> to promote the welfare of the people
> Me, Hammurabi, the worshipful, god-fearing prince;
> to display justice in the land
> to destroy the wicked and the evil...'[12]

[12] *Ancient Near Eastern Texts Relating to the Old Testament*, ed. J. B. Pritchard (1950), pp. 163-180 (Prologue I. 27ff.).

Elsewhere it is Marduk, the god of Babylon, who gives this authority to him:

> 'When Marduk sent me to give the people justice,
> to bring order to the land,
> I established right and justice within the land,
> promoting the welfare of the people...'[13]

The king's duty is set forth in graphic terms. It is he who is

'to stay the strong from oppressing the weak,
to give justice to the orphan and the widow
in Babylon, the city whose head Anu and Enlil raised on high'.[14]

There is evidence also from the Phoenician epigraphic texts that this view of royal responsibility for justice was developed in the Semitic world as a whole. There is, for example, the inscription of Yehimilk, king of Byblos (c. 12th cent. B.C.), in which there is a prayer for the king that his days may be lengthened as he is a 'righteous and upright king'.[15]

In Canaan, the king's responsibility for justice is apparent from the Ras Shamra texts (14th cent. B.C.). These texts are important in this respect as they date from a period far earlier than the Israelite monarchy. In the Legend of Krt, the king is rebuked for his neglect in his duty.

> 'The lad Ysb departs
>   Into his father's presence he enters.
> He lifts his voice
>   and shouts:
> "Hear, O Krt of Te!
>   Listen and be alert of ear!
> Dost thou administer like the strongest of the strong
>   And govern (like) the mountains?
> Thou hast let thy hands fall into negligence
> Thou dost not judge the case of the widow
>   Nor adjudicate the cause of the broken in spirit
>   Nor drive away those who prey upon the poor!

---

[13] Anet, Prologue, v. 15ff.
[14] Ibid., Epilogue, rev. xxiv. 59ff.
[15] Graf Baudissin, *Kurios als Gottesname in Judentum und seine Steele in der Religionsgeschichte*, ed. O. Eissfeldt (1928), iii, pp. 379-463.

Before thee thou dost not feed the fatherless
Nor behind thy back the widow.

. . . . . .

Descend from the kingship that I may rule
From thy sovereignty that I may be enthroned thereon!"[16]

This duty to administer justice which had been the duty of certain judges and officers in the tribes of Israel became the particular responsibility of the king. Yet, in this matter, he represented Yahweh, as justice belonged to the Lord. In the beginning, it was the work of Moses to organize the administration of justice (Exod. 18. 13-23), though the credit for such action is given to his father-in-law, Jethro, the priest of Midian. The rulers appointed over the people were given the responsibility to decide any 'small matter' but every great matter had to be referred to a higher authority. Judges and officers came to be appointed in all the towns when the tribes settled in Canaan (Deut. 16. 18-20). In all cases where homicide, legal right or assault were involved, the parties were required to go to the appointed place, to the priests there and to 'the judge who is in office in those days' (Deut. 17. 8-13). It seems probable that in matters of justice, the practice of tribal justice in the wilderness was carried over into the larger life of the nation as the Israelites became more settled in the land. It is evident also that some places were associated with justice as well as particular people. By a holy well (*en-mishpat*: 'the well of judgement'. Gen. 14. 7) or under a sacred tree (the palm of Deborah: Judg. 4. 5), the judge was given power to speak the proper decision in the cases which were brought before him. The sanctuaries as holy places were associated with judgement as the men of God were there. Prophets were associated with the shrines, where also there were Levites who represented the priestly functions of Moses and Aaron. Among the particular persons, who gave judgement, there were reckoned priests, prophets and other leaders of the people. Noted war-leaders like Deborah fulfilled this duty (Judg. 4. 5). However, it is probable that whilst local elders and leaders did interpret customs for a long period (into the monarchical period), yet at length it was

[16] C. H. Gordon, *Ugaritic Literature* (1949), pp. 82f., lines 39-50, 53-4.

mainly the duty of priests to seek to give such judgements. It was in the sanctuary that oaths were sworn, which were deemed to be holy utterances. When Jephthah became the war-leader of his people, 'he pronounced all his words before Yahweh at Mizpeh' (Judg. 11. 11). The importance of the sanctuary and the priests are expressed in the 'Blessing of Moses', which may well date from the early monarchical period. 'Give to Levi thy Thummin and thy Urim (i.e. the lots of the oracle) to thy godly one . . . They shall teach Jacob thy ordinances *(mishpatekha)* and Israel thy law *(torah)*' (Deut. 33. 8, 10). The standard of Israelite conduct was indeed the law *(torah)*, i.e. the instruction which the priests were supposed to give to the people. Even when the king took over the administration of justice, there is no doubt that he leaned heavily upon the priests.[17] The skill, experience and knowledge of the priests were required to interpret the *mishpat* in Israel, as upon them also the responsibility lay to be the teachers of the *torah* (law).

Nevertheless, it was the peculiar responsibility of the king to see that justice was done. There is reference to the lawlessness which prevailed in Israel before the monarchy was established. 'In those days there was no king in Israel; every man did what was right in his own eyes' (Judg. 17. 6; 21. 25). When David was king, cases were brought to him for judgement. Therefore, when his son Absalom sought to wean away the hearts of the people to make him king, Absalom met the suiters 'beside the way of the gate' and commiserated with them in their legal delays. When these suitors did obeisance to him, Absalom would raise them to their feet and embrace them. 'Thus Absalom did to all of Israel who came to the king for judgement; so Absalom stole the hearts of the men of Israel' (2 Sam. 15. 6).

David's concern with justice is seen in the narrative of the wise woman of Tekoa, who comes to the king pleading her necessity as a widow who has trouble with her sons (2 Sam. 14. 1-20). In similar fashion, Solomon displayed his wisdom in his ability to pass judgement on difficult matters. His treatment of the two harlots who claimed the same child is given as an outstanding example of this wisdom. He ordered that the child in dispute should be hewn in two but his order revealed the true mother

[17] J. Pedersen, *Israel*, III-IV, pp. 160-3.

who was willing to give her child away rather than to see the child destroyed (1 Kgs. 3. 16-28). It was undoubtedly a royal responsibility under each of Solomon's successors to keep harmony in Judah and in Israel by a right judgement in law suits. It is also probable that from time to time reform became necessary as 'time made ancient good uncouth'. This appears to have been the case in the reign of Jehoshaphat, the king of Judah, who appointed certain Levites and priests and heads of families to give judgement 'for the Lord and to decide disputed cases' (2 Chron. 19. 8-11). At an earlier period, a decree of Haremhab (c. 1350-1319) set forth measures to reform the Egyptian judiciary and Jehoshaphat's measures appear to be similar to the earlier Egyptian reforms.[18] Until the Hebrew kingdoms were destroyed, this responsibility for justice remained with the kings.

Whilst it is apparent that justice was the responsibility of the king in all the ancient kingdoms in the Near East, yet it is clear that in Israel the responsibility for justice had a peculiar significance in the light of the king's supremely important place in the social order. The people of Israel were deemed to be a psychic entity, with a corporate personality of their own. This psychic entity found its local focus in the head of the household whose offence caused disaster not merely individually but to the whole unit to which he belonged. This is clear from the sin of Achan (Joshua 7). Similarly, the head of the royal household acted as the focus of the nation, the reigning monarch who was one with his people, as in the case of Ahaz (Isa. 7. 2, 13). Any national disturbance, such as a prolonged drought or an outbreak of plague, was liable to be attributed to the action of the king, as though he were personally responsible (2 Sam. 21. 1-14). Saul's trespass involved not only his entire household but his kingdom as well. When David sinned by counting the people, he was given the choice between three disasters—three years of famine, three months' flight from the enemy or three days' pestilence. When the pestilence approached Jerusalem, David pleaded for mercy: 'Lo, I have sinned, and I have done wickedly: but these sheep, what have they done? Let thy hand, I pray thee, be against me and against my father's house' (2 Sam. 24. 17). In this case, it seems that the plague ceased and so David's house-

[18] W. F. Albright, 'The Judical Reform of Jehoshaphat', *Alexander Marx Jubilee Volume* (ed. S. Lieberman (1950), pp. 61-82.

hold did in fact escape the plague. The action of the king needed to be just because a failure in justice would involve his household and perhaps the nation itself. When later Manasseh acted abominably against the worshippers of Yahweh, there came Yahweh's threat to make Judah an abomination among the nations (Jer. 15. 4).

CHAPTER SIX

URBAN CIVILIZATION AND ITS RESULTS

1. Economic changes in the life of the Hebrew clans. The Canaanite city and its ruling group of elders. The authority of the elders in Israel. Changes due to the new monarchical rule. The appointment of royal officials in the larger cities—as governors, army officers and civil servants.
2. Changes in economic life—reflected in the attitude to landed property. New patterns in agriculture, with enclosures. The deterioration of the position of the small farmer and the disintegration of the family inheritance.
3. Family disintegration seen to be a symbol of the weakening of the ties between Israel and Yahweh. The relationship between commercial prosperity and moral laxity in society and within the family.
4. Moral decline was linked with disloyalty to Yahweh. Religious worship of other gods ('adultery') gave rise to moral practices in conflict with Yahwist ethics. Therefore, religious and moral disloyalty led to social disunity. The prophetic concern for loyalty to Yahweh and social righteousness. Economic injustice as an expression of social dis-unity.
5. The changing conception of Yahweh as a Lord of Nations and of History. His power manifested in Nature and his glory expressed in righteousness. His holiness (separateness) exalted Him above His people—above their disloyalty and even beyond their very survival.

CHAPTER SIX

URBAN CIVILIZATION AND ITS RESULTS

THE settlement of the Israelite clans in Canaan brought about a change in their mode of life. Whereas they had been nomadic and moved from place to place with their flocks and herds, they now came to have settled areas which were already occupied, in some instances, by the Canaanite peoples. Adjustments took place on both sides as the two cultures—the already settled urban or village culture and the nomadic one—had to come to terms with one another. The bulk of the Israelites came to share in village life, with its basis in agriculture, whilst there remained across the Jordan, some elements of the Hebrew people who kept to the old ways and continued the shepherd life. The two Israels remained aware of the fact that they belonged together to Yahweh, yet they followed different ways of life. The conflict between the two Israels is one of the most important in history. The nomad had the simple life, a hard fight with the elements and with wild beasts. The village-dweller lived a secure life with its rhythm of the seasons. The nomad wished to move on—sometimes in a tension between the pleasures of the oasis and the desire to move elsewhere. The village-dweller wanted to remain where he was. This conflict remained as the nomadic Israel never allowed the city or village dweller to forget the first love of Yahweh, which took place in the wilderness. When the people wanted to settle down and dwell at ease in Zion, a prophet of the Lord would come in haste from the wilderness (like Amos) to remind the people that they must move forward to new pastures of the spirit.

There is no doubt, however that changes took place in the outlook of the Hebrew people when they began to dwell in villages after their wanderings. Even before the establishment of the monarchy, some of these changes had begun to take place. The monarchy helped to re-inforce these changes and bring about other changes in due course. The place of the city in the life of

Urban Civilization and its Results 109

the people has therefore to be considered and then it will be possible to determine the changes which took place in the family economy.

Prior to the coming of the Israelites, it is probable that among the Canaanites the city and its surrounding countryside formed an important unit, a local and partially independent community. Thus, Gideon settled in Ophrah, which belonged to the Abiezrites. His activity appears to have been confined to the area in their control. When he sought the help of the two cities of Succoth and Penuel, they gave their several answers as independent communities (Judg. 8). There was a connection between Ophrah and Shechem, where dwelt the maternal kin of Gideon. Abimelech, Gideon's son, secured these two cities and tried to add a third, Thebez (Judg. 9. 50)—to form an extended city monarchy but his attempt was short-lived. On several occasions one city decided to oppose another city in an enterprise, indicating their independence as autonomous units. Thus, the cities of Ziph and Keilah took sides in the war between Saul and David (1 Sam. 23). The city of Jabesh was attacked by the Ammonites (1 Sam. 11). There appears to have been no tribal unit as such to oppose the adversary, so the city itself as an independent community acted with the help of other Israelites.

There is reason to believe that often a single family dominated the city itself, as Shechem was ruled at one period by the Hamor kin (Gen. 34), and the Abiezrites ruled in Shechem. It is probable that the family of Jesse had a prominent place in Bethlehem or that the whole township (in such a small place) was regarded as itself one family (1 Sam. 20. 6). Each city had a common sanctuary, normally a high place nearby (1 Sam. 9. 13, 25). Sometimes the city might be famed as an important place of worship, as was the case of the city of Nob, which was ruled by a family of priests. Such a city community had a strong sense of corporate solidarity, so that Saul put the whole of the city of Nob to the sword because one of their leaders had helped David (1 Sam. 22. 19). Gibeon demanded revenge against the house of Saul, because of the way that Saul had treated them (2 Sam. 21).

In the Deuteronomic laws, there is seen clearly the importance of the city. If a man is found slain in a field, the citizens of the nearest town must declare by certain rites that the city is not guilty of the murder (Deut. 19. 1-9). Among these laws, cities of refuge are mentioned to protect certain types of man-slayers. If a murderer has entered such a city and there is insufficient justification to permit him to stay there, the elders of the city of refuge must hand the murderer over to the messengers of the elders of the man's own city, who in turn will hand over the man to the kinsmen of the slain man for their vengeance (Deut. 19. 12). Elsewhere, it is written that the murderer when he reaches the city of refuge must 'stand at the entrance of the gate of the city and explain his case to the elders of that city' (Josh. 20. 4).

Other instances show that the elders of the city were the authorities to judge cases which were beyond the control of the father of a household. Thus, if parents had a particularly stubborn son, then he must be brought by them to the elders in the gate and then all the men in the city would stone him (Deut. 21. 19-20). In the case of a newly-wedded wife, whose husband had accused her of unchastity, it is the elders of the city who have to decide the matter. If the husband is right, then the men of the city were to stone her before the house of her father. But if her father proves her to be innocent, then it is the elders who have to pass judgement, that the man shall be whipped and then fined the sum of a hundred shekels of silver. This sum was given to the father as compensation for the defamation of his daughter's good name (Deut. 22. 13-21). In cases of appeal, it is the 'elders at the gate' to whom the people turned to make public decisions (Deut. 25. 7-9). It does not seem that these elders were an official body or council but were the grown-up men of the leading families. Numbered among them were the 'men of valour' *(gibbōrē hayil)*, the warriors and the landowners who were responsible for the well-being of the community. The 'city-gate' was the normal place for the elders to gather together to exchange news and come to a common mind on communal affairs. As there would normally be a sufficient number of such men of experience at the gate, so everything of importance took place in their presence there. If a field was bought, then the buyer and seller would go there (to the gate) together to ratify the arrangements before the elders. They served as the witnesses to the legality of the purchase, with all such responsibilities as might accrue with the purchase according to levirate law (Ruth

Urban Civilization and its Results

4. 4, 11). It might well be that in general the whole body of citizens of adult age formed the company of 'the elders'. In some place, a select number might form the council of the elders, as in Succoth where seventy-seven officials and elders are mentioned (Judg. 8. 14). In some cases, it is probable that a single family might dominate the rest of the families, so that it could take all power into its own hands (Judg. 9. 2).

The method of procedure which was used by these elders may be reflected in a small cameo, a brief scene depicted in the Book of Job (29. 7-11). In the square which stood by the city gate, the men of the city are assembled. There they discuss matters of importance, one elder after another. Then there arrives one man of standing, whose authority is particularly respected. Some of the younger men withdraw. The other more senior men are hushed to hear the word of the newly arrived elder, whose judgement is duly accepted and considered to be a source of blessing. Many cities must have accepted the judgement of a particular chief, like Abimelech, though the responsibility rested upon the 'men of valour' as a group.

The powerful and influential men in the community were called by different terms as 'the elders' *(nādhībh)*, 'officials' *(nāghīdh)* or 'chiefs' *(sārīm)*. Such phrases as the 'men of Succoth', 'the elders of Succoth', 'the officials of Succoth' and the 'chiefs of Succoth' appear to be used indiscriminately with reference to the leading men of the town in their conflict with Gideon (Judg. 8. 5, 6, 8, 14, 15, 16). As Israel became established in village life, so every Israelite would live in some definite community to which he 'belonged'. Therefore, the reference to 'elders' would refer to the leaders of his community, the elders of his town or village. It is presumably to these responsible leaders from the various towns and villages that there is reference as the 'elders of Israel' (1 Sam. 4. 3; 8. 4; 2 Sam. 3. 17; 5. 3, etc.). This does not appear to refer to any distinct institution, such as a Senate but rather to the gathering of various responsible leaders from the different communities, which made up Israel. As the term 'elder' signified authority, so in a great house, like that of the king, there were the 'elders of his house' (2 Sam. 12. 17; Gen. 15. 7). A trusted slave might even be regarded as coming within this category because of his authority (Gen. 24. 2). By the time that the records came to be written down in Israel, this practice of government by local elders had become so far accepted that it was taken as a matter of course that in pre-Canaanite days Israel had been governed by elders. It is noteworthy that, even in the case of Moses, the elders are introduced to serve as a link between himself and the people. On the other hand, such an endorsement of their authority, namely, that Moses introduced them into Israel, may well have strengthened their hand as an element in the life of Israel. There is no doubt that the introduction of the 'elders' as an abstraction rather than as the leaders of actual communities points to the later views of the Pentateuchal writers. Such leaders developed naturally out of the earlier organization, where among shepherds the leading herdsmen would be given a moral recognition and assume the authority for decisions.

The brief description of the leadership in a small community, such as we find in the Book of Job, is a step forward from the leadership found in a nomadic community. Among the chiefs, one particular man is regarded with particular respect and his word is honoured above the rest. Such a man would have prominence among nomads, as in the case of Abraham or Jacob, but his word would have a wider influence when the community became more organized in a stable setting. The community was in a better position to enforce its decisions, which may well have been his decisions, over a larger number of people. We lack information about the growth of a governing body in the growingly wealthy cities of the period of the monarchy. It is clear that, in the teachings of the prophets as well as in the law codes of Deuteronomy, the township retained its essential place as the local essential unit of community life, being responsible as a unit for its own local self-government and communal responsibility. From such evidence as we have, the monarchs do not appear to have attempted to seek more centralization but rather they left the inner organization of the towns to the elders and chiefs as the responsible men (1 Kgs. 21. 8; 2 Kgs. 10. 1; 23. 1).

However, the king needed to have responsible local officials who were responsible to himself. This was recognized by Abimelech who appointed Zebul as a *sar* (ruler) in Shechem, when he was absent from the city (Judg. 9. 30). King Solomon appointed royal officials *(nissābhīm)* all over the kingdom (1 Kgs. 4. 7-19), mainly to provide for his household. Their task

Urban Civilization and its Results 113

appears to have been to secure taxes and 'corvée-labour' from all the tribes, save Judah. He also appointed a *sar* (governor) as his representative in larger cities (1 Kgs. 22. 26; 2 Kgs. 23. 8), who appear to have had some authority in the administration of justice but these governors did not necessarily over-ride the authority of the local elders and chiefs. Whilst the king might coerce the local elders to execute his orders and deliver up an innocent member of their community, as in the case of Ahab (1 Kgs. 21) and Jehu (2 Kgs. 10), yet he had to reckon with the authority of the elders and act through it.

On the other hand, the monarchy came to have an increasing influence on the social conditions of the towns. Alongside of the *sārīm*, the chiefs and elders of the old recognized families, a new class of officials arose. These officials were responsible to the king for the maintenance of the army, the supervision of roads, aquaducts, palaces and fortresses which came to be established at strategic points in the land. Among these officials, there were the officers of the army which came to be more fully organized and there were the members of the civil service, who were under 'the secretary' (or chancellor) (Jer. 36. 20). It is natural that this class of 'new men' was most prominent in the capital, in the larger towns and the royal fortresses, whilst life in the villages and in the smaller towns continued as heretofore. In the past the leading men were 'men of valour' or men of property and wealth. With the new centre of authority, the king was able to raise up a man whom he liked and reject one who had fallen into disfavour—irrespective of the man's family or property, in a manner similar to that of other Oriental monarchs. This state of affairs is expressed, with disapproval, in the anti-monarchic account in 1 Samuel: 'He will take the best of your fields and vineyards and olive orchards and give them to his servants' (8. 14). This class who owed personal allegiance to the king lacked the sense of unity with their fellow-citizens and served to weaken the psychic bonds which bound Israel into one. The sense of responsibility towards Israelite brethren began to disappear as a new kind of aristocracy came into being. This aristocracy, known as *hōrīm*, is only known from the period of the Monarchy.¹ There is reference to them as a distinct class in Jer. 26. 11, 12, 16., and it appears that they were buried in a burial place of their own,

¹ J. Pedersen, *Israel*, I-II, p. 39 (note 1, pp. 504-5).

distinct from that of the common people (2 Kgs. 23. 6; Jer. 26. 23). The older families began to feel the pressure of the 'nouveaux riches', for whom the king wished to provide land and other gifts as signal marks of his royal favour.

The economic and social changes which took place may be seen clearly in the attitude to property—an area where conflict arose between the new and the old. The attitude to property can serve as an example of the wider revolutions in thought and practice which took place under the monarchy. The earlier practice has been mentioned with reference to family laws, in which persons as well as things were regarded as the family property. Under the head of the family, the whole of the family possessions belonged together as a totality, a psychic unity. If you acted against a man's property, it were as though you acted against the man himself. Moreover, the head of the family did not own the property, which belonged to the family group, past, present and future. Therefore, it was not in any man's power to alienate any part of the family property or sell it. It would not merely impoverish the family to act in this way but it would be an act of impiety against the family forebears and a betrayal of the future well-being of the group.

It was recognized, however, that a man could become so impoverished that he could no longer maintain the property. This eventuality is reflected in the Law of Holiness, which appoints the next-of-kin to act in this case. 'If your brother becomes poor and sells part of his property, then his next of kin shall come and redeem what his brother has sold. If a man has no one to redeem it and then himself becomes prosperous and finds sufficient means to redeem it, let him reckon the years since he sold it and pay back the over-payment to the man to whom he sold it; and he shall return to his property. But if he has not sufficient means to get it back for himself, then what he sold shall remain in the hand of him who bought until the year of jubilee; in the jubilee it shall be released and he shall return to his property' (Lev. 25. 25-28). In this first part of this passage, the reference is to the responsibility of the next-of-kin to act as redeemer and in the latter part, there is the redemption due to the year of jubilee.

Jeremiah was faced with his responsibility in this matter, as the next-of-kin, when Hanamel, the son of Shallum, his father's brother, came to him and said, 'Buy my field which is at Anathoth in the land of Benjamin, for the right of possession and redemption is yours; buy if for yourself' (Jer. 32. 8). Then, Jeremiah duly weighed out the seventeen shekels of silver and in the presence of witnesses, he signed the deed, sealed it and handed over the money. The intention does not appear to be that Jeremiah had compassion on his cousin who had become poor but rather that it fell to Jeremiah to carry out his duty as the next-of-kin to ensure that the property did not go out of the family. It might well be that sons had their own portion as also the wife might hold her private property but all such holdings really were the possession of the family, so that Leah and Rachel could say to Jacob, concerning the wealth that he had acquired: 'All the property which God has taken away from our father belongs to us and to our children' (Gen. 31. 16). The property is part of the man, who is one with his house.

Sometimes, there was no kinsman to redeem the property. In such a case, the year of jubilee was intended to ensure that the property was kept intact and was retained as the possession of the family. However, the year of jubilee was every fiftieth year and a shorter period was assigned, similar to the old slave law, whereby every seventh year a release took place. 'At the end of every seven years you shall grant a release. And this is the manner of the release: every creditor shall release what he has lent to his neighbour: he shall not exact it of his neighbour, his brother, because the Lord's release has been proclaimed. Of a foreigner, you may exact it; but whatever of yours is with your brother your hand shall release' (Deut. 15. 1-3). It is not explicitly stated that landed property is to be handed back but it appears to be implied. Such a law provided a period of rest after seven years and made an attempt to enable the poor Israelite to start again after this period.

The passage in Deuteronomy seems to provide a means for the restitution of property, so that the weaker Israelite or his family were protected against misfortune and deprivation. It is difficult to know to what extent such provisions were effective, whether at an earlier or a later date. They appear to have a large measure of idealism, which would hardly prove effective against a rising commercial class, which sought to enlarge their stake in the land—a measure which would inevitably mean that they could out-bid or squeeze out the poor man permanently in his times of extreme need.

Nevertheless, whether it is nostalgic desire or an endeavour to continue the old traditions, it is apparent that Ezekiel, in exilic times, has an ordinance which endeavours to establish the right of a family to keep its property over against attempts by some wealthy member to disperse it. Whilst this ordinance has particular reference to the prince, yet it has reference also to other families whose duty it is to uphold the unity of the family. 'If the prince makes a gift to any of his sons out of his inheritance, it shall belong to his sons, it is their property by inheritance. But if he makes a gift out of his inheritance to one of his servants, it shall be his to the year of liberty; then it shall revert to the prince; only his sons may keep a gift from his inheritance. The prince shall not take any of the inheritance of the people, thrusting them out of their property; he shall give his sons their inheritance out of his own property, so that none of my people shall be dispossessed of his property' (Ezek. 46. 16-18). The same writer points out that the prince shall have certain land for his own but he shall not dispossess others of their property (45. 8). Whilst in Deuteronomy, there is to be a remission of debts and the freeing of Hebrew slaves (Deut. 15. 12-13), in Ezekiel this 'release' is extended to cover the return of land as well. It is clear from the passage in the Priestly Code, however, that every purchase of property which alienated family land had to be restored at the end of the seven year period—if such regulations actually reflected enforcible conditions in Israel (Lev. 25. 28; 27. 17ff.).

However, the growth of walled cities did affect the older practice, if one may judge from the succeeding verses in this same passage. 'If a man sells a dwelling house in a walled city, he may redeem it within a whole year after its sale; for a full year he shall have the right of redemption. If it is not redeemed within a full year, then the house that is in the walled city shall be made sure in perpetuity to him who bought it, throughout his generations; it shall not be released in the jubilee' (verses 29-30 in Lev. 25). A careful distinction is made between a house within a walled city and houses in villages which have no walls around them. Houses in such villages were to be reckoned with the fields of the countryside and could be redeemed, that is, they had to be

Urban Civilization and its Results

released when the blowing of the rams' horns of jubilee took place (Lev. 25. 31). The land of Levites, whether it was within the walled cities or outside it was due to be released in the year of jubilee in any case. Common land attached to the cities was to be kept for the use of the common people in perpetuity and was not to be sold (*ibid*, verses 32-34).

Whilst such regulations were calculated to uphold the unity of the family by maintaining the family land in one family for perpetuity, there is evidence that the rise of the Monarchy, in particular, brought conflict with these older conceptions. As this institution became more powerful in Israel, despite the outlook of the Davidic covenant, the king tended to be regarded as a centre of power who had a right to distribute his favours (including the land), irrespective of the older family arrangements. This was the practice in neighbouring kingdoms and it would not be surprizing that the king in Israel should view his position in a similar way. The most outstanding example is seen in the conflict roused by Ahab, the king of Israel, who desired the vineyard of Naboth in Jezreel—a vineyard which adjoined the royal palace. Ahab had no desire to use compulsion because he offered Naboth to state his own price or Ahab was willing to give Naboth a better vineyard elsewhere. The only matter at stake for Ahab was that the vineyard adjoined his territory.

The case was very different for Naboth, in whose answer there is a sense of the gravity of the request. 'Naboth said to Ahab, "The Lord forbid that I should give you the inheritance of my fathers"' (1 Kgs. 21. 3). This made the king sulk and roused Jezebel to take steps to see that the king's will was done. As the daughter of the king of Tyre, a city which was at the height of its power, Jezebel resented this opposition to royal authority, especially if it was upheld by appeal to Yahweh, the God of Israel. Jezebel's answer is clear. 'Do you now govern Israel? ... I will give you the vineyard of Naboth the Jezreelite' (*ibid*. verse 7). By cunning means, the queen has Naboth condemned for blasphemy and put to death. Then the king took over his property. Such action on the part of the monarch may not be altogether typical yet it is possible that the monarch did act from time to time in this fashion. When David fled before Absalom, he was met by the servant (Ziba) of Jonathan's son, Mephibosheth. Ziba brought asses and food for the king, who was told by the servant that Mephibosheth had remained in Jerusalem with David's rebellious son. The king then, without further ado, gave all the inheritance of Mephibosheth (i.e. Saul's inheritance) to Ziba (2 Sam. 16. 4). On David's return from exile, Mephibosheth declares that the servant Ziba's words are a baseless calumny but David does not restore to Mephibosheth his inheritance but instructs that the inheritance shall be divided between Mephibosheth and Ziba (2 Sam. 19. 29). Mephibosheth is grateful to escape alive and makes no protest against this arrangement.

This action on the part of the king was followed by the leading men, who supported the monarchy and paid little heed to ancient inheritance rights. This is made clear in the outcries of the prophets. Isaiah declaims against those 'who join house to house, who add field to field, until there is no more room, and you are made to dwell alone in the midst of the land' (Isa. 5. 8). His contemporary Micah is even more outspoken about the situation in Judah in the closing years of the eighth century B.C. 'Woe to those who devise wickedness and work evil upon their beds! When the morning dawns, they perform it, because it is in the power of their hand. They covet fields, and seize them; and houses and take them away; they oppress a man and his house, a man and his inheritance' (Micah 2. 1, 2). Even the leading men in Judah (the princes) have become, like thieves, in removing the bounds which mark off their territory from that of their neighbour (Hos. 5. 10).

The prophets' protest against the princes appears to have been that these men by their wealth and position have taken advantage of the poor man, buying up his property and thereby breaking the link between a family and its solidarity with its ancient property inheritance. It was not a matter of the cost which disturbed Naboth, it was the sacrilege in allowing the family inheritance to pass out of the hands of the family. Property was not viewed in this light, as a saleable commodity, like buying and selling other common goods. It could not be disposed of without due consideration of consequences. It belonged to the whole family—past, present and future. Therefore, if any man fell on bad times, it rested with the near-kinsman to act to ensure that the member of the family who could afford to buy it should do so. This would make the transfer back to the original owner easier when the time fell due, in the year of jubilee—as has been noted in the Law of Holiness.

The material prosperity, which enabled the wealthy to 'lie upon beds of ivory', eating and drinking luxuriously (Amos 6. 4-6), in their houses of hewn stone (Amos 5. 11), often took place at the expense of the poor. 'You trample upon the poor and take from him exactions of wheat' *(ibid.)* , and 'you . . . trample upon the needy and bring the poor of the land to an end' (Amos 8. 4). It is not clear whether the state exactions on the peasantry and the small farmer were great but there are signs in the direction of the deterioration of the position of the peasantry. The poor farmer in time of need had to turn to the rich man, so that he could borrow money, no doubt at usurious rates of interest. The poor man had to offer some security to borrow this money and thus he was often forced to mortgage his land. Sometimes, he had to offer his own person or members of his family to serve as security. If famine or a bad harvest came, then the farmer faced eviction and, possibly, slavery for himself and his family. The contrasts of poverty and wealth are seen in the account of the wife of one of the prophets and that of the wealthy woman of Shunem (2 Kgs. 4. 1-37). In the case of the first, the wife (now widow) of one of the prophets appealed to Elisha for help because 'the creditor has come to take my two children to be his slaves' (verse 1). In the second story, the wealthy woman of Shunem calls to her husband to send one of the servants with an ass, so that she may go to meet the prophet. The prophet returns to her home where she has had an extension built on to the house, for the benefit of the prophet, when he is in the neighbourhood (verses 10, 20 and 32). (The picture of this wealthy woman may be compared to the account of Abigail, Nabal's wife, who provided very ample fare for David and his men (1 Sam. 25. 18). Nabal was a very rich man with large herds of sheep and goats who had little respect for David or anyone else, so that his wife had to plead with David not to destroy him). There is reason to believe that the great famine in the time of Ahab caused many small farmers to fail. A great drought, to which Menander of Ephesus refers,[2] may well have been the cause of this famine. Menander assigns this drought to the reign of Ittoba'al, of Tyre, and claims that it lasted one whole year.

[2] Josephus, *The Jewish Antiquities*, VIII, 13, 2.

This Ittoba'al (Eth-baal) was presumably the father of Jezebel and ruled c. 887-856. But it is probable that not one famine afflicted the land but periodic famines for one cause or another. Elisha appears to have found a famine in Gilgal through natural causes (2 Kgs. 4. 38) but when Benhadad besieged Samaria, there was also a great famine (2 Kgs. 6. 35), no doubt due to the activities of his marauding army. From whatever cause, the process of dis-integration appears to have taken place so that when Amos refers to the scene a hundred years later, the process had developed very far and called forth the denunciations of the prophet.

The evidence from the legal codes, including some ordinances from the Priestly Code, which date from the Exilic or post-Exilic period, indicates that persistent attempts were made to prevent the dis-integration of the family and its inheritance. The normal line of succession is set forth in the Deuteronomic Code, namely, that the first-born is to receive two-thirds of the inheritance even though the mother is the less beloved of her husband (Deut. 21. 15f.). This regulation safeguarded the right of the first-born, as such, irrespective of the wife by whom he was born. Even so, a distinction was made between the son of a free-born woman and the son of a slave-woman. The slave-woman's son would only inherit if there were no sons by the free-woman. So Sarah is desirous of turning out Hagar and Ishmael (the slave-born eldest son), saying to her husband, Abraham: 'Cast out this slave woman with her son; for the son of this slave woman shall not be heir with my son Isaac' (Gen. 21. 10). In fact, it is stated that Abraham gave to Isaac all that he had (Gen. 24. 36), whilst giving to his sons, by his concubines, certain gifts (Gen. 25. 5-6). It was probable that no man felt happy about the prospect of the family inheritance passing to a slave, as Abraham bemoaned this likelihood (Gen. 15. 3). From the slave son's standpoint, he was placed in the invidious position, that sons of the free-born woman would declare, as in the case of Jephthah (who was the son of a harlot): 'You shall not inherit in our father's house; for you are the son of another woman' (Judg. 11. 2).

It is a matter of interest that, in the book of Job, it is written that 'their father gave them [his daughters] inheritance among their brothers' (Job 42. 15). This appears to have been unusual because the daughter became the possession of another man and another house, to bring up heirs in another inheritance. Yet in the Priestly Code, it is permitted, in certain circumstances, that the daughters may inherit. Thus, it was laid down that, 'if a man dies and has no son, then you shall cause his inheritance to pass to his daughter. If he has no daughter, then you shall give his inheritance to his brothers. And if he has no brothers, then you shall give his inheritance to his father's brothers' (Num. 27. 8-10). If the father has no brothers, then the next of kin shall take possession of the property. This ancient law of inheritance has already been considered with reference to the levirate law and the avenging of justice. It ensured that the propery remained within the family of the husband, however distantly related the connection might be. The dastardly action of the unscrupulous relative is reflected in the story told to David, by the wise woman of Tekoa, who claimed that the family wished to destroy her son, who had killed his brother. If this remaining son was destroyed, then the property would pass to these other relatives (2 Sam. 14. 7). The ordinance that a woman must marry within the tribe of her father, if she inherits her father's property, was presumably to ensure that at least within the tribe, the inheritance remained secure. The wording is interesting, with regard to the daughters of Zelophehad: 'Let them marry whom they think best; only, they shall marry within the family of the tribe of their father' (Num. 36. 8).

The Priestly Code, however old some of its ordinances may be, sought to maintain the standard of family solidarity, which must have been much more difficult when the families were in exile and torn away from the family's former property inheritance. Yet the priestly leaders sought to keep the traditions alive, so that even in the land of strangers such family laws would provide a pattern for life and conduct. It is claimed that on their return from exile, the Jews agreed to maintain the ordinances of the year of jubilee, namely, the remission of debts (Neh. 10. 31), but this passage has been held in question.[1] In any case, in later times, the Jews managed to get round such an ordinance by means of a proviso made beforehand. From such evidence, there is clear testimony that immense importance was attached to a man's inheritance from which he must not be separated.

The weakening of the psychic unity of the family revealed,

[1] J. Pedersen, *Israel*, I-II, p. 89, note 1.

for the prophets, a deeper underlying dis-unity—a straining of the bonds which bound the people of Israel to their covenant-God. The departure of the old family ways showed clearly that the ties, which held the community together in the past, were weakening. This pointed towards the dissolution of the community *per se* and towards its refusal of its mission as the people of God. This insight of the prophets is reflected in their constant allusion to the symbol of divorce which hung over the divine marriage between Yahweh with Israel. It is true that the symbol, no doubt, arose out of Canaanite ritualistic practices, which involved sexual acts as symbolic of fertility rites, as Ba'al was married to the goddess, Anath or Asherah. But the symbol of marriage reached down into the most intimate human relationship and gave a deeper significance to the divine fellowship.

The prophetic insight was based on firm foundations. Before there is a community, there is the family. Before there is a government, there is the family. The family exists to secure certain basic personal as well as social needs, namely, the regulation of sex, the regulation of property and the regulation of youth. As the family seeks to fulfill these tasks, it is in fact already the 'matrix of government'. The form of the family may differ according to the system of rules which prescribes and limits sexual relations but 'the one universal principle is that it (the family) finds its being as well as its specific character within the shelter of a strongly, sanctioned, highly authoritative code'.[4] As the shelter grew weaker, so the specific character, if not the being, of the family was undergoing change to the detriment of the larger community, of which it formed a part. This appeared to be the case in Israel and accounts for the warnings of the prophets. The old family economy in which the labour of the various members of the family contributed to the welfare of the whole served as a pattern for the earlier communal arrangements. Among the shepherd economies, even the youngest member of the family would, at an early age, share in the care of the flock and be left sometimes to face the lion and the bear, as in the case of David. The wool from the sheep provided the clothing which was woven by the women of the family. The women also cared for the provision of the family's physical needs, such as the preparation of the milk and curds (Judg. 5. 25). There is the utmost praise for

[4] R. MacIver, *The Web of Government* (1947), p. 26.

Urban Civilization and its Results 123

the woman, who with administrative ability orders well her household and 'does not eat the bread of idleness' (Prov. 31. 27). The woman has proper control of affairs and so the home is in peace.

But the changing order had brought a different state of affairs. With the growth of wealth, there are more servants to do the various menial tasks in the house. This provides more leisure, especially for the women of the household. This results in the increase of useless idleness on the part of women, who prefer to be an ornament of Society. Therefore, as an illustration of the departure from former ways, the prophet Amos turns scathingly against the women who dwell at ease, at the expense of others' suffering. 'Hear this word, you cows of Basham, who are in the mountain of Samaria, who oppress the poor, who crush the needy, who say to their husbands, 'Bring wine that we may drink!' (Amos 4. 1). In similar fashion, Isaiah threatens with head-scab and nakedness 'the daughters of Zion who are haughty and walk with outstretched necks, glancing wantonly with their eyes, mincing along as they go, tinkling with their feet' (Isa. 3. 16). He proceeds in the same passage to catalogue the useless trinkets—the anklets, the headbands and all the paraphernalia of finery which will be brought to nought. 'Instead of perfume, there will be rottenness; and instead of a girdle, a rope; and instead of well-set hair, baldness; and instead of a rich robe, a girding of sackcloth; instead of beauty, shame' (Isa. 3. 24). Thus, the prophets consider that the standards set by the women have much to do with the health of the social order. The current standards showed the rottenness in Israel.

The denunciations of the prophets of Yahweh brought clearly to light a fundamental distinction between the Canaanite religions and the religion of Yahweh. Canaanite religion, as seen in the Ras Shamra texts, had an elaborate myth and ritual which shows that there was a high degree of literary culture. However, this religion was, at heart, an ethnic one, which had an important fertility cult as a central feature. Whilst the father-god El was nominal head of the pantheon, the chief active deity was Hadad (an ancient Semitic storm-god) or Ba'al, who reigned as king among the gods on a high mountain in the north. Opposite Prince Ba'al, there were a number of female deities, including Asherah (also known as a wooden cult object: Judg. 6. 25; 1 Kgs.

18. 19), Astarte (known in the Bible as Ashtaroth or Ashtoreth) and Anat (who is Ba'al's consort in the Ras Shamra texts, but is known in the Bible only through place-names, e.g. Beth-anath). These goddesses represented the female principle in the fertility cults and no doubt were manifestations of the Great Earth Mother cultus which pervaded the whole of the religions of the Middle East. The goddesses are portrayed as sacred courtesans or as pregnant mothers as well as jealous goddesses of war. The Canaanite ritual represented the sacred marriage of Ba'al with his consorts which served to give fertility to man and beast. In like manner, the myth of the death and resurrection of Ba'al corresponded to the annual dying and reviving of the forces of Nature. The yearly ritual, in its mimetic performance, was believed to bring to life afresh the fertility of the soil, of the flocks and the family. Such behaviour on the part of the gods found its counterpart in their shrines with the use of sacred prostitution, homosexuality and a variety of orgiastic practices, which were deemed to further the fertility process. As Israel became integrated with the local inhabitants in the towns and villages of Canaan, it was to be expected that the local inhabitants should expect a 'give-and-take' in religious matters. Furthermore, to neglect the rites of the local fertility gods was certainly to court disaster.

It is, therefore, not a matter for surprise that, despite the sacrificial cultus on Mount Zion, the 'high places' continued to flourish especially in the Northern Kingdom of Israel. When Elijah fought for Yahweh against Ba'al in the ninth century, there is no evidence that he had any connection with Zion. He fought against the house of Ahab, which was eventually cut down by Jehu, who was anointed by a prophet from the circle of Elisha yet he still worshipped Yahweh in the semblance of a bull (2 Kgs. 10. 31). There is ample evidence that the process whereby Yahweh was exalted above other gods was a long and costly one. In the course of this process, its course changed as the early prophets sought to retain the early tradition of Yahwism against the practices of Canaanite religion whilst the later prophets, in the eighth century, opposed the life of the cities which were filled with social relationships that were contrary to the righteousness of Yahweh.

The passage between the earlier prophets and the later ones

may perhaps be seen in the writings of the prophet Hosea. Hosea was concerned with an issue which links him with Elijah, namely, the fertility of the agricultural life of Canaan. For the ordinary Canaanite, fertility was to be attributed to Ba'al, assisted by his consorts. But in Israel, Yahweh alone was to be regarded as the source of life and energy. This was true for Elisha, the prophet of Yahweh through whom Naaman was healed. Naaman in consequence took two mules' burdens of earth to worship Yahweh when he returned to Syria (2 Kgs. 5. 17). So too, for Hosea, an Israelite cannot sacrifice to Yahweh outside of Canaan and, in another land, can only eat unclean food (Hos. 9. 3f.). Canaan in this same verse is called the land of Yahweh, which makes it clear that the prophet considered that Yahweh had fully taken possession. This was recognized by the people of Israel who went up to worship Yahweh at Gilgal and Bethaven (4. 15) and brought their flocks and herds for sacrifice (5. 6; 8. 13). Nevertheless, Hosea reproaches the people because in fact they neglected Yahweh and worshipped the Ba'alim. The prophet expressed this truth with the symbol of marriage. The use of the symbol of marriage was not new. As the rites connected with Ba'al were fertility rites, by which Ba'al as husband gave fruitfulness to the earth and to his people, so the Yahwist prophets regarded such practices for Israel as fornication and adultery since Yahweh was the true husband. This use of expressions denoting adultery is found in the early strata of the record, as seen in the J material. 'You make a covenant with the inhabitants of the land ... and play the harlot after their gods and sacrifice to their gods and when one invites you, you eat of his sacrifice' (Exod. 34. 15). In the later Holiness Code, there are warnings against playing the harlot with foreign gods (Lev. 17. 7; 20. 5). From such false loves, there could only come sorrow.

Hosea's use of this metaphor was made the more poignant by its reflection of his own domestic situation. Whatever may have been the ultimate situation within his home, there can be little doubt that he was faced with the decision to love a wife who had been or was unfaithful to him. There was a prophetic symbolism in his experience of this unfaithfulness. In the same way, Isaiah expressed the nakedness of Israel by going about naked (and barefoot for three years) and Jeremiah wore a rope and a yoke to denote the coming bondage of exile (Isa. 20. 3; Jer. 27. 2). Such action was the externalization of the message that filled their souls and gave intensity by the psychic connection between thought, word and action.

With reference to Israel, the people are figured as the wife of Yahweh and the mother of the Israelites. As a faithless wife, she had gone after various lovers, believing that they gave her bread, wine, oil, flax as well as silver and gold. But she pursued such lovers in vain because it was in fact her true husband, Yahweh, who was responsible for providing all the physical needs of her people. 'It was I who gave her the grain, the wine and the oil and who lavished upon her silver and gold which they used for Ba'al' (Hos. 2. 8). The people of Israel are rebuked because they attend the feasts of Ba'al, at the new moons and the other appointed feasts (2. 4ff). They worshipped others' gods with their offerings (3. 1), with sacrifices and incense to idols and Ba'alim (11. 2). In particular, Hosea condemns the calf of Samaria, an image which the hands of men have made (8. 4-6). Both priests and people tremble before the calf of Bethaven, whose glory shall be carried away by Assyria (10. 5-6). In speaking of this image, the speaker says dramatically, 'Yea, the thing itself shall be carried to Assyria, as tribute to the great king' (verse 6). The prophet's claim that the people's tribute to Ba'al is the hire of a harlot is forcefully expressed in the statement: 'You have loved a harlot's hire upon all threshing floors' (9. 1). In fact, the more fertile the land appeared to be, the more altars were built. 'Israel is a luxuriant vine that yields its fruit. The more his fruit increased the more altars he built; as his country improved he improved his pillars' (10. 1). Presumably, the latter refers to female objects of worship as tribute to the fertility goddesses. The ancient objects of pre-Canaanite worship were everywhere revered and so the people worshipped and sacrificed on the tops of the mountains and on high hills, under the oak, the poplar and the terebinth (4. 13), in Gilgal, and in Bethaven (4. 15), in Gibeah (10. 9) and Gilead (12. 12). The reverence to Ba'al is expressed by the skill used by the craftsmen in silver and by the kisses which men bestow upon these images (13. 2). Nevertheless, the people still offered sacrifices from their flocks and herds to Yahweh (5. 6), yet He did not heed them, 'he has withdrawn from them'.

This clear picture, which Hosea draws, indicates the measure in which Canaanite worship and practises continued to live on in the midst of the Israelite occupation. Far from the older inhabitants and their ways being blotted out, the practice of intermarriage and steady integration of populations resulted in the acceptance by Israel of rites and moral ways which the true Yahwist prophets heartily condemned. In fact, it may well be that the moral issues of these other forms of worship were the central point of their condemnation. Hosea connects together closely the immoral ways and the false acts of worship. Whilst Hosea condemns the false ways of the people ('there is swearing, lying, killing, stealing and committing adultery; they break all bounds and murder follows murder'; 4. 2), yet he condemns the priest in particular, because the priest withholds the true knowledge of Yahweh, so that the people are due for destruction. Men and women alike have adopted 'adulterous' ways, the men have sacrifices with cult prostitutes and the women share in harlotries (4. 4-14). Such profanities have taken place that Hosea claims that Ephraim (Israel) is incapable of returning ('Their deeds do not permit them to return to their God. For the spirit of harlotry is within them and they know not the Lord': 5. 4). Such practices are foreign to the worship of Israel and has resulted in 'alien children' (5. 7), whilst Ephraim mixes himself with the peoples and aliens devour his strength (7. 9). With the multiplication of altars in the Northern Kingdom, so the torah of the true God has become 'a strange thing', however many commands Yahweh gives them (8. 12). The cults in Canaan have become a snare for Yahweh's people, leading Israel into paths which were contrary to His torah and knowledge. This apostasy by prince, priest, prophet and people arose out of the fact that 'they have broken my covenant and transgressed my law' (8. 1).

Hosea foresees that dire consequences must be the cost of such apostasy. Already the land mourns in its distress (4. 3) and Israel is a useless vessel among the nations (8. 8). Yet Israel will not find satisfaction in such ways, because, by forsaking Yahweh, they will find that 'threshing floor and winevat shall not feed them, and the new wine shall fail them' (9. 2). The blessedness and fertility which they believed would come by devotion to Ba'al shall in fact be denied them—'Ephraim's glory shall fly away like a bird—no birth, no pregnancy, no conception' (9. 11), even the sons who do grow up shall be taken away. Furthermore, deserted altars are to be pulled down (12. 11), overgrown with thorn and thistle in a time of destruction (10. 8). Yahweh will withdraw himself until in their distress they seek him (5: 15). Nevertheless, the prophet never loses sight of the Lord's lovingkindness. He is the same Lord, who led them forth from the land of Egypt. 'I am the Lord your God from the land of Egypt; I will again make you dwell in tents, as in the days of the appointed feast' (12. 9). With great tenderness, the early steps of Israel are recalled before apostasy arose. 'When Israel was a child, I loved him, and out of Egypt I called my son.' Despite their sacrifices to the Ba'alim 'yet it was I who taught Ephraim to walk, I took them up in my arms' (11. 3). In another change of metaphor, the prophet recalls the Lord's care. 'Like grapes in the wilderness, I found Israel. Like the first fruit on the fig tree, in its first season, I saw your fathers. But they came to Ba'al pe'or and consecrated themselves to Ba'al and became detestable like the thing they loved' (9. 10).

With such tenderness and yet with a piercing clarity, the prophet reveals the state of the nation. It is apparent that there was much devotion to the Ba'alim of Canaan and this had resulted not merely in a large measure of religious apostasy but in moral degradation. In fact, political and national disaster would follow this separation from their fount of blessing. Heavy responsibility lay upon the shoulders of the princes and the priests who should have guided the people in the way of the knowledge of the Lord. The general depravity has eaten away the heart of the nation, so disaster will follow. 'Ephraim has given bitter provocation; so his Lord will leave his blood-guilt upon him, and will turn back upon him his reproaches' (12. 14). The sense of inevitability hangs over the scene. The dissolution of the community, in the form in which they have known it, was about to take place. Yet the prophet does not leave without a message of hope a nation which has acted so foolishly. Yahweh will seek Israel afresh, as in the days of old, so that Israel will recognize her true 'husband' and a wider covenant with all nature will be established—a lasting relationship of righteousness, truth and love (2. 14-20). The moral claims of Yahweh are closely knit with religious duty, so that the religion and morality of Israel henceforth march forward together.

An older contemporary of Hosea, the prophet Amos, gives a similar picture of the destiny which awaits the two kingdoms.

Urban Civilization and its Results 129

Judah will be destroyed by fire and its strongholds in Jerusalem shall be destroyed, whilst the Northern Kingdom of Israel will not be strong enough to save its life (2. 5, 14). The destruction of the altars and the palaces will not be delayed (3. 14f.) and the people and their sanctuaries will perish (5. 4-6, 16). Whereas the people looked forward in hope for a day in which Yahweh would send them triumph over their opponents, they can only expect a day of darkness and gloom (5. 18-20).

The strong link between faith in Yahweh and right relationships within the kindred of Israel is brought out strongly in the teaching of this prophet. Israel is to be punished because 'they sell the righteous for silver and the needy for a pair of shoes' (2. 6). Their religious practices only show more clearly their disobedience to his commands (2. 7-8; 4. 4-5), therefore all their offerings will be unacceptable to him (5. 21-22). The close link with the order of the physical world is made clear in that Yahweh has tried to bring Israel back into the way of righteousness, by means of punishment in terms of drought, famine and the plague, even so far as to give rain to one city and withhold from another (4. 6-11). Nature is seen as the instrument in the hand of Yahweh, so that he can alter the normal course of things to express his anger ('I will make the sun go down at noon': 7. 9).

The message of Amos is concerned to bring out the glory of Yahweh, who is offended when Israel exalts herself (6. 8). Because Israel has been specially called ('You only have I known of all the families of the earth': 3. 2), therefore she is to be punished for her iniquities. In a sense, other nations have their place in Yahweh's concern, such as the Ethiopians, the Philistines and the Syrians (9. 7), and greater peoples have in fact perished (6. 2), so Israel cannot take for granted that her position is secure. Yahweh is seen by Amos to be concerned in the fate and morality of neighbouring peoples (1. 3—2. 3). The Lord is exalted over the nations, bringing them from their original homes (9. 7). So he seeks his true Israel within Israel—his loyal ones, the prophets (2. 11).

Thus, Amos teaches that the glory of Yahweh will be revealed among the nations, because justice and righteousness are part of his nature. Yet, on the other hand, the true Israel is revealed by a likeness in nature and character to him rather than by birth.

Yahweh's independence of his people was more clearly seen, whilst his connection with other nations and their destiny became clearer. He who is Lord of Nature (4. 13; 5. 8) is Lord also of righteousness, whether in Israel or in her neighbours. If Israel, who is his chosen, shows herself to be unrighteous, then she shall suffer the more for her disobedience. In fact, it appears as though the Lord calls upon the empires around Israel, namely, Egypt and Assyria, to assemble on the mountains of Samaria that they may witness the violence and robbery there.

This cleavage in purpose and character between the Lord and his people presents a problem for this prophet and for later ones. Previously, as the Lord was one with his people, so they served as an entity to be one with him. As the father of a household found himself fully expressed in the family entity, in a psychic unity, so the Lord and his people formed a psychic entity. Their defeat was his defeat. Their triumph was his triumph, even though it was recognized that their disobedience might foil his plans. But with his exaltation amid his people's failure, it now seemed as though he could survive yet his people could be utterly wiped out. Could those who embodied his purpose be utterly destroyed? Yahweh was still Lord in Zion but what of Israel upon whom disaster was so swiftly to fall? This problem remained to be answered. The holy community was divided in its loyalties and affection, though it was recognized that some in Israel, especially the Lord's prophets, had remained faithful. Perhaps there is an element of hope in the closing verses in Amos, when the prophet looks forward to that day when the Lord will raise up the booth of David which is fallen (9. 11). It is open to doubt that the last three verses of hope can be attributed to Amos. But hope was not dead and was re-awakened in a number of different directions.

CHAPTER SEVEN

THE VALUE OF THE INDIVIDUAL

1. Individuation and individuality. The concept of self-identity. Personal distinctiveness in legal attribution of guilt. Changes in the forms of punishment in dealing with persons, with particular reference to the treatment of slaves.
2. Later law-codes and justice for the individual. Love for one's neighbour expressed in the cultus. Religious basis of legal obligation. The growing link between the demands of Yahweh and the common law.
3. The conflict between popular tradition and custom versus royal authority. The prophets' support for the common people. Prophetic demands for the personal obedience of monarch and subject alike. The inner core of loyalty expressed in individual devotion.
4. Yahweh's relationship with mankind as Creator. Man's place in creation within the framework of dependence on Yahweh. The peril of human pride. Human worth rooted in divine purpose, yet subject to the claims of righteousness. Human blessedness as the result of obedience to divine law.
5. Man's solidarity with his fellows. Man's relationship with Yahweh, in Israel, sought to avoid an inchoate cosmopolitanism as well as an exaggerated nationalism. Yahweh's care for those who lay outside of Israel. The rise of individual devotion and responsibility in the teaching of Jeremiah and Ezekial. The rational, moral and religious grounds of human responsibility.

CHAPTER SEVEN

THE VALUE OF THE INDIVIDUAL

ONE of the most important of the new directions was the discovery of the individual. It is a matter of considerable consequence to discover the period when the individual really began to emerge. The polarity between individuality and collectivism is found in all communities, although, in primitive communities, collective responsibility is much more prominent than individual responsibility. From the early materials in the Old Testament, as we have seen, it is the family and the kin which have the prominent place in the scheme of things, whilst the consciousness of the individual ego remains weak. It is therefore of great importance to discover wherein man's essential individuality lies. There has been much discussion whether man is essentially a collective being or an individual one. If the latter is true, wherein does man's individuality lie.

It is a matter of plain experience that there is a distinction between individual existence and individual distinctiveness, between the concept of individuation and that of individuality. Individual existence (or the concept of individuation, as Natorp calls it) is seen in the use of terms, namely, 'this' object is not 'that' one. Even though a fluid may be composed of many similar atoms, yet each atom is 'another atom' compared with the others. In the same manner, the various leaves on an apple tree may be similar in shape, colour and size, yet they are separate in the matter of existence from one another. A robin may be very similar to another robin yet it is clear on a frosty morning, that there are two as they try to take from one another such crumbs as they find. Such individuation may be of little consequence in many cases, especially where the species is considered to be the important factor. In the case of sheep, it is the type of sheep, its wool, its breeding powers and like factors which are important. Any sheep of the species, which fulfills the conditions, may be acceptable. Yet such is not the case with man.

The Value of the Individual

Individuation does not provide much of a clue to the sense of self-identity, which pervades man's actions. Two important factors are involved, among others, in the selfsameness—'that no human being can be exchanged for or confused with any other'[1]—namely, the peculiarities and particularities of the human species *per se* and the sense of identity of the individual self within that species. Various attempts have been made to identify the characteristics of the human species, biologically, intellectually and culturally. It may well be true that 'man is a tool-making animal' and a 'political animal' and 'a law-making animal', yet these characteristics fall short of a satisfactory identity of the self-consciousness of the individual self. Particularly, from a religious standpoint, some further point of reference is necessary—namely, a reference to the higher claim on his personality to which a man is responsible for his actions. Whether in religion or as a citizen, 'the basic phenomenon peculiar to man is the consciousness of responsibility'.[2]

It has already been made clear that, for primitive man, the sense of responsibility was mainly felt as collective responsibility, whilst the consciousness of individual selfhood remained comparatively weak. A society had to gain a considerable measure of integration and security before the individual could break out of the collective restraint and express himself as an individual person. The social recognition of this emancipation of the individual consciousness is not easily identified in its origin but it does appear probable that, among ancient civilizations, it is in the legal constitutions that the recognition of the responsible individual may most clearly be seen. The culture which first gave such recognition, in any fullness, was no doubt the Hellenic one, where the city state in Greece expected each full citizen to exercise his judgement and fulfill his responsibility to the *nomos*, by discussion, by the vote or veto and by the acceptance of public office.

However, the Greek conception of individuality might be summed up in the ancient statement, *principium individuationis est materia*, which is essentially pantheistic and monistic whilst in Democritus it is atomistic. Individuality in terms of persons requires more than a material base, even though much of our

[1] E. Brunner, *Man in Revolt* (1947), p. 280.
[2] W. Eichrodt, *Man in the Old Testament* (1951), p. 9.

individuality (in terms of freedom of self-determination) is 'given', namely, our physical individuality, our psychical structure and inborn talents and capacities. Moreover, every individual person has a history which links him with his family and his race as well as his present environment. This has clearly been seen in regard to the individual Israelite.

It is therefore a matter of importance to discover the ground on which is based man's distinctiveness as a person. In Israel, before the conception of citizenship could have any force, a man had to have a place in the community and it is in the attribution of guilt that a man's individual responsibility began to be seen in a decisive manner. In place of the earlier collective responsibility and retribution, the Book of the Covenant (Exod. 20-23) recognizes the individual as a moral subject, who can act with knowledge and intention in the choice of his actions. It is the owner of the ox, which has been known to gore in the past, who must die if his ox gores a man or woman to death (Exod. 21. 29, 36). The moral personalism ('Thou shalt' and 'Whoever') of the law in the Book of the Covenant is remarkable in the evidence it gives, if indeed it reflects the conditions which belonged to the early years of the settlement in Canaan. The term 'whoever' may cover a man or woman, a full citizen or a sojourner, so that it is the guilty person who is to suffer and, not his kin, for the murder, the kidnapping or the cursing involved (Exod. 21. 12-17). Guilt is removed from the category of an objective fate, which drags the doer down with it, into the realm of conscious and voluntary responsibility, which must be borne by the one who has carried out the deed.

The importance of the attribution of guilt is reflected in the changes which took place in the forms of punishment. It is not easy to discover the date at which such changes take place but there is a sharp contrast in the fact that whilst neighbouring peoples still inflicted death for crimes against property (e.g. the theft of a sacred object from the royal palace, among the Hittites, was punishable by death), yet capital punishment was abolished in this Israelite code for crime against property. If a man steals an ox or destroys another's stacked grain by fire, then he shall make restitution in full (Exod. 22. 1, 3b., 6). If he is unable to make restitution for his theft, then he is to be sold for his theft but there is no indication that his life must be taken. A man's

The Value of the Individual

life, even that of a guilty man, is regarded as more important than property. It is evident that capital punishment has not been abolished altogether, so that a sorceress must be put to death, as also one who lies with a beast or sacrifices to another god (Exod. 22. 18-20). But a man has been differentiated from property and comes to have a higher value.

This enhanced conception of the person, over against the thing, is seen clearly in the treatment which is to be given to slaves. It is still recognized that 'the slave is his master's money' (Exod. 21. 21), but if the slave dies under his master's rod, then the master is to be punished, though if the slave lives on a day or two, the master goes unpunished (verses 20-1). But if the slave is attacked by his master and loses an eye, then the slave is to be set free. If the slave has a tooth knocked out, then he is to be set free 'for the tooth's sake' (Exod. 21. 27). In these regulations to which reference has already been made (cf. p. 58), it is clear that a more humanitarian approach has found a place in the code of law. Whilst a Hebrew slave was to be set free in the seventh year and to depart alone, yet more consideration was to be given to a female slave. 'She shall not go out as the male slaves do' (Exod. 21. 7). She should be permitted to be redeemed by her family (who had sold her) or (if designated for a son) treated as a daughter or be permitted to go free but she must not be sold to a foreign people (Exod. 21. 7-11). If she has been taken into the household and designated by the master for himself, then, when the master takes another wife, the slave-girl's food, clothing and other rights were not to be diminished. This recognition of the personal value of a female slave, at such an early period, is remarkable, especially as the almost unlimited power of the owner over the slave was recognized throughout the ancient world.

This early awareness of the individual, which amounts at times to a concern for him, was re-inforced in the law-codes of succeeding generations. The basis for justice for the individual does not rest on the appeal of force, which threatens the owner who does not recognize any personal rights of his slave—whom he can use as though the slave were a 'thing', an 'It'. The appeal lies increasingly on the loyal acceptance of the law, by all parties. Thus, it is rooted in the sense of personal responsibility. This is expressed in the 'Thou shalt' of the divine Law-giver but such a divine command again is based, not on force, but on love for the Lord. This is only expressly set forth in the Book of Deuteronomy, which appeared during the generation previous to the downfall of the Judean State in 586. The Law Book, which encouraged King Josiah in his reform in 621 B.C., did state clearly the ground for obedience to the commandments, namely, in the *Shema*—'Hear, O Israel: The Lord our God is one Lord; and you shall love the Lord your God with all your heart, and with all your soul, and with all your might. And these words which I command thee this day shall be upon your heart' (Deut. 6. 4-6). This devotion of the heart lay behind the words of the prophets and possibly made the figures of marriage and adultery fitting descriptions of the disloyal heart, whether of the people or of the individual.

Similarly, when the law became elaborated for the purposes of the cult, describing the various ordinances connected with the proper administration and celebration of the cult, namely, in the priestly law of the Book of Leviticus, yet the fundamental importance of the individual choice is not overlooked because it is expressed in care for one's neighbour, 'You shall love your neighbour as yourself: I am the Lord' (Lev. 19. 18), a love which in fact embraces the stranger as well as the native Israelite (Lev. 19. 34.) This evidence from the law-codes is such that Eichrodt claims that 'it may be affirmed without exaggeration that in no other people of the ancient East is the sense of the responsibility of each member of the people so living, and the personal attitude so dominant. The explanation lies in the religious basis of the Law of Israel.'.[1]

As Eichrodt points out, the civilized peoples of the ancient East normally believed that the gods were concerned with justice, so that when an Assyrian or Babylonian king came to power, he claimed that the god who called him to power also endowed him with authority to administer justice. However, it was the king's power and justice which the sovereign sought to secure by the help of the gods, whilst, in Israel, legal obligation had a religious basis. The king was called upon to administer a law which he had been given in the cultic observances of the people. He, like his people, was under a religious obligation to carry out the legal behests of the Lord. As the king was never essentially deified in

[1] W. Eichrodt, *Man in the Old Testament*, p. 13.

Israel, he could never claim to be on an equality with the gods or over-rule their authority with regard to the law. Therefore, in regard to the Law, even the king had no other court of appeal but by repentance and forgiveness, when he broke it, as David himself recognized (2 Sam. 12. 13).

Moreover, the Law which in Israel originated in the cultic ritual, with its 'Thou shalt', did not merely remain in the cultic ritual but came to cover the 'common law' (the ordinary legal tradition) of the local courts of the villages and towns. Rather than being confined to the appointed place (the Ark and its Shrine) and to the holy officials (priests and prophets), who summoned the people to obey the Lord of the Covenant (Deut. 27. 14-26), the local traditional law is transformed into a channel of instruction in the ways of Yahweh. This consecrated the civil law and made disobedience to the Law not merely a moral offence but a religious offence.

This had an important result from the viewpoint of the individual. It meant that the Law came to be regarded in Israel as not merely a royal concern (important as that was) but reached down to the ordinary members of the community, who were placed under an unconditional obligation to the divine Lawgiver. The Law-giver had a concern for and interest in the ordinary Israelite, with a particular concern for those who were the more defenceless in the community, namely, the stranger, the widow and the orphan as well as the Levite (Deut. 14. 29). This concern of the Lord was a living experience for Israel, which could never take its existence as a people for granted. As a unit, Israel had only to recall that it had been a band of slaves who were lifted out of the Slough of Despond and were created a people, powerful and self-conscious, because, in his loving-kindness and for his own sake, the Lord had given them the Covenant-relationship, expressed in the Law and the promises. The divine demand upon them was 'from the beginning embedded in a history of this God with his people'.[4] Eichrodt claims that this divine demand 'was laid with such exclusive power on the individual' but such a claim can be over-pressed, since the evidence appears to point to a divine command, which was felt to be a corporate obligation for a long period—long before it came to have a fully significant place for the individual. 'The exclusive

[4] Ibid., pp. 16-17.

claim on the individual' rested on the individual as an *Israelite* rather than on him as an individual with worth as such. The day of the recognition of the individual even in Israel took a long period to mature. Nevertheless, the early strata in the law-codes of Israel, from the time when Israel entered Canaan, began to differentiate the individual from the mass of society and to give him a measure of responsibility and obligation, not merely towards his fellows (as a member of society) but towards the divine Law-giver, whom he approached in worship. His personal acts were within the purview of the Lord and the opinions of the elders were the concern of the Lord as well.

The extension of the concern of the Lord into the day-to-day judgements and ordinances of the local community did not take place without considerable resistance, especially on the part of the rulers, who desired to establish their own authority in matters of Justice. This is apparent from the early days of the monarchy as may be seen from the occasion when Saul disregarded the ancient law of the ban, pronounced by Yahweh's prophet, against the Amelekites (1 Sam. 15). Similarly, Saul failed to obey the divine ordinance with regard to sacrifice. Such acts by Saul amounted, in fact, to an attempt to place the monarchy outside the duty of absolute obedience to the divine commandments, even though such obedience was expected from the ordinary Israelite.

Moreover, the divine sanction which was given to popular traditional laws (such as the sanctity which was attached to the family inheritance) appeared to the politically successful ruler as an unwarranted and intolerable limitation on the normal rights of a sovereign. It meant that another law ran through his kingdom and that the sovereign, like his subjects, had to bow to it. This limitation was probably felt more keenly in the Northern Kingdom of Israel than in the Southern Kingdom of Judah, where the Davidic conception of the covenant in loyalty to Yahweh probably retained a larger measure of acceptance. Nevertheless, even in the Southern Kingdom, under Manasseh and Ahaz, there is seen the triumph of Assyrian justice, with religious and political conceptions which went with it. The severest struggle took place in the North, where the politically brilliant rule of the House of Omri came as the climax in the development of the Northern Kingdom. This royal house sought

The Value of the Individual

to assimilate the law and religion of their kingdom to that of the surrounding Canaanite-Phoenician world. Ahab, of the House of Omri, who was married to Jezebel, the daughter of a successful neighbouring king, found that his wife's standards and those of the prophets of Yahweh were so deeply in conflict, that the triumph of the one could only be by the extermination of the other, so Elijah killed all the prophets of Ba'al (1 Kgs. 18. 40).

Nevertheless, it is clear from the Old Testament record, that the powerful authority of the monarchs did not overawe the devoted Yahwist prophet and priest, who remained uncompromising in their loyalty to the pre-eminent commands of Yahweh. Jezebel might endeavour to break the opposition by destroying the prophets of Yahweh, yet still those in high places gave them food and shelter (1 Kgs. 18. 4) and there still remained a great company (seven thousand) who had not bowed the knee to Ba'al (1 Kgs. 19. 18). The viewpoint of the loyal Yahwist is seen in the so-called 'royal code' in Deuteronomy (17. 14-20). This code expresses a limitation on the royal prerogative, the king's authority and control, which would have been intolerable in any of the neighbouring oriental states. Such a passage demonstrates the strength of the Israelite devotion to the Law which had its basis in a belief in God—One Who bound together as 'brothers' (king and shepherd alike) the whole community of Israel. (It is a matter for regret that there has not survived adequate evidence from Moabite and Ammonite law codes to provide light on the strange and peculiar stance of Israel which arose out of her faith.)

Whilst Saul might endeavour to take (divine and human) affairs into his own hands, yet Samuel's unequivocal demand rings out as a challenge to any leader who dared to challenge the authority of Yahweh over Israel. 'To obey is better than sacrifice and to hearken than the fat of rams' (1 Sam. 15. 22). This demand was re-iterated again and again. Such a demand made the ritual offerings meaningless unless they were accompanied by a personal obedience, which was offered with the gifts to God. But personal obedience was not merely true in respect of the king but also in respect of the subject who also had to offer 'sincerity of heart' to the Lord. Here lay another road along which the individuality of man was able to travel to a place of responsibility—in the presence of the Lord. As the sons of Jesse passed before Samuel, the prophet was reminded that it was not appearance or stature but on the heart, that the Lord looked (1 Sam. 16. 7). Sincerity of heart is a personal attribute and it serves as a refrain which is carried forward by the psalmists. 'He leads the humble in what is right and teaches the humble his way . . . Who is the man that fears the Lord? Him will he instruct in the way that he should choose' (Ps. 25. 9, 12). 'The friendship of the Lord is for those who fear him and he makes known to them his covenant' (verse 14). Whilst it has to be borne in mind that such expressions of devotion, in which the singular personal pronoun is used (such as 'I', 'me', 'he'), may well have a corporate reference (as the offering of devotion by Israel), yet the use of such personal terms, together with the use of such terms as loving-kindness, thankfulness and trust, gave opportunity for the growth of individual initiative in the approach to God—an initiative which came to fulfilment in due time.

The law of Israel which bound king and subject and made personal demands on all alike served as a protection for Israel (or the remnant of Israel) in the days when her political success came to an end and both the kingdoms were shattered. It was the endeavour of the prophets to preserve the inner core of devotion (corporate and individual) to Yahweh against all who would weaken that devotion by the syncretistic worship of other gods. The record in the historical books shows the care with which the writers and editors (whether one or many) chose their material to outline the steady prophetic witness to a loyalty and service which belonged alone to Yahweh. To ensure this devotion, the prophets were prepared to face any cost, even that of life itself. At length, the community (in terms of a political unit) broke in pieces, part of it was hewn down by the sword and part was scattered like chaff to the four winds and part was destroyed in the fire which demolished Jerusalem (Ezek. 5. 2), yet a small number survived to become the bearers of the covenant. Then there was seen the importance of the earlier devotion, as the cult-community which remained true still had the rule of the Lord of the Covenant wherever they might be called to fulfill it.

It may indeed be claimed that the works of the prophets saved the faith for the individual as well as for the community but

The Value of the Individual 141

before we explore further their contribution to the development of the individual's faith, it is well to turn to certain basic issues which stand behind faith in Yahweh from the beginning—issues which have a close bearing on the place of man as man, namely, the belief in Yahweh as Creator and as the Source of the solidarity of mankind.

Whilst the Covenant-relationship made Israel deeply aware of the acts of God, yet it was not only in history that the divine might could be seen but also in the work of creation. The God who had acted in calling Israel, 'He is God; there is no other beside him' (Deut. 4. 35). This gave a validity to the physical universe of which he is the Transcendent Ground. He does not arise out of the natural order (as Mithras emerged from the tree) nor is he a demiurge who constructs the world out of existing materials as in other creation-myths of the Middle East. On the contrary, he is absolutely free in his activity and calls the world into existence as the expression of his will alone. This hiddenness in the divine action makes it impossible for man to claim that he is other than part of creation. Man cannot subsume himself simply under some natural principle of species and classify all that there is, so that the ultimate reason of all creation can be proved. To grasp the whole plan is possible to the absolute Creator alone. Herein the majesty and power of the created order were never under-estimated as may be seen in the early creation story in *Genesis* 2 as well as in the Psalms which extol the work of creation, such as *Psalms* 8, 19 (which opens with the majestic words: 'The heavens are telling the glory of God; and the firmament proclaims his handiwork'), 29, 104 and 148. So too a similar viewpoint is set forth in the priestly account in *Genesis* 1 and in the speeches of the Lord in the Book of *Job* (38-41). No attempt is made to claim a natural kinship between the Lord and his creatures. To fathom the eternal thought and plan is beyond the creature, so the Lord is God, 'wholly other', beside whom there is no other.

The belief in the Creator does, however, lead on to an important aspect of the doctrine of man. Whilst man is a creature and is in continual dependence upon the Maker of all, yet the Creator Himself has a unique relationship with man. 'It consists of God's honouring man, and him alone of all creatures, by addressing him and confronting him as a "Thou".[5] The Lord of 'all worlds that are' manifests his willingness to communicate and enter into communion with man who thus is ranged in part with God in confronting the rest of creation. This realization, that man is not simply part of the order of creation but has qualities which enable him to rise above the rest—in fact to have lordship over other parts of creation—is evident even in early Israel's thought. In the earlier account of creation (Gen. 2), a clear distinction is made between man and the rest of the animals. Man is created first and then placed amid the good things which God makes. Man's control is expressed in his power to give names to all things yet he was not to sink to the level of the sub-human for a 'helper'. It was a woman, one like himself, who was to share in the responsibility with him. This 'separateness' between man and the rest of creation is described by the later priestly writer, in significant terms: 'So God created man in his own image, in the image of God he created him; man and female he created them' (Gen. 1. 27). Thus the writer expressed his conviction that man has a significance and place which is other than that of other animals. Man has a destiny and responsibility which he alone can discharge in the cosmic purpose of God. Dramatic utterance is given to this conviction in Psalm 8. 'When I look at thy heavens, the work of thy fingers, the moon and the stars which thou hast established; what is man that thou art mindful of him . . . ? Yet thou hast made him little less than God . . . Thou hast given him dominion over the works of thy hands; thou has put all things under his feet' (verses 3-6). Such a proud position might well lead man into the supreme sin in Greek tragedy, namely, *hubris* (pride), but the other Psalms (19, 29; 104; 135 and 147), to which reference has been made, testify to the work of the Lord's hand in creation, so that to the Lord alone belongs praise for all that has been made. Whilst God has necessarily to stand over against his creation, man cannot stand with him absolutely but can stand at a further distance from Nature, because he shares God's image. Such a conception of man's place in the natural order has a number of implications. Since all nature is God's creation, so all that God has made is good and the world is seen as no longer hostile to man, with fearful nature-gods of variable moods. Man now is set free from fear of his

[5] W. Eichrodt, *Man in the Old Testament*, p. 30.

The Value of the Individual

environment, so that he may have a responsible place in the creative activity of God, sharing in the achievement of the divine will and goal.

Nevertheless, as Greek drama noted only too well, *hubris* (man's presumptuous claim to almightyness) is a constant threat to man's well-being. Man cannot take the resources of nature and use them simply as he wishes. There are laws of the natural world and there are intricate inter-relationships between the several activities in the different orders within nature and it ill behoves man with his limited knowledge of the whole to act as though all things were entirely his own. The Hebrew was well aware of his limitation of knowledge as we find set forth so dramatically in the Book of Job (38-41), where the Lord defends his position as the One to Whom the whole is known. 'Where were you when I laid the foundation of the earth? ... Who determined its measurements—surely you know!' (38. 4-5), to which Job replies: 'Therefore I have uttered what I did not understand, things too wonderful for me, which I did not know' (42. 3). In similar fashion, the Wisdom of God, which is beyond the knowledge of men, is described in personalized terms in *Proverbs* (8. 22-31) as well as in *Job* (28. 12-23). If the creative purposes of God are separated from their divine source and the laws of nature are viewed simply as mechanistic regularities, then man finds it hard to reach any clear conception of his destiny. This is brought out clearly in the pessimistic tones of the writer of the book of *Ecclesiastes*, who even though he saw all the work of God, yet believed that 'man cannot find out the work that is done under the sun. However much man may toil in seeking, he will not find it out; even though a wise man claims to know, he cannot find it out' (Eccles. 8. 17). In his view, life is over-shadowed by vanity and purposelessness. Wisdom is beyond the reach of man though it may lie within the mind of God.

Despite such limitations, the place of man *vis-à-vis* nature is brought out clearly in the Old Testament as part of the relationship between the Creator and his creatures which is referred to as a covenant in the promise to Noah (Gen. 9. 9). Man has to respect the life of the animal world and of the land and has to act within certain limits which are placed upon his activity. These include the offering of the first fruits to the Lord (Exod.

23. 19), breeding cattle of like kind (Lev. 19. 19) and yoking beasts of like kind (Deut. 22. 9f.). In the latter two references, there is also a prohibition on planting together different kinds of seeds. Thus, man was taught his responsibility in the care of creation. He had to show respect to the various orders in nature and in particular, there was special abhorrence when man failed to respect such orders. In such cases as when man attempted to have intercourse with lower orders in the animal world (Lev. 20. 15), both man and beast are to be put to death. In due time, when Canaan came to be held in special honour as the divine inheritance, then man had a special responsibility to exercise true human behaviour there. Since the life of nature in this land was the gift of Yahweh, man had to make due response to Yahweh in his use of it (Jer. 2. 7; 3. 1f.). If man failed to use such provision aright, then he must expect to be 'vomited out', where the land had been defiled (Lev. 18. 25). Herein, the act of God as Creator is linked with His work as Redeemer and it ill betides man to believe that he can live without responsibility towards Yahweh in either capacity.

On the other hand, the Hebrew Psalmist is often found linking together the work of God as Creator and Redeemer. When Yahweh sends forth His spirit, the earth is created and all living things receive their food (Ps. 104. 27-30), yet in the same psalm the writer prays that sinners be consumed from the earth (verse 35), as the Creator also wills righteousness as the Redeemer. In the Psalm 105, the stress lies on the work of the Lord as Redeemer. 'Remember the wonderful works that he has done, his miracles and the judgements he uttered' (verse 5). Therefore, man can face the natural world with assurance as a home which the Lord has provided but, at the same time, man can face his fellows and history with assurance, since the same Lord is strong to redeem.

These two aspects of the Lord's activity serve as a guide to man in his goal. As Creator, God has placed man in a veritable garden of the Lord. Man is a husbandman, to cultivate and guard the good things in the garden. This cannot be done without toil, in fact, without great toil—which is regarded as a curse due to man's disobedience (Gen. 2. 15). Yet in his work, man can work with the Lord's blessing since he has been commissioned to 'be fruitful and multiply and fill the earth and subdue it' (Gen.

1. 28). Since man's blessedness lies in the doing of the Lord's will, then contrariwise, in man's refusal lies his curse (Isa. 48. 22). This is amplified in later days, when the commandments of the Lord had been filled out in fuller measure, but the central conception remained the same. The Lord willed blessedness in obedience but a curse would result from disobedience (Deut. 11. 26-28). Disobedience might involve either (or both) the denial of allegiance to Yahweh as Creator or Redeemer—in any case, such denial spelled disaster and death for disobedience.

It is not therefore a matter for surprise that the ends of moral action are defined in terms of practical blessedness, namely, natural goods which mark a man in the eyes of his fellows. Such natural goods included earthly possessions, many children, longevity, friendship, wisdom, beauty, honour and political freedom—indications of physical, mental and spiritual wholeness. It was only to be expected that if a man sought to do the Lord's will, then the natural good things in life would fall to his lot. 'The rewards for humility and fear of the Lord is riches and honour and life' (Prov. 22. 4). There was no place for the contrast made, in extreme ascetic views, between the natural life (with delight in physical good) and the spiritual life, which alone is given value. To depreciate the material aspect of life in the interest of the spiritual is to create a dichotomy which was alien to the thought of the Old Testament Hebrew, who believed that God had made all things (material and otherwise) and had seen that they were good. Yet, such an appreciation of life's material blessings were within the conception of responsibility to the Creator, who was also Redeemer, so that irresponsibility in the use of these material things was ruled out. This became a problem of some significance for Israel when life's good things became a temptation to disloyalty to Yahweh. In particular, a man's special gifts might prove a source of *hubris*, which led him to act against the divine purpose—as in the case of Absalom, who won many hearts by his youthful beauty; of Michal, the king Saul's daughter, who was proud of her royal dignity and of David, with the kingdom as his possession.⁹ The increase in wealth and elaboration of the external trappings of economic success easily led to a strong belief in one's own ability, on the one hand, and in continuing well-being as inevitable on the other. Pleasure and power,

⁹ W. Eichrodt, *Man in the Old Testament*, pp. 46f.

irrespective of the demands of justice and morality, could replace the belief in responsibility towards Yahweh. Therefore, the prophets spoke out forcefully against such a betrayal of the divine mission of Israel—such irresponsibility would dissolve the bonds which knit the nation together and deny to every man the very goods which he desired. Thus the emphasis came to fall, as we have seen, on the use of such good things within the obedience which is due to Yahweh. If he demands the destruction of the unclean thing, then woe betide the man who hangs on to it.

If a man continued to seek the will of God, then he could expect to find blessing. Such blessing would bring joy to man and also to God. It is in praise and with shouts of joy that the morning stars sang together with all the sons of God in the beginning (Job 38. 7), so joy continues to be a hallmark of the divine handiwork (Prov. 8. 22-31) and of the man who pleases God (Eccles. 2. 26). A man and his household is able to rejoice in the blessing of the Lord in all his labour (Deut. 12. 7; 14. 26). Likewise in the festivals (Lev. 23. 40) and appointed feasts (Num. 10. 10), man could rejoice before the Lord in gratitude for all his goodness. Even in the evil day, when the wicked man seems to flourish, yet the righteous man can rejoice in the protection which he finds in the Lord (Ps. 5. 12). Similarly, there is rejoicing in the deliverance which the Lord will give to his people (Ps. 14. 7). The servants of the Lord can look forward in the hope that his steadfast love will give satisfaction and joy will fill the days (Ps. 90. 14). Such a firm conviction that joy has part in God's purpose for man in his life here gives to the individual man the assurance that the pleasures of life are not to be dismissed but are to be used within the purpose of God.

The recognition which is given to man in the whole created order is complemented by the solidarity which exists between men in relation to one another. There is in fact an attempt made to overcome the natural divisions which are liable to create hostility and even destruction. There is, for example, the division between men and women which is recognized in a surprising equality, even though only in principle. In the older tradition, woman appears as the fulfilment and completion of man, by the Lord's act (Gen. 2. 18), whilst, in the priestly record, woman's creation in the image of God is acknowledged, so that woman

The Value of the Individual

shares with man in a special destiny of grace (Gen. 1. 27). This gave a divine sanction to marriage and lifted up this institution among social relationships, closing less worthy doors.

The conception of Yahweh as Creator is extended to embrace not merely the physical order, with man's place in it, but also to provide an explanation for the relationship of peoples to one another. As all men are created by the One God, so all peoples are members of one great family. Such a concept appears to be unique in the literature of Eastern peoples, so that in Genesis 10 there is a list of the nations, among which is Israel, which is proud of its special place within the solidarity of humanity as a whole. This solidarity is very marked. Israel is unable to boast that she is outstanding in natural ability or greatness in comparison to other nations. There is no evidence that some races are 'naturally inferior' or slave-races which are less than human, as the Greeks tended to regard the 'barbaroi' beyond their borders. However exclusive the priestly writer may have been in his outlook in his attempt to exalt Israel, yet the relationship between all peoples (non-Israelites included) and God was regarded as a covenant of mercy (Gen. 9. 16).

The Hebrew conception of the unity of mankind served, as Eichrodt has pointed out, to safeguard the Israelites against two 'pressing dangers" Humanity does not get lost in a 'perverted cosmopolitanism, to which the individual's responsibility to his own nation is a matter of indifference'. Secondly, humanity is not destroyed by an exaggerated view of the nation or state, which often blazed up in Israel when political misfortune overtook them. The first danger was overcome by the powerful combination of individual responsibility and the life of the community (later the nation), since this combination called upon the individual to take his full share in the normal and natural institutions of society, namely, the family, the community and the State, within which the individual had his part in forwarding the growth of the holy people of God. Moreover, the very command to 'love his neighbour as himself' served to emphasize his duty to his immediate neighbours with whom he had relationships and had to live his life from day to day.

The second danger is evident in the challenge which came from national exclusiveness. The people of Yahweh, who served

[7] W. Eichrodt, *Man in the Old Testament*, pp. 36f.

him under the covenant, could not easily forget that their unity, in the early days, arose out of the amphictyony, which was a sacred one and was centred on the covenant-relationship. Their various charismatic leaders constantly reminded them that the promises were dependent upon obedience. They could expect naught but sorrow and disaster if they allowed any other claim to take precedence over their loyalty to Yahweh. Nevertheless, when the monarchy grew strong, there was a natural growth in national feelings, which encouraged the people to believe that the divine promises would bolster up their national claims and bring them political success. They came to believe that they could use the covenant as a religious support for power politics, with condemnation in military terms of the surrounding nations, which had to submit to Israel in the time of her strength. In this way, there remained the ever present danger that the Lord of all might would be regarded as a national god, whose work was to see that his people prospered and that other nations (which opposed his people) would be humiliated. It is in this light that the prophets' fight against the royal interest needs to be seen. The attempt to bring down the purpose of Yahweh to an identification with the political success of Israel had the corollary that if God had to rule all lands then it would mean Israel's glorification. The disaster that befell the monarchy and the State in the two kingdoms at least served to vindicate the teaching of the prophets, for whom righteousness and obedience were of more consequence than national glorification. As the exiled community in Babylon emerged from the blows to their political fortunes as well as to their faith, they looked forward with new insight into their mission among the nations. The national hopes were not dead that a new state would rise and be a glorious one but there also arose a more universal viewpoint, which found expression in the book of *Ruth* and *Jonah*. These books reveal a conception of Yahweh as a God of mercy, whose concern reaches out to the heathen nations and gives to the non-Jew a place in his purpose. In the book of *Jonah*, even Ninevah (the capital of the cruel Assyria)—'the bloody city, all full of lies and booty—no end to the plunder! (Nahum 3. 1)—comes within the loving concern of God, whose compassion covers also the cattle in the city (Jonah 4. 11). In the book of *Ruth*, the Moabitess (Ruth) has her place as an ancestress of the great king David.

The Value of the Individual

Similarly, in the Psalms, the Lord is praised not only as the King of Israel but as Lord of all the earth—'Declare his glory among the nations, his marvellous works among all the peoples . . . Say among the nations, "The Lord reigns! . . . he will judge the peoples with equity"' (Ps. 96. 3, 10; cf. Pss. 97 and 99). The kingdom of the Lord is universal and his rule is to be established over all peoples. At the same time, in the post-exilic community, the nationalist and particularist hopes were kept alive (Isa. 66. 18f.; Zech. 9. 11-11. 3; Obad. 15ff.).

Both these beliefs, namely, that Yahweh is Creator who has given man a creative relationship with himself and that Yahweh is the Source of the solidarity of mankind, served to strengthen the conviction that God expects the individual man to show responsibility towards himself and other men. Such beliefs confirmed those rights and responsibilities which belonged to the individual man under Yahweh's covenant-law. Nevertheless, as the national community, with its strong cultic unity, came to break up under the pressure of Babylon, so the prophetic message tended to accelerate the development of the individual who by choice could become part of a new community. This new community grew out of the loyalty of those committed men and women who offered their individual devotion to God to continue the covenant. This individual devotion, as we have seen, had its roots in the legal codes and beliefs of Israel, but it was fostered by the prophetic teaching, which was so often opposed to national policy. As the individual voice of the prophet was raised up against the actions of king and court, so an individual's faith was hammered out on the anvil of experience. This was particularly true in the case of Jeremiah whose lead was followed by Ezekiel.

The prophet Jeremiah was not insensitive to his place in the heritage of the people of God. As a member of a family, which had cared for the Ark, as priests, in the days before the kingdoms were established, Jeremiah would be trained to be keenly conscious of the vocation of Israel. Nevertheless, his family in Anathoth were no doubt also keenly critical of the national cult, which centered in Jerusalem and which was served by priests, whose leading family had ousted his own from a position of leadership. Despite this hereditary conflict between two families of proud lineage, Jeremiah appears to have supported the reformation, sponsored by king Josiah and the priesthood in Jerusalem (Jer. 11. 6), but such support by Jeremiah resulted in antagonism from his own townsmen who threatened his life unless he ceased to prophesy (11. 21). Not only did Jeremiah suffer from this estrangement from his own townsmen and kinsfolk but he felt that his vocation demanded that he should not marry and have children (16. 2), since, with the collapse of the nation, there would follow deadly diseases, with famine and the sword. As with the other prophets, acts of symbolism played a large part in Jeremiah's message, setting forth in dramatic and forthright manner the truths which he wished to impress on the people. Jeremiah was convinced that his people had deserted Yahweh, 'the fountain of living waters and hewed out cisterns for themselves, broken cisterns, that can hold no water' (2. 13). Such desertion would result in disaster for Israel—'Have you not brought this upon yourself? ... your wickedness will chasten you and your apostasy will reprove you' (2. 17, 19). Yet the prophet was a sensitive soul who loved his people, so at times he shrank from the burden of his own message but when he restrained himself, his message burned within him as 'a burning fire', shut up in his bones, until he could no longer hold it in (20. 9). For a long period, he was called upon to lash his people, who were to drink of the cup of the Lord's wrath, which would make all the nations drunk and reel in lust and battle (Jer. 25. 15ff.).

As he became increasingly estranged from the national cult, so his loneliness increased. Although he had supported the reform under King Josiah, in the hope that the kingdom might 'ask for the ancient paths' (6. 16), yet he came to realize that the people did not have any real intention of seeking the paths of righteousness and peace, so that only evil could result from such obtuseness and heedlessness (6. 17-19). Moreover, Jeremiah, like his prophetic predecessors, condemned the ritual practices which were the people's expression of devotion. 'Your burnt offerings are not acceptable, nor your sacrifices pleasing to me' (6. 20), claiming that such offerings were not part of the original covenant. The Lord gave no command concerning burnt offerings and sacrifices (7. 22). His concern lay with matters of obedience—if they obeyed his voice and follow his commandments, then they would go forward in blessing. For Jeremiah, his people's great need was that of cleansing—'to remove the

The Value of the Individual

foreskin of their hearts', 'O Jerusalem, wash your heart from wickedness, that you may be saved' (4. 3, 14).

This experience of Jeremiah led him and succeeding thinkers into two paths of development. On the one hand, the intensity of his loneliness drove him into any inward seeking for a closer communion with the God, who spoke so powerfully through him. When all the world (his world) was opposed to him, with powerful interests trying to stop his message, he turned to God who had called him to undertake so difficult a task. So his religion became an individual possession which he had to hold, not in common with his people, but despite their endeavours to turn him away from his true path. From the anvil of his inner life, under the hammer-blows of his message and of his times, there was wrought out a faith of pure devotion, which saw that the individual soul must give account of itself to God. Quoting the old-time adage, 'The fathers have eaten sour grapes, and the children's teeth are set on edge', Jeremiah claims that 'every one shall die for his own sin; each man who eats sour grapes, his teeth shall be set on edge' (31. 29f.). The prophet looked forward to a new day when a new covenant will be established between God and the house of Israel and the house of Judah—a covenant unlike the marital one which they broke because this new relationship will take the form of an inner law which will be written on their hearts. Moreover, this covenant will be such that it will no longer be communicated through exalted figures (priest, prophet and king) but will be open to the least of the people as well as to the greatest. Thus, the vision was implied of a universal God who was seeking to communicate himself to the individual—an insight which would lead in due time to the 'priesthood of all believers'. Jeremiah's conception of the new covenant (Jer. 31. 31-34) was one path from which fruitful development came.

On the other hand, Jeremiah's insistence on inner cleansing, for which no ritual practice could act as a substitute, led to a new conception of worship, namely, to a religious faith in which there was no external cult. Such a faith would have been well nigh impossible for the ancient believer, since his cult, his community and himself were all part of one offering. The prophetic witness against the ritual sacrifices (or, as some claim, against the abuse of such ritual practices divorced from moral responsibility) prepared the way for the worship of the synagogue, when the book of the Law in its Ark held the central place, with stress on circumcision, on the Sabbath and 'sacrifices of thanksgiving' in place of the animal sacrifices of an earlier day. Such a mode of worship could provide a channel of approach to the most High God for the individual, for whom (like Jeremiah) 'the heart knows its own bitterness, and no stranger shares its joy' (Prov. 14. 10). The Exile separated the Jews in Babylon from all the acts of worship which had meant so much in earlier times. The King in Mount Zion had ceased as a political reality, since the earthly Mount Zion had been destroyed. Yet the hope of David's house, and the restoration of the monarchy lived on in the hearts of the exiles. More important still, the faith in Yahweh—a faith which had begun to have universal implications had begun to be transformed to become a message which would be a means of redemption for all nations, with Israel's very suffering as a channel by which this message might reach the hearts of all men.

Ezekiel was concerned too about the divine Justice. He quoted the same proverb, as Jeremiah (above), and then declared that 'the soul that sins shall die' (Ezek. 18. 4). He then outlined the individuality of justice, namely, that 'true justice between man and man' and walking in the statutes of the Lord will bring a man honour even though as father he may begat a bad son or as son he may be heir to a bad father. Men asked, 'why should not the son suffer for the iniquity of the father?' (verse 19), to which Ezekiel replies that the son who does that which is lawful and right, he shall live. 'The righteousness of the righteous shall be upon himself and the wickedness of the wickedness shall be upon himself' (verse 20).

Thus, Ezekiel sought to remove men from the shackles of corporate guilt which had held his people over the centuries. His message sought in fact to lift from their hearts the dead weight of a fatalism, which threatened to inhibit all endeavour. They could no longer lay at the door of their heritage the sorry state in which they lay, blaming the transgressions and sins of former days (Ezek. 33. 10). They regarded themselves as 'dried up bones, whose hope is lost' (Ezek. 37. 11). But the prophet brought fresh vigour and life into his people by reminding them that even if, in the past, a man had been wicked, yet the Lord would have mercy upon that man, if he turned from his wickedness to walk

The Value of the Individual

in the paths of righteousness. In like manner, the Lord would have mercy on his people (despite their fathers' behaviour), if they followed his commandments (33. 11). Each generation, yea each man, may have a fair chance as he stands before the bar of God's justice. Thus, Ezekiel and Jeremiah encouraged individual Jews, who were cast down with the political misfortune of their people, to find fresh resources in their faith and to affirm afresh their loyalty to Yahweh, who ruled above the passing currents of the affairs of men and yet within them was Lord of all.

The claim that 'the basic phenomenon peculiar to man is the consciousness of responsibility'[8] raises the important issue as to whom or to what is man responsible. In the Greek cities, the free citizen thought of himself as primarily responsible to the nomos which was shared by all, with some recognition that he was responsible also to the gods of the nomos. At a later time, among the Greek philosophers, as also among her dramatists, it was the moral law (*Dike* or *Fatum*), to which man was responsible and which he was liable to break by his '*hubris*'. Responsibility appears, however, to be a necessity for full human development and much appears to depend on the nature of the authority to which man feels a measure of responsibility.

Whenever the Greek ideal of man has raised its head afresh, there has been a re-affirmation of man's individuality but whether such an ideal can continue to be upheld apart from a sense of relatedness to a larger reality may well be questioned. This idea awoke afresh with the Renaissance, but although 'the Renaissance began with the affirmation of man's creative individuality; it ended with its denial'.[9] It is difficult to uphold so lofty an ideal unless the basis is firm and deep in a superhuman reality. Furthermore, it has been claimed that rationalism is truly concerned with man's nobility and place, rather than with 'unreal metaphysical ideals'. Certainly, rationalism has striven hard to establish the important place of the individual in society and in the world. During the period of the French Revolution, rationalism sought freedom of thought, of speech and assembly, all of which were products of a hard-won toleration. It also sought to uphold the rights of the individual with its desire for

[8] W. Eichrodt, *Man in the Old Testament*, p. 11.
[9] N. Berdyaev, *The End of Our Time* (1919-23). Eng. trans. (1933), p. 54.

democracy *(Liberté, Egalité, Fraternité)*. Nevertheless, such ideals were proclaimed more as moral ideals than as essential facts. On rationalistic grounds, individualism is hard put to find grounds for demonstrating man's supremacy. On the one hand, his individualism may destroy the community whilst on the other hand, it is not difficult for man to sink to the level of the animals. Reason may provide man with capabilities to lift him above other animals but will it provide the motive-power and an adequate goal? What is the criterion for reason? Self-love or society? What if it should prove that the two should turn out to be the same? Alexander Pope extolled man's acquisitive powers, with all the rest of human instincts, in his conception of a deist God, who left the powers of Nature to proceed without further effort on his part. The rest could be left to rational man. So Pope wrote:

> 'Thus God and Nature linked the general frame
> And bade self love and social be the same.'[10]

The Age of Reason in the eighteenth century enabled men to develop their individualism, with a vicious penal system to support the well-being of higher status groups in society. Thus, property was protected and the poor were in destitution, through lack of effort or downright badness. It was easy to see the reasons for the lack of social concern, even in England where the fierce fires of religion had not caused so much disaster as on the Continent. Yet even when rationalism became caught up later in the rationalistic liberalism, man did not really find himself carried beyond himself. He may well have tried to find a key to relatedness but he still searched in vain, until the totalitarian revolt revealed again man's irradicable social belongingness—a super-individual whole into which his selfhood has to enter and find fulfillment. 'This relatedness is not only the object but the root of his being.'[11] If he does not find the key, then man's very individuality may wreck havoc in atomizing society. There has been ample opportunity for men to see the fruits of individualist theories, since, in the economic area, such theories are characteristic in the 17th to 19th centuries in Western Europe, from the days of John Locke to those of Herbert Spenser. In the

---

[10] Alexander Pope, *An Essay on Man*, Ep. 111., 11. 317-8.
[11] V. A. Demant, *The Religious Prospect*, pp. 113, 119.

The Value of the Individual

psychological field, the individualism of David Hobbes led to an atomism which in its extreme form is philosophic anarchism.

An ancient and logical alternative position to the exaltation of human reason is the philosophical theory of naturalism. Naturalism may have various meanings. It may refer to a method of approach to the understanding of phenomena, an empirical use of observation and experiment. It may mean a theory of the universe in which all things, including mind, God and matter, are held to belong to the natural order. For its use in philosophic theory, it may be held to mean any philosophy according to which physical or material things and processes are considered ultimate. This eliminates any belief in any outside control. Nature itself is conceived to be uncreated and eternal. Such a non-theistic perspective is not new. Leucippus, Democritus and Lucretius formulated theories of dogmatic materialism which in the case of the first two thinkers date back to the fifth century B.C. The attempt to reduce all formula and phenomena to quantitative terms reduces the individual man to matter, such that the transcendence of man's intelligence becomes a perennial problem. Despite the attempt of Julian Huxley to present a naturalistic humanism, in his book *Religion Without Revelation*, it is difficult to avoid the dilemma, which was stated by Francis Bacon: 'They that deny a God destroy man's nobility, for certainly man is of kin to the beasts by his body and if he be not kin to God, by his spirit, he is a base and ignoble creature.'[12] The claim by Feuerbach, Freud and Huxley that religious aspirations are solely due to the primitive and inveterate tendency of man to personify the forces of the universe around him, allowing no place to divine revelation, still leaves man with the problem of his ideals and aspirations. Are these ideals related to objective conditions in any fundamental way? Are they merely the fruit of natural processes and the interplay of man in society, without any 'down-rush from the Super-conscious', as Bishop Gore claimed? The facts of human existence present the same amoral face as Nature herself unless there is the element of value which transends them. The claim that religion has provided an open door to value by emphasizing the life of the spirit gives hope.

It is in the realm of value that man is most himself. 'The fact that man can transcend himself in infinite regression and cannot

[12] Francis Bacon, *Essay* 16 ('Atheism').

find the end of life except in God is the mark of his creativity and uniqueness.'[12] It is strange that to find his individuality a man has to look beyond himself, since to have himself alone may well leave him in a land of shadows which is a form of hell.

> 'What is hell? Hell is oneself,
> Hell is alone, the other figures in it
> Merely projections. There is nothing to escape from
> And nothing to escape to. One is always alone.'[14]

Calvin defined the death of the soul as to be without God, 'to be abandoned to oneself'.[15] Therefore, the very emancipation which was given to the individual when he was set free from the bonds of an all-embracing communal unity presented man with problems. There was the problem of his relationship with the cosmic order ('The One Whom men call God'), that of his connection with his fellows and perhaps, most intimately, that of the significance of his own personal self-identity. If man has to stand vis-à-vis God and vis-à-vis society, did not his very solitariness separate him from part of his own being? Kierkegaard did not believe so. He dedicated his book, *Purity of Heart is to Will One Thing*, to 'hiin Enkelte' *(That Solitary Individual)*. His English translator translates the dedication in this way, because Kierkegaard 'means the individual separated from the rest, the individual as he would be if he were solitary and alone, face to face with his destiny, with his vocation, with the Eternal, with God Himself who has singled him out'.[16] It may be claimed that Descartes sought to separate the individual 'I' in man from all the medley of experience and that he made it the starting point for his system. Yet he did not press on beyond the point where man has the capacity to think *(Cogito ergo sum)*. Kierkegaard went further and sought to uncover the central core of the self, from which choice and responsibility springs—where the centre itself comes face to face with reality. 'The consciousness of one's eternal responsibility to be an individual is the one thing needful.'[17] So intense was this emphasis upon the individual

---
[13] R. Niebuhr, *Nature and Destiny of Man* (N. York, 1949), p. 123.
[14] T. S. Eliot, *The Cocktail Party*, p. 98.
[15] H. Quistorp, *Calvin's Doctrine of the Last Things* (1955), p. 75.
[16] S. Kierkegaard, *Purity of Heart is to Will One Thing*, Eng. trans. by D. V. Steere (Harper, N.. York, 1956), p. 15.
[17] Ibid., p. 16.

The Value of the Individual

that Kierkegaard regarded any form of 'social salvation', whether by group, by tribe, by race, by class or by nation as an act of spiritual betrayal. As Reinhold Niebuhr would point out, it is the individual who is capable of self-transcendence and of experiencing *agape*, whilst society is not capable of self-transcendence and cannot realistically strive for a higher goal than justice.[18]

The discovery of the individual, however, does not automatically out-mode all previous views on the significance of the social groups to which man belongs. Man had emerged, in the days when the kingdom of Judah came to an end, from the group into a place of new responsibility as an individual before God and man. This responsibility provided a starting-point for new thinking. In one sense, the significance of the community *continued* to develop as an important aspect of Israel's thought but in another sense, it was a fresh starting-point as the individual's share in the promises was not merely the result of his birth (in physical Israel) but also subject to his personal loyalty to the demands of Yahweh to whom he now had a more individual responsibility. The Exilic writers and the leaders who followed gave emphasis to the community of the faithful who had a vision of the mission of Israel which could embrace all the nations.

[18] Reinhold Niebuhr, *Moral Man and Immoral Society* (Scribner, N. York, 1923), pp. 257ff.

CHAPTER EIGHT

THE EXILE AND ITS AFTERMATH

1. The mystery of the survival of Judaism. The problem of their suffering as reflected in the book of Job. The rise of certain institutions to new importance in the exiled community. Their aspirations and hopes in the visions of Ezekiel.
2. Yahweh's rule over the nations in the prophecies of Second Isaiah. Israel's suffering as a preparation for her divine mission. Her place among the nations—the Suffering Servant. Vicarious suffering and sacrifice.
3. The return from exile. The leaders and their visions. The early return and relationships with their neighbours. The later return party and the hardening of nationalism. The solidarity of Israel and the new Jerusalem. The viewpoint of Ezra and Nehemiah. Voices of protest.
4. The experience of the Exile and Israel's faith. The exaltation of Yahweh over the nations. The rise of intermediaries, with particular reference to angelology. The use of symbolism. The teaching of the apocalyptic writers. The place of the book of Daniel in the maintenance of Jewish unity. Judaism's solidarity upheld by devotion to the Law.

CHAPTER EIGHT

THE EXILE AND ITS AFTERMATH

A SIGNIFICANT part of the mystery of the Jewish community lies in its survival. There is no doubt that the army of Nebuchadnezzar took no half measures in their treatment of Jerusalem. By fire and slaughter, they razed the cities of Judah to the ground and Jerusalem itself was burned and scarred for long years to come. It was, however, not merely the physical damage which was extensive. The Southern kingdom had held on to the belief that Yahweh had chosen Mount Zion to be his eternal earthly seat and had given to David the promise of successors who would reign for ever in Jerusalem. Whilst many of David's successors had not lived up to expectations and had not kept true to the covenant, in the way that David had done, yet there always remained the hope that the ideal scion—perhaps the newly-born prince or the next successor—might prove to be the king under whom the beneficient rule of Yahweh's righteousness might be established. Thus the promises made to David would become realized in the true community of Israel which would be faithful to Yahweh. Such a fulfilment for the nation was accepted without question. There was no need to ask further questions, such as—what lay beyond such a wonderful reign, if such a king came and did not live for ever? 'Nebuchadnezzar's battering rams of course breached that theology beyond repair.'[1] There could be no return with assurance to such a national hope and even the prophets who had proclaimed it were regarded as guilty of vain talk and foolishness (Lam. 2. 14).

The damage which was wrought to the state and its institutions was not confined to those elements in the national life. Religion was a living part of the very institutions themselves and therefore the status of Israel's God became a matter of question. Whilst the community had long been monolatrist, it had not

[1] J. Bright, A History of Israel, p. 328.

The Exile and Its Aftermath 161

denied that other gods existed. However, for a long period, it is probable that in Judah there were many who were monotheists who denied the existence of other gods. They may not have formulated their beliefs as monotheists but they held that the gods of other nations were 'no gods', since there was one God alone in the world. However, such a belief in one God received a serious reverse when it became apparent that Judah was to be overwhelmed, like her neighbours, by the might of Babylon. What place must be given to the gods of the Babylonians when it was so evident that these gods bore their protégés, especially Nabopolassar and his son Nebuchadnezzar, forward with such eminent success? Such mighty gods could not be so easily dismissed. It is evident, in fact, that some Jews thought that it was wise to leave the worship of Yahweh and to turn to the worship of more successful divine beings. They returned to the worship of the Queen of Heaven (Astarte), pouring out libations to her and making cakes bearing her image (Jer. 44. 15-19). Other Jews were inclined to question the divine justice (Ezek. 18. 25; Lam. 5. 7), especially as the punishment seemed so severe, however great the iniquities of the fathers had been. Perhaps the greater number of those who were faithful were overcome by the sense of disillusionment, a feeling of hopelessness, in the face of such disaster. It seemed that it was to no purpose that Yahweh had chosen Israel, which had been swept away like many other peoples (Isa. 63. 19). With such a destruction, due to iniquities, it seemed that they must die as a people and lose their identity (Ezek. 33. 10). It were as though Yahweh had repented that he had ever called Israel and, on account of their transgressions, they had been cut off from their place in his purposes. As they looked forward, there were no signs of hope, no prophetic word (Ps. 74. 9f.), so that their enemies scoffed at their faith. It appeared as though the law had passed away from them and no vision could be expected to come to any prophets who remained in their midst (Lam. 2. 9). Such thoughts of despair must have been accentuated by the contrast between the wealth and culture evident in Babylon and the poverty of Jerusalem, which they had formerly regarded as the centre of their world.

It may well be possible that the book of Job belongs to this context. The figure of Job himself, as a fabled righteous man of an earlier period, and the material in the book probably belong to an earlier period, since the descriptions often have the freshness of one who has shared in the life of a small Israelite community. Thus, in Job 29, there is the picture of the respected chief of a small community—one whose word is treated with great respect as he gives his judgement on the matter under discussion.[2] It is perhaps an idealized picture of how affairs used to be conducted in an earlier day. However, even though the material is older and belongs to the stream of tradition of small community life, there can be little doubt that the issue posed by the book of Job belongs to the period of the early exile, when possibly the book was brought together and its message had a particular pertinence to the situation. In the first place, it recognizes the significance of the individual who makes his plea in regard to the divine justice. Although the figures in the book may well represent different schools of thought, yet they speak as individuals, which is significant. Above all, the book reveals Job as one whose individual conscience seeks justice over against the judgement of his community. Moreover, in the close of the book, Yahweh vindicates the faith of Job whose integrity has remained clear throughout all his unwarranted sufferings. In the second place, the plea also expresses the concern of the community in the light of the intensity of the blow which has fallen upon them. In fact, they want to know, why does God fail the righteous? After all, in the book itself, Job is a leading member of his community. The community depends on his righteousness and if he is struck down, then the community receives a serious blow. Jerusalem had seen the 'good figs' (the first exiles) carried away and the house of David had suffered in this disaster. There seemed little hope when even the righteous, the heirs of the covenant, were treated in this way. The exile brought this issue to a sharp focus and God's honour was involved.

The problem was, in fact, not a new one as is seen by the pleas in the prophets. It is present in the teaching of Jeremiah: 'Righteous are thou, O Lord, when I complain to thee; yet would I plead my case before thee. Why does the way of the wicked prosper? Why do all who are treacherous thrive?' (12. 1). Jeremiah pleads that these wicked and prosperous ones should

[2] Pedersen, *Israel*, I-II, 26; 36; 363ff. cf. S. Terrien, *The Interpreter's Bible* (G. A. Buttrick, ed. (T. Nelson and Sons), pp. 884-891) and p. 111 above.

The Exile and Its Aftermath 163

be set aside and destroyed. Also there is the plea of Habakkuk: 'Thou who art of purer eyes than to behold evil and canst not look on wrong, why dost thou look on faithless men and art silent when the wicked swallows up the man more righteous than he?' (1. 13). It is a matter of controversy when the passage from Habbakuk should be dated. Many scholars have identified the violent and unjust ones with the Assyrians and so date the passage in the last quarter of the seventh century when Babylonia was reasserting her independence. Verses 5 to 11 describe the rise of the Chaldeans. However, Duhm dates the passage at a later time, namely, as describing the conquests of Alexander the Great. However, it may be held that the verses 2 to 4 in Chapter 1 may refer to internal disorder in the reign of Jehoiakim, whose behaviour was criticized by Jeremiah (22. 13ff.). Therefore, it may well be that the record in Habakkuk reveals a long standing problem in the mind of faithful Israelites who sought to understand the justice of God.

The interpretation of events which was given by Jeremiah and Ezekiel enabled the Jewish community to re-think and readjust itself to the new situation. The fact that Jeremiah, when disaster was at its worst in the siege of Jerusalem, believed in the future of his people and purchased a piece of family property in Anathoth (Jer. 32)—such an act revealed his deep conviction that Yahweh's ultimate purpose for Israel had not been defeated. A clear distinction was made between national hopes and the redemptive action of Yahweh. To enable the latter to take place, the prophets believed that merited punishment and a purging of heart were needed to take place to fit Israel to become the better instrument in the Lord's hand.

Out of the dust of disaster, however, a new community did in fact arise. The old stress on the nation and the cult were replaced by a new kind of loyalty, namely, an allegiance based on tradition and law. In the case of tradition, great emphasis was given to the ancient institutions, particularly the Sabbath and circumcision. The strict observance of the Sabbath became a clear mark of the faithful Jew, who thus expressed his devotion to the covenant. The significance of this observance of the Sabbath is made clear in a number of passages which date from the period of the exile and post-exilic times (Jer. 17. 19-27; Isa. 56. 1-8; 58. 13f.). This institution was marked out to be a perpetual sign, which had been instituted from the beginning of Creation (Gen. 2. 2f.). It was the 'sign' that Israel was the chosen and holy people of Yahweh (Exod. 31. 12-17; Ezek. 20. 12). Circumcision served also as a mark of the true Jew. The practice of circumcision was used among some of Israel's neighbours, though it has not been found among the Philistines, possibly because they were a Greek people who disliked such physical disfigurements. It also was not used among the Babylonians. However, from an early period, among the Israelites, circumcision was regarded as 'a sign of the covenant' (Gen. 17. 11). Such outward marks, which gave the Jewish man and the Jewish community a distinct identity, became very important. Added to these practices, there were others which concerned ritual cleanness (Ezek. 4. 12-15; 22. 26; 44. 23). The Holiness Code (Lev. 17-26) appears to have close connection with this period, with points of contact with Ezek. 40-48. This relationship is an intricate problem, however, since there are also points of contact with the earlier D Code (which contains the bulk of the present book of Deuteronomy). A careful distinction is made between clean and unclean practices, in the ethical and ritual spheres. The case for their codification in this period appears to be strong.

The community found fresh strength in the remembrances of the acts of Yahweh in the past. They drew nourishment from the past to quicken their hope for the future. Whilst the Deuteronomic historical corpus (Joshua to 11 Kings) was probably composed before the fall of the state, when records were available, yet this corpus received additions and was no doubt adapted to the situation of the exiles.[2] Similarly the sayings of the prophets were preserved and additions made to them. Perhaps even more important was the priestly collection of cultic laws which became the so-called Priestly Code. Such a collection which set down in definitive form the Temple practices in Jerusalem became all the more important when the cult practice itself had ceased. This collection, together with the Priestly narrative of the Pentateuch (P), formed an important element in the development of the Torah, the Law which became the sheet-anchor of the Jewish faith in later days. The community in seeking to hold on to its past was looking forward to the day when Yahweh would act again in redeeming his people.

[2] J. Bright, A History of Israel, pp. 330-1.

The Exile and Its Aftermath

The Jewish community came to believe that its exile was an interim, a belief that was nurtured by the visions of the prophets, such as Ezekiel's vision of the re-awakening of the valley of dry bones (Ezek. 37). The people were homesick for their homeland in Jerusalem (Ps. 137); they looked for judgement on proud Babylon, which was to be destroyed (Isa. 13. 1—14. 23), which is an indication of the way in which older material was taken to serve as a doom oracle on Babylon. The yearning of the Jewish people for restoration is seen in the prayer that present trials may come to an end (Isa. 63. 7—64. 12). The hope of many exiles is probably reflected in the writings of Ezekiel, who in part expressed his people's desires and in part served to focus their expectations in the coming days. The ancient belief in the Davidic covenant remained among them (Ezek. 34. 23f.; 37. 24-28). Perhaps the release of the former king, Jehoiachin, from prison by the son of Nebuchadnezzar (2 Kgs. 25. 27-30), may have raised the hopes of the exile that his position might be restored to him. The former king was given a place of honour, being permitted to eat at the emperor's table. He was not allowed to return home nor were his people. Other exiles had their dreams of the earlier days, when Israel was an amphictyony, pledged as a tribal league in close allegiance to Yahweh. In the book of Ezekiel, chh. 40 to 48, the prophet looked forward to a reconstituted state, which would have a secular prince (presumably of the house of David), who would be a staunch upholder of the national cult. But the real power was to be the Zadokite priesthood, since it was to be a theocracy, whose representatives were to take the utmost care to keep the ritual laws and ensure that the holy presence of Yahweh should abide in the restored Temple from which all contaminating elements were removed. There Yahweh would be enthroned to reign for ever. Whilst the vision of Ezekiel did not correspond with reality, since he placed the tribes in an artificial location in Western Palestine only (ch. 43. 13—48. 29), yet this vision greatly helped to shape the hopes of the Jews. Whilst the new Jerusalem might exist, for many, solely as an act of faith, yet it served as a focus for those who wanted to return when the opportunity came.

The Jewish community, like other exiled groups which had been torn from their homes, did not have to wait very long for fresh grounds for hope. The Babylonian Empire was short-lived.

After the death of Nebuchadnezzar in 562 B.C., there was grave internal friction. The throne changed hands thrice in the course of seven years. Such a situation invited other aspirants to power to try their hand. In particular, Babylon was threatened by the rival state of Media, where there was overt conflict with Babylon. But in Media, internal revolt broke out when a vassal king of Anshan (Cyrus) rose against the king Astyges of Media.

Although Nabonidus (king of Babylon) supported Cyrus in his revolt, it was not long before it was realized that Cyrus was the real danger. After defeating his overlord, Cyrus went on to defeat the king of Lydia and so gained possession of Asia Minor. Then he moved to the East across Parthia as far as the Jaxartes and eventually he turned his attention to Babylon which was like a ripe plum ready to fall when he approached the city. This triumphal progress filled the exiles with excitement and exhilaration, as the conqueror drew nearer. The feelings of the Jewish community are vividly reflected in the prophecies of the prophet of the Exile, who is known as Second Isaiah as his prophecies are found in the book of Isaiah, chh. 40 to 55. These writings date from a period before and possibly during the fall of Babylon (539). His vision provided a powerful stimulus of faith to his people.

This prophet lifted the eyes of his people above the events which were taking place around them. He expressed his faith in Yahweh as not merely the God of Israel but as the Creator of all things, whose power was beyond human resources or any human likeness (Isa. 40. 12-26). He made explicit the monotheism which had long been implicit in Israel's faith. In consequence, he treated with satiric irony the pagan gods around him (44. 12-20), making fun of them as pieces of wood and metal (40. 19f.; 46. 5-7), whose prophecies were nothing and could accomplish nothing (41. 21-24). Moreover, it was Yahweh who was guiding events (41. 2-4), who had in fact raised up Cyrus (as 'his anointed') to subdue the nations (45. 1). Among men, there was Yahweh alone who was the first and the last, beside whom there was no god (44. 6). From this lofty conception of Yahweh as Lord of History, this prophet saw clearly the purpose of the people of Israel. Abraham and Jacob had been called to serve his purpose of old (41. 8-10). His people were the witnesses of his saving hand in the midst of the nations (43. 8-13). Nevertheless, Israel had

The Exile and Its Aftermath

suffered on account of her sins (42. 24f.; 48. 17-19), yet there was no surrender of his purpose but merely a purging of his people to refine them and try them by the fire of affliction (48. 9-11).

This prophet considered that the conquests of Cyrus were under the hand of Yahweh, who would accomplish his purposes through him (44. 24—45. 7). It was evident that in this respect Cyrus was the unwitting agent of the God of the Jews and yet in the decree that enabled the Jews to return, he regards himself as the benefactor, provided by their God, if we may trust the wording of the decree in Ezra 1. 2f. As Israel trusted in their redeemer, so Yahweh would restore again the waste places of Zion (Isaiah 51. 1-16). The vision of the prophet took the form of a new deliverance from a bondage, such as Israel had previously known in Egypt. It was a new exodus (43. 16-21) and the Lord would provide a new highway through the desert which would blossom and flow with water (40. 3-5; 49. 9-11; 55. 12f.). Such a deliverance was in fact an even greater event than the previous Exodus, so that it could only be likened to the demonstration of power which was evident in the time of creation (51. 9-11). As for Israel, his redeemed would return and they would realize again that his covenant remained with them (54. 9f.). This covenant is not a 'new' one, since he had never removed his love from them nor had he divorced them (50. 1). In fact, Abraham had been promised an innumerable seed and now that promise was to be brought to pass (54. 1-3) but in an even wider context. 'Your descendents will possess the nations and people the desolate cities' (54. 3). There is reference to the Davidic covenant but there is no large stress given to his house's place, except as leader of the people. It is Yahweh who is exalted as king as in the primitive days, when he led his people in the desert. He would lead his flock through the desert to Zion (40. 1-11) and there establish his kingly rule (51. 17—52. 12). The Israel which would be established would have his Spirit in fuller measure and acknowledge his lordship over them (44. 1-5). Moreover, Yahweh's rule would not be confined to 'the preserved of Israel' but also reach out to other nations (49. 6), whose wealth and worship would be offered to him (Isa. 49. 14ff).

This renewal of the covenant, but with the further affirmation that the nations of the whole earth were to share in Yahweh's rule, was not new. The universalism which is implicit in monotheism had been suggested by earlier writers (Gen. 12. 1-3; 18. 18 and Amos 9. 7). It had found expression also in the Deuteronomic history (I Kgs. 8. 41-43). But in the great prophet of the Exile, proclaiming his message at the heart of a great empire, there is the clearest expression in explicit terms that Yahweh rules over all the earth. It was one thing to have such a message but it was quite another to accept the implications of such a message. However, the Old Testament teaching on the solidarity of mankind (which arose out of the awareness of the group as it expands to include the world), since all were the descendents of one man (Adam)[1]—such teaching prepared the way for the belief that the solidarity of the human race in sin called for a universal Redeemer—in whose purpose Israel had so large a share.

In this task of redemption, a new insight came from this prophet. He believed that Israel's very history was evidence of the greatness of Israel's God ('Let all the nations gather together . . . Who among them can declare this and show us the former things?' Isa. 43. 9). In her very existence, Israel was the witness of the power of his might. Yet to be the Servant of Yahweh was a costly obligation, it involved a measure of suffering which thus gave meaning to the mystery of Israel's current plight. Whilst there has been much discussion relating to the 'Servant Poems' in this part of the book of Isaiah, yet there appears to be strong reasons for believing that these poems are an integral part of the prophet's message and of his thought. The poems are found in chh. 42. 1-4 (5-9); 49. 1-6 (7); 50. 4-9 (10-11); 52. 13—53. 12. It should also be made clear that interpretation is sometimes difficult, yet the message of Yahweh to the nations flames out clearly. In the first poem, the Servant, who has been chosen by Yahweh and endowed with his Spirit, has been called to give, with unremitting devotion, Yahweh's law to the nations. In the second poem (Isa. 49. 1-6), the Servant proclaims that he has been called, from the time of his conception, to bring Israel back to Yahweh—a thankless task yet one in which the Lord would justify his servant. The return of Israel is linked with God's purpose of giving light to all nations. In the third poem (Isa. 50. 4-9), the Servant is true to his destiny, despite ill-treatment, as he is confident that the Lord will vindicate him.

[1] R. P. Shedd, *Man in Community* (London, 1958), p. 72.

The Exile and Its Aftermath   169

In the important final poem (Isa. 52. 13—53. 12), the Servant looks forward to a final triumph. Despite his disfigured form and the marks of suffering, he believes that his innocent behaviour will have a vicarious quality and will cause his opponents to acknowledge that their sins were being borne and expiated. Nevertheless, the Lord would cause him to prosper and enable the Servant to have numerous offspring and to see the triumph of the divine purpose.

Whatever may have been the origin of this concept of vicarious suffering, it is closely linked to the whole sacrificial pattern of the Old Testament, which sought to restore holiness to the group (within which the individual had his place). Also the sacrificial system provided a way for the part to represent the whole, the individual unit to act on behalf of the group—ideas which found an expression in the servant (Israel) who suffered for and on behalf of the sins of the nations. It is also not clear whether the prophet himself had a particular individual in mind (namely, Jeremiah, Jehoiachin, or some other) yet it is beyond doubt that the writer sought to re-kindle hope in the hearts of the Jewish community. Outside of the Servant Poems, the figure of the Servant is always Israel and even within them (Isa. 49. 3) but the figure in the Poems themselves appears to fluctuate between the individual and the group, a practice which has so large a place in early thought. Israel, as a community, and the true Israelite are alike called to be God's instrument of redemption.[5]

The vision which was transmitted by this great prophet became a focus for the eyes of the pious Jew in later times. However much he might resist the universalist aspects of the prophet's message, yet the Jew was shown by the prophet's teaching that suffering was not purposeless or futile but might be lifted up into the plan of God and serve his redemptive purpose among men. Humility and patience in waiting for the fulfilment of the fullness of God's time became a characteristic quality in pious Jewry. It was the mark of the *Chasidim* (the meek) as well as those who succeeded them as interpreters of the Law, namely, the Pharisees.

[5] cf. C. R. North, *The Suffering Servant in Deutero-Isaiah* (2nd. ed. Oxford, Clarendon Press, 1956), where the various issues raised within these poems are reviewed in detail.

The victorious progress of Cyrus continued until the whole of the Babylonian Empire came under his control. In the first year of his reign in Babylon (538), Cyrus issued a decree which permitted the Jewish Community to return home and the cultus to be re-established in Jerusalem. There are two versions of this decree, in Ezra 1. 2-4 and in Ezra 6. 3-5. The latter version is part of a collection of Aramaic documents (Ezra 4. 8—6. 18) and was probably preserved by the Temple authorities in their archives, where it became available to the Chronicler for his narration of events. This memorandum of a royal oral decision (a *dikrona*: Ezra 6. 2) permitted the Temple to be rebuilt and made provision that the expenses should be defrayed out of the royal treasury. Certain stipulations were made about the building and the vessels taken by Nebuchadnezzar were to be restored to their place in the Temple. Such a fulfilment of their hopes must have soon stirred up the Jewish community to act on this permission. It is probable that influential Jews were in the court and encouraged Cyrus to be generous to the Jews, whilst, from the viewpoint of Cyrus who contemplated the invasion of Egypt, it was a distinct advantage to have a community under obligation and loyal to himself who were so close to the borders of Egypt. A return party began to prepare themselves for the journey to Jerusalem where it was hoped that a new day might dawn for a new nation. The leader of the first return party was Sheshbazzar, a prince of the house of David. It is not possible to compute the number of those who accompanied him.

The political status of the returned community, during the early period of the return, is not at all clear. Whilst an Aramaic source (Ezra 5. 14) claims that Cyrus appointed Sheshbazzar as 'governor' *(pehah)*, yet that title is not in itself clear. He may have been governor of a separate and reconstituted province of Judah or deputy governor of the district of Judah under the governor of Samaria, or merely a royal commissioner in charge of a specific project, such as the settlement of the exiled community in its old home. It appears probable that Sheshbazzar had some political authority in so far as his nephew and successor, Zerubbabel, is designated as 'governor of Judah' by his contemporary, Haggai the prophet (Hag. 1. 1, 14). Under these two men, the Temple foundation was laid again.

The fortunes of this returned community were seriously at

The Exile and Its Aftermath

odds with the glorious anticipated visions of the great Prophet of the Exile. The Jews had a succession of poor harvests and bad seasons (Hag. 1. 9-11; 2. 15-17). They lacked adequate food and clothing (Hag. 1. 6), so that their morale reached a very low ebb. It is evident that the ruling party in Samaria resented the intrusion of this company of Jews, especially if their own political authority was reduced thereby, whilst the Jews who already lived in the South did not view with pleasure this influx from the East (Ezek. 33. 24). When the returned Jews began to draw apart from their neighbours and enforce ritual cleanness (Hag. 2. 10-14), then relationships would naturally deteriorate into open violence when public safety was threatened (Zech. 8. 10).

Some indication of the low morale of these returned Jews is seen in the prophecies in Haggai, in Zechariah and in Isaiah, chh. 56-66. The hopes of a great and triumphant return, with Yahweh ruling all nations from Zion, was clearly far from their actual experience. Their hope remained, so that Trito-Isaiah looked forward to a great gathering of Jew and Gentile alike, as Yahweh's people, to rejoice in a cleansed and beautiful Zion (Isa. 56. 1-8; 60. 1-22), where tidings of redemption and justice would be proclaimed (ch. 61). His message looked forward to a new creation where longevity and blessedness would abide (65. 17-25). The present sorrows of Israel could be regarded as the birth-pangs of a new nation (66. 7-14). Whilst such promises would certainly buoy up the spirits of the disconsolate people, it was not easy for many of the people to share the prophet's vision. Many felt that in fact the Lord had deserted his people, who wandered in darkness and injustice (Isa. 59. 1, 9-11). Some of the people prayed continually to God to act on their behalf (cf. Zech. 1, 12; Ps. 44. 23-24).

We have only glimpses of the life and thought of the new community. The urge to secure land and to establish a new home must have created problems which aggravated relationships with the older established inhabitants and among themselves. Some were willing to treat others ruthlessly and yet retain a 'pious' concern, which roused the prophetic wrath (Isa. 58. 1-12; 59. 1-8). It soon became clear that the community had within itself diverse elements, which became more clearly differentiated into two main polarities, namely, those who were sincere and devoted worshippers of Yahweh and were upheld by the prophetic ideals and those who were soon closely attached to the practices of their pagan neighbours and among whom syncretistic practices became prominent. As the records have been handed down by those who belonged to the first group, it is natural that our knowledge of the second group is given to us in terms of the prophecies in which the prophet inveighed against the syncretism of an unfaithful people (Isa. 57. 3-10; 65. 1-7, 11; 66. 3-4). This unfaithful segment of the people, who were prepared to adjust their cultic practice, if not their belief, to that of heathen neighbours, was deemed by the prophet to be unworthy of the care and loving kindness of the Lord. It also raised the issue whether some separation was necessary within the Community—a weeding out of the unfaithful elements so that the faithful could be more clearly defined.

It is not surprising that there was a real fear among the more devoted leaders of the exiles lest the spiritual integrity of the community would be undermined by the assimilation of pagan practices which were part of the every-day life of their neighbours. (Every spiritual community has to face this peril in one form or another!) Some leaders were inclined to view the foreigners with compassion, especially when such foreigners were willing to accept the demands of the law (Isa. 56. 1-8). In some cases, there was in fact an eager looking forward to the bringing in of the offerings of the nations, including them also among the priests of the Lord (Isa. 66. 18-21; Zech. 2. 11; 8. 22f.). 'And some of them also I will take for priests and Levites' (Isa. 66. 21). Yet there was also a strong current of opinion who held heathen practices in abhorrence and therefore suspected the contaminating influence of all foreigners (Hag. 2. 10-14).

The spiritual lethargy of the people is manifest in the delay which took place in the building of the Temple. The mission of the community could hardly survive without some focal point of worship. Whilst their God was now revealed to be too vast to be contained in earthly temples—'the high and lofty One who inhabits eternity, whose name is Holy' (Isa. 57. 15)—yet it was clear to the Jewish leaders that the symbol of worship expressed in the Temple was clearly necessary for their survival as God's people. Therefore, eighteen years after their return from exile, spurred on (in particular) by Haggai and Zechariah, the people resumed the task of re-building the Temple. This work was

The Exile and Its Aftermath

completed by March, 515 B.C., when the Temple was dedicated with great rejoicing (Ezra. 6. 13-18).

The prophecies of Haggai and Zechariah probably belong to the period, in early 520 B.C., when Darius, successor to Cambyses, was fighting against a series of uprisings in the Persian Empire. His rule was threatened by rebellions in Media, Elam, Parsa as well as in Armenia and further east. It is natural that the hopes of a revival of the promises made to David entered into the preaching of the prophets. The nations might be cast down but the Lord would raise up the son of the house of David, namely, his servant Zerubbabel, to accomplish his purposes (Hag. 2. 20-23). Such Messianic hopes, however, had very little foundation in fact as Darius showed that he was a strong monarch, who was well able to cope with the rebellions. Yet the risings may also be reflected in the prophecies of Zechariah who hoped that these upheavals might be the forewarnings of the intervention of Yahweh to establish his triumphant rule (Zech. 2. 6-13). In apocalyptic visions, he describes the anticipated victory of Yahweh who will return to Zion to establish his throne there (Zech. 1. 7-17; 8. 3). The prophet urged the people to complete the building of the Temple (1. 16; 6. 15), even urging those who had remained in Babylon to flee from coming trouble to Zion, where many nations would join themselves to Zion where the Lord had his dwelling-place. The prophet sought to strengthen the hand of Zerubbabel, claiming that God's spirit would enable the prince to complete the Temple work (4. 6b-10a) and that the 'Branch' (the scion of David's line) would shortly appear (3. 8). There can be little doubt that in this reference to the 'Branch' (cf. Jer. 23. 5f.), Zachariah is referring in veiled language to Zerubbabel, who, it was hoped, would occupy the throne of David. Both these prophets were declaring the pre-exilic theology, which was based on the centrality of Zion, with its connection with the Davidic dynasty, both of which were the chosen of Yahweh. Moreover, the community was regarded as the chosen and true remnant of Israel (Hag. 1. 12, 14; Zech. 8. 6, 12), in the same way as Isaiah had anticipated the remnant as the hope of Israel. Both these prophets looked upon Zerubbabel as the awaited scion of the house of David, the one who would fulfil the ancient promises. It is not known how far Zerubbabel shared these views. He does not appear to have committed any disloyal act so that Darius confirmed the decree of Cyrus and the local satrap, Tattenai, was instructed to give assistance for the building of the temple and the maintenance of the cult. There can be no doubt that prayers for the Persian king were included in the services of the new Temple, as well as sacrifices which would demonstrate loyalty to the dynasty which had enabled the building to be built. Whilst there were many Israelites who were not interested in the settlement in Jerusalem, especially those who lived at a distance in Samaria, yet for the 'Remnant', this Temple provided a focus of faith and served as a centre for the revival of allegiance to Yahweh. Whilst many blows might be struck at the Jewish faith in coming days, yet this centre acted as a rallying-point to which the faithful could return to renew their loyalty. It is evident, however, that the dedication of the Temple was not followed up in the way that Haggai and Zachariah had hoped. The throne of David was not re-established and the promised hopes were not fulfilled as that generation had hoped. Zerubbabel does not appear again and may have been removed from power as a possible danger. The incipient growth of royalist feeling might well have proved unacceptable to the Persian power.

This early period of return reveals the unsettled state of the Jewish community, which could hardly expect to create afresh a national state in the old form. It was not clear how the future of the community should be shaped if indeed Yahweh still was to use the 'remnant' for his mission. It was also not clear whether the ancient promises made to David were to find fresh meaning in some future day. The failure on the part of the returned exiles to re-establish the throne of David may well have caused a lack of enthusiasm on the part of many exiles to return home to Judah. There is no evidence that many Jews wished to leave their home in various parts of the Persian Empire even though there were probably accessions of Jews to Judah from time to time (e.g. Ezek. 4. 12). There is very little light given to us with regard to the fortunes of the Jewish Community in Jerusalem from 515 to 450 B.C. Local affairs were administered from Samaria, with the Persian governor living there. In Jerusalem, the high priests were in a position of leadership.

There seems to have been considerable friction between the

Jews and their neighbours. The provincial officials were often officious and overbearing in their demands, which caused ill-feeling (Neh. 5. 4, 14f.). At the same time, relations with neighbouring peoples were severely strained. Edom had been driven out of their land by the pressure of the Arabs (cf. Mal. 1. 2-5) and had occupied much of southern Palestine to a point north of Hebron. The perfidy of Edom in failing to help Judah in the hour of her trial had created acute bitterness between them (Obad. 1-14). The prophets of Israel looked forward to a Day of the Lord when the enemies of Israel would be destroyed and among these enemies, Edom was included (Obad. 18). It was because of the very insecurity of their position, that the nobles of Judah appear to have taken the step to fortify the city by re-building the walls, in the reign of Artaxerxes 1 (Ezra 4. 7-23).

At the spiritual centre of their life, there is, however, some evidence that the morale of the people was low. This may be seen from the prophecies of Malachi and from the memoirs of Nehemiah which date from a little later period. The priests were not unwilling to offer sick and injured animals to Yahweh (Mal. 1. 6-14), treating their sacred office with little respect and showing partiality in the teaching of the law. The Sabbaths were neglected and used for business (Neh. 13. 15-22). As the people neglected to pay their tithes (Mal. 3. 7-10), so the Levites were forced to leave their sacred duties and to seek elsewhere to make a living (Neh. 13. 10f.). It began to be questioned whether there was any value in being loyal to the faith at all (Mal. 2. 17; 3. 13-15). This neglect of faith led to a failure in public and private morality, so that divorce became prominent (Mal. 2. 13-16). The employers of labour were quite ready to cheat their employees of their wages (Mal. 3. 5), whilst the poor, who had mortgaged their lands in time of trouble or drought, found themselves reduced to servitude (Neh. 5. 1-5). Perhaps even more dangerous, in the long run, was the growing tendency for the Jews to intermarry with Gentiles, since such intermarriage brought a closer association with foreign worship (cf. Mal. 2. 11f.). The children of these 'mixed marriages' ceased to care for the affairs of Judah. Many of them could not speak its language and therefore there was a serious threat to the integrity and continuity of the chosen people, 'the remnant' in Jerusalem.

Considerable attention has been given to the situation in Judah, on the return of the exiles, because this situation prepared the way for the changes in the Jewish community which took place under Nehemiah and Ezra. These changes became determinative in the life and purpose of the community for the centuries to come. There was a closing of the ranks to provide a stiffened protection from the world around them. It also enabled the Jewish 'remnant' to resist the temptation to permit doctrinal changes into the inner core of its faith, when Hellenism came like a great wave to engulf all the current beliefs of the Near Eastern peoples. The situation when Nehemiah and, later, Ezra came to pull the Jerusalem community together was a serious one, in that their morale was low, amid a mixed culture which threatened to remove many of the most distinctive elements of the earlier faith and practice. It was an open question whether this people were to provide a message and mission for the world as the chosen people, as their fathers believed, or whether they were to be sucked into the vortex of peoples, who had become attached to the land of Palestine after the Assyrian invasions— peoples who had lost their distinctive identities and ways of worship in a medley of cults and practices. It was a time when the significance of this particular community concept was being challenged. What did it mean to be 'the people of God'? What were the demands which such a claim involved? How was this people to express its difference from other local and related peoples who, in so many ways, were akin to themselves? Did the earlier promises mean anything any more? These were the questions which needed to find a radical answer.

The re-organization of the Jewish Community took place through the energetic endeavours of two men, who led their people along a path, which was to be pursued for many centuries to come. It may well be claimed that Judaism has followed the same or a similar path to this day. These two men were Nehemiah, the administrator and governor, and Ezra, the priest. The work of these two largely over-lapped but they were complementary to one another, in that the political endeavours of Nehemiah received religious and devotional significance through the work of Ezra.

It was in the third quarter of the fifth century that the Jewish community received the new vision which, in large part, saved them from disintegration and preserved them as a community of

The Exile and Its Aftermath

devotion to Yahweh. It was probably about the year 440, that Nehemiah reached Jerusalem with authority from the Persian monarch, Artaxerxes I Longimanus (465-424), to build the city wall. Prior to this date, Nehemiah (the king's cupbearer) had heard from his brother of the deplorable conditions in Jerusalem and so had requested from the king that some action should be taken. His request was more than granted and Nehemiah appears to have been appointed governor of Judah (Neh. 5. 14; 10. 1), which was made a separate province with independence from Samaria.

Nehemiah's task was accomplished under very great difficulties. The city needed physical security if the community was really to do more than exist. Many attempts were made to thwart his plans, so that the governor had to work secretly and rapidly to carry out the work. Among the powerful opponents he had to face was Sanballat, the governor of the province of Samaria. Sanballat was a Yahwist, as also was Tobiah, the governor of the province of Ammon in Transjordan, but these men were galled by the fact that the more orthodox leading Jewish families in Jerusalem, including Nehemiah, regarded them as little better than heathen as their Yahwism was mingled with other syncretistic elements. Another powerful opponent was Geshem, 'the Arab', who appears to have governed the province of Arabia, which was nominally under Persian control (Neh. 2. 19; 6. 1, 6). These opponents, together with friends and families, with whom they had inter-married within the city, sought to delay the developments in Jerusalem, by a variety of different means. Externally, marauding bands of Arabs, Ammonites and Philistines (Neh. 4. 7-12) made raids on the countryside around Jerusalem, terrorizing various towns. Nehemiah had to withdraw some Jews from the environs of the city, to protect them and to assist the city. Whilst the work went on, the workers were divided into two shifts—one group stood on guard whilst the other group was working on the walls. Internally, there were attempts to delay Nehemiah's work by sending him letters to shake his morale and to lower his position in the eyes of the people (Neh. 6. 10-14). By dint of devotion and courage, the walls were eventually completed and dedicated with solemn ceremony (Neh. 12. 27-43). Thus, the Jewish community in Jerusalem had a measure of external security within which they could develop their own manner of life—free from the interference which would make religious observances lax. It is evident that Nehemiah raised up opposition from those who were less strict in their devotion and who had intermarried with the neighbouring peoples.

Nehemiah's first term of office as governor came to an end in 433 (Neh. 5. 14), when, after a period of twelve years, he had to return to the Persian court. It is possible that during his period away from Jerusalem, he may have discussed the religious and political situation of Jerusalem with the Jewish leaders in Babylon. In any case, when he returned to Jerusalem for a second term of office, Nehemiah took energetic steps to clear up some of the laxity which he found in religious matters. Tobiah from Ammon had been installed in the Temple, living in a room which was properly used for cultic purposes. Nehemiah instructed that the goods of Tobiah should be thrown out into the street and the room cleansed of pollution (Neh. 13. 4-9). He restored the room to its proper use. With like energy, Nehemiah took steps to see that the tithes were paid to enable the Levites to carry out their duties without the necessity of seeking other employment. The city gates were shut on the Sabbath to prevent business on that day. He took vigorous steps to stop inter-marriage with foreigners. In the case of the grandson of the high-priest, who had married the daughter of Sanballat, Nehemiah acted so firmly that the young man fled from Judah to Samaria.

Nehemiah's measures were taken to meet various situations as they arose—situations which seemed to him to threaten the solidarity and integrity of the community. He was a practical man of affairs yet he had firm religious convictions in his loyalty to God and his people. It is therefore not surprizing that when the priest Ezra came from Babylon and sought to reform the religious life of the Jerusalem community, the governor Nehemiah supported Ezra and placed his seal on the plans which the priest introduced (Neh. 8-9; 10. 1). Nehemiah's part in the Judahite community was to preserve the political identity of the returned exiles, to give them status and a cleaner administration which served as a good foundation for the work which Ezra sought to do.

Ezra was concerned primarily, if not entirely, with the religious affairs of the community. He was anxious that the inner

The Exile and Its Aftermath

life of the returned exiles should be entirely devoted to the Lord of Israel. He came armed with a copy of the law, together with a rescript from the king which gave him authority to enforce it. He did not have the same political and administrative authority as Nehemiah had had but he did have the needful authority to regularize religious practice. However, the term 'religious practice' was a wide one since it covered those aspects of secular life which impinged on the sacred order! Whilst Ezra could not enforce the religious affairs of the whole area of the satrapy of Abar-nahara, in which Jerusalem lay, yet he could bring all the cult activities of the Jewish community in Jerusalem into conformity with the law which he brought. This he sought to carry out with energy and authority. He probably came to Jerusalem about the year 428. He was particularly shocked by the manner in which many leading families, including the high-priestly family, were involved in mixed marriages and he took drastic action. He chose the path of moral persuasion as the means to bring home to their consciences the evil of their ways. He wept and confessed the sin of the congregation before Yahweh, so that the people came to acknowledge their transgressions (Ezra 10. 1-5), in acting against the law. They agreed to make a covenant to put away their foreign wives and children. They also encouraged Ezra to go on with his task and they would support him.

This moral victory by Ezra enabled him to re-establish the Jerusalem Community on the deeper foundation of Mosaic Law. When the people bound themselves by covenant to live according to the law (Neh. 9. 38; 10. 29), they specifically agreed to refrain from marriage with foreigners as well as from work on the Sabbath. They also agreed to allow the land to lie fallow and to forego the collection of debts in the seventh year, whilst they were to levy on themselves an annual tax for the upkeep of the sanctuary. Tithes were to be offered more regularly, in accord with the commandments of the law (Neh. 10. 30-39). Thus, it seems that, within a year of his arrival, Ezra had brought to fulfilment much of the religious work for which Nehemiah had striven. His work laid a firm foundation which enabled Israel's faith to stand the storms which smote the community in succeeding centuries.

The central significance of Ezra's work lay in re-ordering the life of Judaism about the law. Whilst the Temple had been rebuilt as a centre for worship and the returned community had begun to establish itself as a unit (under Zerubbabel and then Nehemiah), it was clear that full nationhood as a sovereign state was practically impossible within the Persian empire. There were two dangerous possibilities—namely, that Israel's strength would be whittled away on futile nationalistic attempts at revolt or that she would be so acculturized to her pagan environment, that she would cease to count as a distinctive force and become disintegrated as other communities had done. It was needful that a firm framework should be given to the community to enable its inner life to remain inviolate—this was provided by the basis of law.

It is not altogether clear what the law-book, which Ezra brought from Babylon, contained. It may have been the Priestly Code or some collection of laws whose content we may be unable definitively to outline but it is probable that, by Ezra's time, the Pentateuch had reached its completed form—to become *par excellance* the Torah, the rule in faith and practice of the life of Israel. If this was the case, then Ezra's law-book may have been the completed Pentateuch. Certainly this book had the authority of the religious leaders in Babylon, who continued to exercise an important place in Judaistic affairs, as well as support from the Persian court which permitted this form of spiritual autonomy among this strange people.

Thus, from a political community, 'Israel' became a newly defined entity, namely, a community which was based upon a religious law. In place of the former national entity, or of those who were descendents of the Israelite tribes or even those who were inhabitants of the old national territory, the remnant of Israel were now seen to be those who rallied round the law. It should be recognized that the solidarity of Israel did not wholly depart from the hereditary and even monarchical foundations of earlier days, since they conceived that there was a continuity throughout their whole history, yet now spiritual factors played an even more significant part. These factors included the rites of initiation into the community and those which helped to integrate the people of Judaism and define the gap between Israel and the Gentiles. There was always the fear lest those of Israel who lived among the heathen, especially among the Diaspora,

The Exile and Its Aftermath   181

might lose their Hebrew identity by intermingling with the heathen. Hence, the horror of inter-marriage, which is evident in the books of Ezra and Nehemiah and also in the Book of Jubilees (in the Apocrypha).

With the Law as the central and integrating factor, other elements of religious life became re-interpreted and re-inforced. There were still the Temple and the cult but there were also the synagogue and the path of righteousness, which were exalted as means of expressing devotion to the Law. The Law served not merely to bind Israel together but also to cut off those within the covenant from those who were outside it. This separation came to be expressed in the rites of initiation and incorporation into Israel, which were in fact three in number, namely, by circumcision, baptism and sacrifice.[6] Circumcision was a mark of separation which distinguished Jews from Gentiles (cf. Gal. 2. 7-9), so that when Gentiles (as Christians) received circumcision, it meant to the Apostle not merely a physical act but no less than a reversion to Judaism from the faith in Christ, which he had preached. 'Circumcision was considered to be in effect a ticket of admission to the World to Come and . . . its benefits were irrevocable."[7] Thus, this rite separated the Jew from the non-Jew and was a badge of the Jew's part in the covenant, which would ensure his part in the World to Come. Baptism also had a part in enabling the homeborn (and later the proselyte) to enter into the covenant. The baptism under John appears to have carried a new significance when it signified a general need for moral cleansing, which went beyond the ceremonial cleansing of rabbinical practice. Sacrifice was continued in the Temple, until A.D. 70, since such offerings as two doves were regarded as the expression of devotion to Yahweh. All these acts were part of the cult but were all fulfilled in obedience to the Law which God had given to Israel.

The note of separation became increasingly dominant in the thought of Judaism. It was on this account that inter-marriage was regarded with horror, as no better than fornication (Jub. 30. 7-10), since it made very real the danger that the Jew became like the Gentile. The book of Esther expresses the fierce desire among the Jews that they must keep together in common loyalty

[6] R. P. Shedd, *Man in Community*, pp. 49-50.
[7] *Ibid*.

to one another. On the other hand, those Jews who departed from the Law were regarded with high contempt, as 'the wicked', the 'ungodly', the 'scoffers' as indeed they were the 'lawless ones' who consorted with the Gentiles (1 Macc. 1. 11). The profoundest contempt was felt for the Samaritans. They were placed lower than the Edomites and Philistines, by Ben Sirach (Ecclus. 50. 25f.) as a people who were particularly abhorrent to God. This abhorrence towards the Samaritans deepened as the years passed. It was in fact a more blatant case of the 'hot indignation' which seized the godly Jew, when he saw 'the wicked who forsake the law of the Lord' (Ps. 119. 53). This was also accentuated by the rival sanctuary which was set up by the Samaritans on Mount Gerizim.

The separation which took place between the Jew and his neighbour was in part due to his intense pride in the Jewish community and its mission. As the heirs to the promises of God, there was an intense pride in the possession of the Law (Ps. 147. 19-20. 'He declares his word to Jacob . . . He has not dealt thus with any other nation'). It was they alone who were privileged to be the people of God (Ecclus. 17. 17) and their city was the Holy City, which was the centre of the earth (Jub. 8. 19). Their language was used by God in creation (Jub. 12. 25f.) and their mission, as God's holy people, could never be brought to fulfilment if they became like unto others or mixed themselves with other nations (Jub. 22. 16). It may well be claimed that their pride was not merely nationalistic for their own sake but also had a large measure of responsibility and concern for other nations. If Israel was true to her mission, then God's will would be preserved among the nations.

Whilst the national pride of the Jews burned with a fierce intensity as is apparent from the book of Esther and the books of the Maccabbees, yet it would not be true to say that Israel completely lost sight of her mission to bring the light of God to the nations of mankind. A monotheistic faith had been proclaimed by 'Second Isaiah' and his message was not lost on his successors. The prophets of the Return looked forward to the day when many nations would flock to Zion (Zech. 2. 11; Isa. 56. 1-8; 66. 18-21 and Mal. 1. 11). Therefore, even amid the exclusiveness of the godly and law-abiding Jews, there was a place for the proselytes, who were given fair (even equal) treatment (Lev. 24. 22). There

The Exile and Its Aftermath

remained a measure of concern for the ingathering of the nations, who (so it was believed) would in due time turn to Israel's God. Thus, in the second Temple, the universal kingship of Yahweh was proclaimed and faith in his ultimate triumph found its place in the cultus (cf. Ps. 9. 7f.; 47; 93; 96-99). The Book of Jonah shows that there were those in Israel whose compassion for even those who had sorely used Israel (such as Assyrian Nineveh) was real. Such Jews took seriously the mission of Israel to the world and were also conscious of the need to bring sinners (even beyond Israel) into the ways of God. There appear to have been others who felt that the God of Israel had a place in the life and worship of other nations, as fragments indicate (Isa. 19. 16-25; Psalm 87). Whilst, Judaism drew increasingly into herself, the spirit that was concerned for the nations dwelt in chosen spirits over the years.

Thus, between the Testaments, there continued to be the belief that the time would come when all nations would turn to Israel's God (e.g. Tobit 13. 11; 14. 6f.; 1. En. 10. 21f.); that God would care for them with his tender mercies (T. Levi 4. 4) and that righteous Gentiles would be saved together with those of Israel (T. Napht. 8. 3). The importance of their witness before the nations was recognized (Tobit 13. 3f.) as well as the evil influence of unworthy behaviour which brought dishonour to God (T. Napht. 8. 3.). In fact, there were some Jews who recognized that some Gentiles had fine qualities which might bring Jews into judgement (T. Benj. 10. 10). Therefore, proselytes were received into Israel and were to be found in most of the communities where the Jewish communities lived.

Such devotion to Yahweh reveals that monotheism had completely carried the day in Israel. The old pagan gods were consigned to limbo and idolatry was treated with scorn (Ps. 135. 15-21; Ep. Jer.; Jub. 21. 3-5). It is clear that whilst Jews might be warned against moral laxity in sharing in the activities of the Gentiles, even in astrology and magic, yet Judaism had effectively overcome the threat of idolatry as far as her own inner life was concerned. The strength of this internal victory was sorely tested during the Seleucid period, when Antiochus IV (Epiphanes) (175-163 B.C.) sought to Hellenize the Jewish subjects under his rule. Under the Maccabean leadership, the Jews refused to compromise or temporize with the acceptance of any foreign deities.

Furthermore, when Persian sources (as well as Greek) introduced dualistic tendencies into the life of Israel, such tendencies found it hard to establish a footing in Jewish thought because the belief in One Supreme Power had been so well and truly established.

The lofty teaching of Second Isaiah had confirmed the teaching of the earlier prophets, who had taught that righteousness is not the concern of one nation but of all nations. Above all, righteousness was the concern of Yahweh and he would show forth his righteousness among the nations. Therefore, his people and other nations could depend upon him as his rule governed all in accord with his law, which is eternally valid, immutable and firm (e.g. Jub., passim). All events are within his foreknowledge (Ecclus. 42. 18-21) and guided to the consummation of his purposes, yet the individual remained fully accountable for his choices, since God would reward each according to his deserts (Ecclus. 15. 11-20; 35. 12-20; 39. 22-27). It was recognized that the ways of God are unsearchable (cf. Ecclus. 3. 21-24; 18. 1-14; 39. 12-21). Whilst there are many things which man can know by means of discovery and books, yet the beginning and the end of things remains in the hand of God (Eccles. 3. 11; 8. 16f.).

A further instance of the exaltation of Yahweh is seen in the development of intermediaries, since it was unfitting to approach their deity with familiarity. There was hesitation in regarding God in anthropomorphic terms (despite the requirements of a personal relationship) and so angels and intermediaries came to be stressed to bridge the gulf between God the All-Pure and Righteous One and man the sinner. There was reluctance to utter the divine name and a number of alternative terms (the Lord; the God of Heaven; Lord of Spirits; the Head of Days and the Great Glory) came to be used in place of the term Yahweh. Most popular was the Most High God.

The popularity of this appellation of the Deity is apparent from the numerous references to it, namely, twenty-five times in the Book of Jubilees, thirteen times in Daniel, forty-eight times in Ben-Sira as well as frequent usage elsewhere.[8] A similar tendency was that of the substitution of some attribute or quality of the Deity for his name, such as, the Divine Wisdom, the Divine Word. The importance of this last development lay in

[8] R. Charles, *The Apocrypha & Pseudepigrapha of the Old Testament*, (Oxford, 1913), Vol. 11, p. 67.

The Exile and Its Aftermath 185

the tendency it gave towards the personification of the quality in question. In the book of Proverbs and in Ben-Sira, Wisdom is frequently personified. Whilst this use may be at times a poetical device, yet it is evident that it has a more literal use in such examples as Proverbs 8 (especially verses 20-31); 9 and Ecclus. 1. 1-10 and 24. 1-34. From a slightly later period, the same tendency is seen in the Wisdom of Solomon 7. 25-27; 9. 9-12 and in 1 Enoch. 42. 1f. and elsewhere. There is a possibility that such a personification of an attribute or quality may be attributed to Hellenistic (if not Hellenic) influence in the Middle East. However, it appears to be probable that this tendency in Jewish writings may be more closely attributed to the Canaanite religious writings such as are found in the Proverbs of Ahiqar, which is dated about the sixth century.⁹ The Jewish use of Wisdom lifted the concept out of the realm of a subordinate deity (such as the Canaanite goddess of wisdom may well have been) but prepared the way for the later development in the direction of Jewish Gnosticism, in which Wisdom was regarded as an emanation of of the Deity. Such a concept is already present in Wisdom of Solomon 7. 25f. In the main, Wisdom served as a synonym for the divine eternal law. Closely linked to the concept of the Divine Wisdom, there was also the concept of the Divine Word, which has its roots in Semitic rather than Hellenic thought. Whilst this latter concept is less prominent in Hebrew thought yet it is found in writings somewhat earlier than the Christian era, e.g. Wisdom of Solomon 18. 15f. It served as a seed for the later development of the doctrine of the Logos (John 1. 1-4, 14) and allied thought (Heb. 4. 12f.; 1 John 1. 1).

More prominent in the rôle of intermediaries were the angelic agents, who were elaborated into a hierarchy. Whilst Yahweh had his attendents from an early period (even within the patriarchal records), yet it is only within the post-exilic period, that Judaism gave added emphasis to these heavenly visitants who brought the message of the great king to his people. In the book of the prophet Zechariah, the angel of the Lord instructs the prophet to rouse the people in Jerusalem to complete the Lord's house (Zech. 1. 9-17). Again, it is the angel of the Lord who encourages the prophet to strengthen the hands of Zerubbabel to complete the work on the Temple. In the hierarchy, some

⁹ cf. J. Bright, A History of Israel, p. 435; also Pritchard, ANET, p. 428.

angels came to have specific names, in particular, the four archangels (Michael, Gabriel, Raphael and Uriel) who are frequently mentioned (Dan. 8. 16; 10. 13; Tobit 3. 17; 5. 4; 1 En. 9. 1., etc.). As in many other matters, *seven* came to have special significance. In Zechariah 4. 10, there is reference to 'these seven are the eyes of the Lord which range through the whole earth', so in Tobit 12. 15, Raphael is described as 'one of the seven holy angels, which present the prayers of the saints'. In 1 Enoch 20, the seven are each given a specific function and called 'the angels who watch' (cf. Dan. 4. 13, 17, 23). Under the leadership of the archangels, there were a vast host of angels—'a thousand thousands and ten thousand times ten thousand' (as in 1 Enoch 60. 1)—through whom the Lord carried out his activities in Nature and with men. This development which brought all other beings within the monotheistic control of Israel's God nevertheless provided a threat—an ever-present one in primitive faiths—namely, that lesser gods or deities seek to fill the gap or to intrude between man and the High God. In Judaism, the High God remained as a living centre of personal worship in contrast to other faiths such as in popular Chinese belief and in Hinduism, where the lesser beings became more significant (because they were more accessible) than the High God.

Another important aspect of the exaltation of the Most High is evident in the use made of this concept of Yahweh by the apocalyptic schools. The apocalyptic literature is 'essentially a protest literature'.[10] 'The whole movement is the expression of a persecution complex', which looked forward in hope to a Golden Age to replace their utter lack of faith and hope in the present and at the same time presented 'a theodicy whereby Yahweh's dealings with Israel might be shown to be righteous'.[11] If Yahweh was righteous and kept his *'chesed'* (covenant-love) to a thousand generations (Deut. 7. 9), then to whom could be attributed the 'whips and scorns of time' which fell upon the Jewish nation? Faced with the demands of a thorough-going monotheistic faith (as expressed in Deutero-Isaiah), the apocalyptic writers had to find some powerful source for their present evils whilst upholding the transcendent power of Yahweh. They managed to do this

[10] S. B. Frost, *Old Testament Apocalyptic* (London, 1952), p. 4.
[11] Ibid., p. 18.

The Exile and Its Aftermath

by attributing the evil of this world to the sin not primarily of men but of angels. These angels are the *'bene elohim'* who appear in Genesis 6. 1-8, as more-than-human beings who married the fair women of earth from whom were born the giants, half-human, half-divine. It was indeed the wickedness of these *'bene elohim'* to whom the evil of these days is due and in their power men are helpless. But the faithful ones must not lose heart because the end (the *eschaton*) is not yet. When the present Age has run its course, Yahweh will vindicate his justice; He, who had created the angels and permits their present control, will at the End destroy them.

Such an interpretation of history sprang into especial relevence when powerful blows were directed against the Jewish faith. It is against the background of this earlier growth in the belief in the exalted place of Israel's God and the pressure of dire present emergency, that the Book of Daniel throws light on the faith of Judaism during the period of the persecutions of Antiochus IV (Epiphanes), c. 166/5. The attempt by the Hellenistic Syrian monarch to bring Judaism into line, in ways of worship, with his other dominions brought a fiery trial on the Jewish people who treasured the Law and were upheld by the pious group (the *Chasidim*: 'the pious ones'), from whom probably both the later groups of the Pharisees and the Essenes emerged.

Against the blandishments and threats of a powerful king, typified in the Book of Daniel under the figure of Nebuchadnezzar, the faithful Daniel and other well-favoured loyal Jewish associates were upheld by their faith until the day when God vindicated his faithful ones and made the proud Nebuchadnezzar eat straw like an ox. The writer is a visionary who seeks to reinforce the failing spirits of his fellow-countrymen who might doubt God's rule and power. The rise of world powers is symbolized in the form of a great image. 'This image, mighty and of exceeding brightness, stood before you (the king), and its appearance was frightening. The head of this image was of fine gold, its breast and arms of silver, its belly and its thighs of bronze, its legs of iron, its feet partly of iron and partly of clay.' This image is suddenly smitten by a stone (cut out by no human hand), which breaks the feet of iron and clay. In consequence, the entire image is broken in pieces and 'became like the chaff of the summer threshing floors' (Dan. 2. 31-35).

In the interpretation of this vision, which came to the king, Daniel points out that the various metals of the image signify the rise of kingdoms, which will replace one another but there will come at length a divided kingdom—partly of iron and partly of clay. This kingdom shall be partly strong and partly brittle. Then the stone will fall which will destroy the divided kingdom, because iron does not mix with clay. To replace these kings, 'the God of heaven will set up a kingdom which shall never be destroyed, nor shall its sovereignty be left to another people. It shall break in pieces all these kingdoms and bring them to an end and it shall stand for ever' (Dan. 2. 44). With such assured tones, the writer of the book sought to strengthen the hand and confirm the knees of his countrymen. The present troubles were not a failure of the divine purpose but an indication that this purpose was coming to its fruition. God had command of events. Whilst Antiochus might believe that he could bring the Jews to obedience, yet his term of power would soon end. The attitude of trust towards God which such faith engendered is given classic expression in the reply of Shadrach, Meshach and Abednego to the king Nebuchadnezzar, who demanded that they should serve and worship the golden image which he had set up. 'O Nebuchadnezzar, we have no need to answer you in this matter. If it be so, our God whom we serve is able to deliver us from the burning fiery furnace; and he will deliver us out of your hand, O king. But if not, be it known to you, O king, that we will not serve your gods or worship the golden image which you have set up' (Dan. 3. 16-18).

By means of a series of visions, the apocalyptic writer looks forward to the downfall of overweening pride which exalts itself against the Most High. In Chapter 7, the great powers are symbolized under the form of four great beasts. The last of these powers which troubled the earth was seen to be the beast which had ten horns (the Seleucid kings), among whom there sprouted a little horn (Antiochus). 'In this horn were eyes like the eyes of a man and a mouth speaking great things' (Dan. 7. 8). Similarly, a two-horned ram (the Medo-Persian empire) was overcome by a he-goat from the west (Alexander), which had a conspicuous horn which was broken and became four (the states which followed Alexander's death). Out of these states a little horn arose which exalted itself even against God. The blasphemy

The Exile and Its Aftermath

against the Most High is evident in that he (Antiochus—the little horn) persecutes the Saints (7. 21), defiles the Temple, takes away the continual burnt offerings and abolishes the Law (7. 25; 8. 9-13; 9. 27). Such defiance on the part of Antiochus must inevitably bring its dénouement, 'until its decreed end is poured out on the desolator' (9. 27).

As the divine plan unfolds, so the doom of Antiochus is certain. He is granted a little time (7. 25; 11. 36; 12. 11)—then despite the fact that 'in his own mind he shall magnify himself' and 'without warning he shall destroy many . . . he shall even rise up against the Prince of princes; but by no human hand, he shall be broken' (8. 23-25. cf. 11. 40-45). The reason for his destruction lies in the fact that God is about to act on behalf of his people. The seer depicts the 'Ancient of Days', seated on his throne of fiery flames, who decrees the destruction of the beast. The dominion of all the beasts is taken from them and an everlasting kingdom is given to 'one like a son of man'. 'All peoples, nations and languages should serve him . . . his kingdom . . . shall not be destroyed' (7. 9-14). This 'son of man' represents 'the people of the saints of the Most High' (7. 22, 27), whose faithfulness will be vindicated and rewarded. 'Their kingdom shall be an everlasting kingdom, and all dominions shall serve and obey them' (7. 27). Elsewhere, for example in 1 Enoch, this 'son of man' is deemed to be a pre-existent heavenly deliverer but this development came later. In the meanwhile, further assurance was given to the saints by the writer's insight that 'many of those who sleep in the dust of the earth shall awake, some to everlasting life, and some to shame and everlasting contempt' (12. 2). This insight came to have increased significance for the Chasidim, who, as the later party of the Pharisees, came to believe firmly in the doctrine of the resurrection. Thus, even the fear of death was removed for those who were loyal to the purposes of God. Therefore, God's kingdom spanned the chasm of death. The close solidarity of the fortunes of the 'saints of the Most High' and the righteous rule of God over men became ever more closely intertwined as expressed in the law which came to be regarded as eternal and immutable. The Maccabaean War made it crystal clear that the Jews had either to be a gathered community, separated by the Law from all others, or they would disappear as an entity. This realization made many Jews hate any and every contact with

Gentiles, who were regarded as 'the dogs of the Gentiles'. This tendency was accentuated because those Jews who advocated closer ties with Hellenism often were swept away from their Jewish faith and embraced aspects, religious and cultural, in Hellenism which were opposed to Judaism. Therefore, the note of separatism became dominant in the writings of Judaism. They were to be a 'holy people', set apart for God but set apart from other nations, with whom inter-marriage was forbidden.

Nevertheless, tensions remained within post-exilic Judaism because it was recognized that God had a concern for the nations, as their Creator and as their Righteous King. This Kingship over history which was exercised through the Law made it possible for those who were non-Jews (who accepted the Law) to be acceptable to him. In the flesh, such non-Jews did not belong to Judaism but by walking in the Law, they showed that they belonged to the true Israel. Such men were honoured above those who were Jews (according to the flesh) but failed to keep the Law. These latter were 'the wicked', 'the ungodly' and the 'lawless' ones. Proud of itself, Judaism as a whole kept true to the Law as God's rule.

CHAPTER NINE

HEBREW THOUGHT AND LATER THEORIES OF SOCIETY

1. *The Pastoral Tradition in Israel. The rôle of the shepherd vis-à-vis the agriculturalist. The tension of two cultures amid one people. The function of the prophet in Hebrew society and his impact on political thought. His status before the king and the people.*
2. *The theocracy in Israel. The amphictyony and its influence on later thought. The monarch's relationship with the deity. The theocracy which survived the Exile. Its peculiar spirit.*
3. *The alternatives to theocracy. (a) The Individualist Doctrine of Society and of Government. Its varieties and forms. (b) The Collective Doctrine of the State. Society as an organism. Collective and collectivist views.*
4. *The basis of social unity. Individual values and basic unity. The grounds of solidarity in Judaism. Democracy—as a goal of social and individual expression. Characteristics of modern large-scale society. Conditions for the democratic organization of large-scale society. The significance of the doctrine of Man in relation to democracy.*

CHAPTER NINE

HEBREW THOUGHT AND LATER THEORIES OF SOCIETY

THE age-long connection with pastoral society appears to have remained unbroken within Israel. The place of Abraham as the hero-father of the faithful is a very significant one, as has already been seen. Throughout her history, the loyalty to the shepherd tradition continued. It was the gift of the shepherd Abel, which was acceptable rather than the offering of Cain, the agriculturist. It was from the same tradition that there came the greatest of her kings, a man 'after the Lord's own heart', David, who left his flocks to be anointed king. Too little attention has been given to this strand in Israel's life—a strand which came to be expressed most forcefully through the mouth of the prophet. It was from his care of the flocks (as well as from his sycamore trees) that the Lord called Amos to bring the Northern Kingdom into the paths of righteousness.

Interwoven with this shepherd-tradition, there was the common loyalty to Yahweh which was shared with the agriculturalists who lived in Canaan. Whilst the agriculturalists were aware that they depended on the rainfall and this rainfall gave fertility, which was Yahweh's gift, yet there was, in more settled conditions on the land, a greater temptation to believe in one's own self-sufficiency ('I cultivated this land and I made it flourish'). Furthermore, the earlier agriculturalists who preceded Israel as dwellers in Canaan had their own gods and were not willing to deny the efficacy of these gods when Israel came. Yahweh may come to be first among the gods but that did not mean that he was the only god who was to be worshipped. For the shepherd, who moved from place to place, he knew that the mighty heavens and the earth were the work of Yahweh's hand. He might find other peoples who worshipped other gods but he was free to move away from them to set up shrines in his own way for the one God in whom he believed.

Hebrew Thought and Later Theories of Society 193

The common loyalty to Yahweh which was shared between the two traditions came to be a source of conflict. As with a marriage, a common bond between two partners can prove a running conflict where both partners are hurt in endeavouring to escape from one another. Both traditions were aware that they belonged to one another but they were also free to exalt their own separate traditions over against one another. In this pattern of Israel's development, it is evident that those who wrote down her records and sought to shape her destiny were deeply imbued with the shepherd-tradition, which was the older strain in the national stock.

The place of the prophet as a representative of this older element needs to receive much more attention. It is clear that he was closer to the priestly element than was formerly believed. Many prophets were attached to temples and carried out cultic rites and rituals. The prophet and the priest were not vis-à-vis one another in the religion of Israel. Nathan the prophet and Zadok the priest stood together to support Solomon in his accession to the throne. The fact that Nathan the prophet was there is the significant one. Throughout the period of the kingdoms, the prophet played an important role in the political life as well as in the social and spiritual life of the people in the North and the South. How large a place and how significant was his political and social rôle is not altogether clear. Presumably, because religion played so large a part in the life of the nation, then all her religious representatives had an important place in all social activities, including political action. Whilst the figure of the prophet is very prominent in many societies, as may be seen most clearly in Red Indian and in Islamic cultures,[1] yet it is doubtful whether any nation has looked to the prophets for guidance in the same measure as did Israel. The peculiar quality about the guidance of the Hebrew prophet lay in his powerful ethical stress in religious matters. When he came into the political arena, he came with a religious authority and an ethical power which appears to be lacking in other prophetic groups in other nations. Moreover, this ethical emphasis came to have an increasing place in the message of the prophets as a whole, so that there was a notable ethical development. This appears to be different from the ethical element in the teaching of Islamic prophets, among whom ethics played an

[1] C. Dawson, *Religion and Culture* (London, 1949), pp. 70, 73-82.

G

important part (as in the case of the prophet Mohammed himself), yet with a lack of ethical development in later generations. The temptation for any ethical system to remain static—as a 'rationalization' of the original standards of the charismatic leader who set the religious movement in motion—besets every religion. The sole escape from such a static condition appears to lie in some doctrine of revelational religion and a belief in a doctrine of the Spirit. Such doctrines allow room for fresh conceptions to enter in succeeding ages. Development becomes possible. Religious leaders do not then always have to be looking back to a charismatic leader but forward to new horizons of light. Herein the prophet prepared the way for the New Testament and believed himself to be the agent of the Spirit of God in his day. In Israel, the ethical note in his teaching apparently came earlier than among other nations' prophets (with the possible exception of Zarathustra). The Hebrew prophet went into every sector of social life and gave the Word of the Lord in terms of immediate significance and relevance to his contemporary situation. The political sectors was part of his concern, so his ethical criteria came to bear on his judgment of treaties, foreign alliances, the influence of marriage with foreign princesses and all the intricacies of the diplomatist's skill.

It is a source of wonder (and indeed of amazement) that there is lacking evidence that prophets did not seem to have wielded such influence in neighbouring kingdoms, such as Moab and Edom. There were prophets, presumably, in Tyre and Sidon, and in most countries of Asia Minor since prophetic movements of various kinds have emanated from this area in succeeding centuries, namely, the Mystery Religions of the early Roman Empire and the Montanist Movement in the second century. It is therefore the more regrettable that we have so little evidence in political affairs of schools of prophets in the kingdoms around the frontiers of Israel, during the period of the kings in Israel. Ethbaal, the father of Jezebel and king of Tyre, may have been a prophet of Ba'al as well as a royal priest. Of the influence of prophets in the neighbouring kingdoms, there seems to be little (some would claim—none) influence of such prophetic leaders in matters of State. Certainly, the prophets of Israel appear to have been drawn from various classes of society—though the older less class-conscious shepherd element in Israelite society appears

Hebrew Thought and Later Theories of Society 195

to have been most fruitful in providing the charismatic type, seen in the prophet.

The writers of the two books of the Kings make it clear that the Yahwist prophets would withstand any attempt by king or priest who would lessen the influence of Yahweh over his people. When the might of the king increased, such a king was held in honour only in so far as he was devoted to Yahweh. Though he might, on the other hand, be a powerful monarch, such as Jeroboam II of Israel, yet he was given little place if he permitted bull-worship in the Northern Kingdom. The king in Israel was deemed to be in covenant with a greater king to whom loyalty had to be shown. In Babylon, Assyria and Persia, the emperors were the earthly rulers for the gods of the states they ruled and the glory of these gods was considered co-extensive with the lands they ruled. The morality of these gods was also closely similar to the recognized moral codes of their peoples. In Israel, Yahweh was ever greater than his people and his moral demands marked him out as leading them on to new heights of moral and religious behaviour.

Thus, there developed in Israel a theocracy which exceeded that of other nations by its intransigence and comprehensiveness. Theocracies may differ in various ways. The head of a theocracy is not hereditary as in the case of a monarchy nor is placed in power by a political *coup-d'état* but rather is elected by a priestly caste or college. This head may be regarded as pre-eminent over the temporal power, which looks to the guidance of the priest-ruler as the vice-regent of God. This is the position which was taken by Boniface VIII in his Bull, *Unam Sanctam* (1302). He asserted the absolute supremacy of the Papacy. All beings must obey it. All monarchs were required to believe this tenet as 'necessary to salvation'. Boniface VIII denied that king or Council had authority without him.

Another form of theocracy sought to combine the functions of a monarchy with the absolutism of divine rule, as in the case of the Sultans in Turkey who were heads of the civil order as well as the caliphs of the Moslem world. The caliph, as the successor to the prophet Mohammed, was believed to have that close knowledge of the divine law, thereby making obedience to him a part of the subject's devotion to Allah. A further form of theocracy, in fact a more complete one, was seen, until recently, in Tibet, where the Dalai Lama as a re-incarnation of a form of the Buddha exercises priestly rule over his subjects. His function as ruler of the civil order was regarded as part of his priestly responsibility. This gave him an absolute control in affairs temporal and spiritual over the lives of his subjects.

But, among such forms of theocracy, it was the form in Judaea which proved most potent in the West because it entered into Western thinking through Judaeo-Christian thought. The Jewish people became convinced of their chosen place, their election, by the God of the nations, who had joined them to himself by an age-long covenant. It was this doctrine that was expressed through the amphictyony and held the tribes together. When the tribes sought to be like other nations and to have a king, then the concept of the divine king over his chosen people was modified. It was modified but it was not given up completely. The line of David, in particular, did attempt to keep the covenant between David and Yahweh. In the North, many other elements (various local gods and agricultural cults) served to dilute the loyalty to one God. The later monarchy saw a long struggle between the prophets and the monarchy to hold the loyalty of the people. The prophets fought hard to keep the nation true to the allegiance due to their invisible overlord. In the South, some kings aided the prophets, especially kings Hezekiah and Josiah. These kings were themselves assisted by political events (namely, the political weakness and dynastic quarrels within the Assyrian Empire) but they made a stalwart attempt to assert the overlordship of Yahweh. Although these kings sought to reform the faith of Yahweh's people by a return to earlier practices, such as the regulation of feasts and the celebration of the Passover, yet in effect the result was, particularly in the case of Josiah, a change to a new principle (possibly implicit far earlier)—the centralization of worship on Mount Zion in Jerusalem. Throughout all the changes the underlying allegiance to their covenant-Lord remained firm.

The disappearance of the monarchy did not vitally affect the relationship between Yahweh and his people. The teaching of the prophets had prepared the nation for the period of severe national crisis, which the Exile involved. The exaltation of the righteousness of Yahweh made the destruction of the political

Hebrew Thought and Later Theories of Society 197

structure of a disobedient nation understandable. When the political structure had disappeared, his righteousness and his faithfulness were not affected by the nation's debacle except that his covenantal love shone more clearly in dark days. In fact, national disaster served to exalt his position. Their disaster through disobedience, at the hands of foreign nations, revealed the truth that other nations were the instrument of his care (in discipline) of Israel. When these great powers (such as Assyria and Babylon) had carried out his purposes, then they would be cast aside. Thus, even amid the depression which inevitably accompanied the experience of exile, the exiles from Judah still retained a living belief in the ability of Yahweh to use this period for his redemptive purposes. In due time, he would show his hand and reveal the path for his chosen people. This hope is evident in the teaching of Jeremiah, who bought his plot of land as a token that the day of restoration would come. Under Ezekiel, the hope was fanned into a flame. Beside the waters of bitterness, the Lord set down his chariot and would lead back his people to a restored Temple and a purified land. As the exile continued, many hearts must have questioned the Lord's ability to show his power over the great power in Babylon which ruled them. However, fresh fuel was added to the flame of hope by the message of the great Prophet of the Exile. He had no doubt that the gods of Babylonia would be overcome and that the Lord would use the conquering Cyrus the Mede to show his power. Events established the faith of this prophet in that Cyrus gave the exiles permission to return to Jerusalem, under the leadership of a scion of the house of David, Zerubbabel. Although the difficulties were enormous, both from the standpoint of the hardships of the return journey and also from the hostility of those who already were established in Judah, yet the promise of exaltation for the chosen people at the price of obedience remained among them. The Lord's righteousness had now been clearly revealed. He had not forgotten them nor had he forgotten his ancient sanctuary on Mount Zion. He had restored Israel to Zion and so the later prophets encouraged the people to work hard to restore the Temple and to carry out their religious duties. This would enable them to be further used as the instrument of his will. Despite many setbacks, the faith which contained this promise continued to hold together the returned community.

This faith became crystalized in the form of the sacred law-book, which became an object of extreme reverence. The elaborate ritual precautions taken by the scribes to ensure the purity of the text also served to emphasize the pre-eminent place which this book came to hold in the affections, the life and the worship of the Jewish Community. The priestly-law, the Torah, was in the nature of a compromise between the priestly and the prophetic standpoint. Whilst the records were clearly a depositum of the prophetic schools, especially in the Deuteronomic element, yet it was the priestly authors who brought the final compilation of the Pentateuch together, providing in particular the ritual laws in Leviticus and their own emphasis in various places. Although this law had to adjust itself to the law of the State, especially when the latter was a foreign power (Persia, Syria and Rome), nevertheless the obedience of the Jewish people primarily to their divine law did not waver. The Maccabaean War is a clear expression of their devotion to the demands of the Torah, when the Syrian King, Antiochus IV (Epiphanes) endeavoured to en-enforce foreign ways of worship and practice upon them. As in the case of the three Jewish leaders in the Book of Daniel, their reply to the royal challenge was clear: 'Our God whom we serve is able to deliver us from the burning fiery furnace . . . but if not, be it known to you, O king, that we will not serve your gods or worship the golden image which you have set up' (Dan. 3. 17-18). It was this quality of faith which enabled this people to endure through the hardships of their history—a quality of faith which depended on the assurance of his rule and of their election in his purposes.

The form of theocratic rule of the Hebrews was closely modelled on the patterns of the ancient world, which normally recognized the tripartite classification of states, namely, monarchy, oligarchy and democracy. Herodotus gives an account of an argument between seven leaders of Persia who sought to determine a constitution for their country.[2] They discussed the three forms mentioned above and although each form had its advocates, they decided for monarchy by a majority of one. Plato, in his *Republic*, describes the three forms but discussed also their abuse.[3] In the case of a monarchy, it may degenerate into tyranny. If you establish rule by an aristocracy, this form may degenerate into

[2] Herodotus, Book III, 80-83.
[3] Plato, *Republic*, Bk. VIII, 545c and Bk. IX, 576b.

Hebrew Thought and Later Theories of Society 199

an oligarchy, whereas if you seek to establish democracy, this may well become a 'mobocracy'. Aristotle follows Plato closely, but prefers to use a term 'polity' to refer to a constitutional 'rule of the many' (namely, rule by the middle classes) in contrast to 'democracy', which he is inclined to suggest means 'control by the poor'.⁴ These thinkers serve as examples in political thought, since their discussion of the tripartite classification has been accepted by later thinkers ever since. Political philosophers have enlarged and expounded their views through the centuries.

According to this classification, the Hebrew form falls within the category of a monarchy which has a monarch with absolute demands. This ruler can brook no rival in the allegiance of his subjects and may treat his rivals ruthlessly when his honour is at stake. This conception comes out clearly in many passages in *Judges*, *Joshua*, the books of *Samuel* and the books of *Kings*. Much of the criticism, which has been levelled against the moral practices of the prophets, is in fact directed against these ancient conceptions of the honour due to the absolute demands of a divine king. It was for this purpose that Samuel hewed King Agag of the Amalekites in pieces (1 Sam. 15. 33) and Elijah killed the prophets of Ba'al (1 Kgs. 19. 40). These foreign political and religious leaders represented a threat to the sovereignty of Yahweh over his people. Therefore these opponents, in accord with the standards of that age, had to be destroyed. If the Israelite king, as in the case of Saul, demurred in carrying out the decree of Yahweh, then Saul himself came under the decree of destruction. This brings out forcibly the sovereignty which Yahweh held over Israel. When, in due course, the political leadership declined and the state organization in the North and the South disappeared, the sovereignty of Yahweh remained firm and deep in the faith of his people.

Nevertheless, the theocratic order of the Hebrew people had a spirit which was peculiarly its own. As has been pointed out, in particular regard to the prophets, this spirit subordinated considerations of class and gave an unusual sense of unity to the people as a whole. This is evident also in the Deuteronomic and Levitic codes of law, which provided for the needy members of the nation. The Jubilee Year enabled a man to take up his citizenship afresh and to remind the creditor and the debtor that a Hebrew is still a Hebrew who must be treated with the fellow-

⁴ Aristotle, *Politics*, Bk. IV.

feeling which Yahweh expected between brethren. Similarly, whilst the Hebrew king might be exalted among his fellows, yet this king had to bear in mind that he ruled over brethren. 'You may not put a foreigner over you, who is not your brother' (Deut. 17. 15). The egalitarian attitude which was part of the pastoral heritage, wherein each shepherd exerted his independence vis-à-vis all other shepherds, remained as a stubborn opponent against every attempt by royal prerogative to establish the usual oriental despotism over the Israelites. The royal recognition of the poorer shepherd's rights is vividly brought in the parable by which Nathan the prophet admonished King David's adultery with Bathsheba. Even a royal shepherd must respect the rights of poorer brethren, particularly in Israel because the Lord kept watch over the right acts of his people. The common realization that all shared in the heritage has pervaded Hebrew activity and made even the meanest Jew proud that he is part of the chosen people. The greatest service to the Jewish cause was rendered, so it is claimed, by 'the many little obscure Jewish communities through the ages, persecuted and despised, who kept alive the flame of purest monotheism and the supremacy and divineness of the Moral Law'.[*] This service was carried out in many lands and amid many cultures, in freedom and in servitude, but always with the awareness that the divine Kingship made all Jews one in a living brotherhood. Within the present generation, there has been an outstanding expression of such brotherhood in the help poured out by Jews to help Jews who suffered under the terrors of National Socialism. International Jewry has poured out millions of dollars and pounds to assist needy fellow-believers, some of whom have been settled in the State of Israel. Theocracy became a precious heritage which contrasts strongly with other forms of Society and of the State.

The leading forms of alternative views may be divided into those which emphasize the Individualist Doctrine of Society and of Government in contrast to those which stress the Collectivist Doctrine of Society and of the State. For those who are concerned to uphold the rights of the individual, government is regarded as though it is a necessary evil but it was to be watched carefully lest such government will interfere unduly with individuals. In-

[*] *The Legacy of Israel* (ed. by E. R. Bevan & C. Singer) (Oxford, 1927), pp. 515-6.

Hebrew Thought and Later Theories of Society

dividualist theories vary in their view of the extent of individual rights. From the seventeenth to the nineteenth centuries, individualism flourished in Western Europe, from the time of John Locke to that of Herbert Spencer. For John Locke, the Law of Nature is objective and *a priori*—a principle which preceded the formation of government. This Law of Nature he thought to be expressed in the rights of individuals, namely, a man's life, liberty and estate. It was therefore for the protection of these rights that the need for a *sovereign* arose and government came to be necessary. The Law of Nature was often violated by criminal and anti-social acts and also even those who accepted this Law differed in their interpretation of it, therefore it was the duty of the sovereign to safeguard this Law. A good sovereign will uphold the Law of Nature but if the ruler failed to do so, then it is the duty of the people to remove him from his place of authority, because he has betrayed his trust. Thus, John Locke justified the Glorious Revolution of 1688 and his view of the 'Law of Nature'—as embodied in written constitution (to which both the President and the Congress are subject)—came to have wide acceptance especially in the United States of America.

John Locke considered that 'Men being ... by nature all free, equal, and independent, no one can be put out of this estate, and subjected to the political power of another, without his own consent, which is done by agreeing with other men to join and unite into a community for their comfortable, safe, and peaceable living one amongst another, in a secure enjoyment of their properties, and a greater security against any that are not of it'.[1] This empiricism assumes a premise of individualism which it is very difficult to substantiate. In the view of some, Thomas Hobbes' view is closer to experience, when he described man's life, in the state of nature, as not 'free, equal and independent' but 'solitary, poor, nasty, brutish and short'.[2] For Hobbes, the lack of security and power (a lack of strength) demanded a 'sovereign', a man or assembly which would, by contract, act on behalf of all for their peace and common defence. Apart from such contract, 'the condition of man ... is a condition of war of everyone against everyone'.[3] Thus, the State (for him) originates in, and is maintained by, calculated self-interest.

[1] J. Locke, *The Second Treatise on Civil Government*, VIII, 95.
[2] T. Hobbes, *Leviathan*, XIII, para 8.   [3] *Ibid.*, XIV, para. 4.

Whilst the individual may have, in some primaeval time be it assumed, given up his individual rights for the sake of existence in a community, yet it is not within the experience of anyone that such a contract exists today. We are born into a community which does, in fact, do many things contrary to our wishes. We are involved in conflicts in which the individual has little knowledge or interest. Therefore, individualism appears to be a weak base for community.

The discussions in the seventeenth century ranged around the political liberties of the subject. In the eighteenth century, these discussions took a practical turn in the controversies which involved the person of John Wilkes, with particular reference to the liberty of the individual before the law. In the aftermath of the original Industrial Revolution, it was John Stuart Mill who gave powerful literary expression to the 'limits of the authority of society over the individual'.[9] Whilst the individual is in society, he has obligations to that society. Mill's words on the matter of contract are strongly in contrast to those of Hobbes, when Mill wrote, 'Though society is not founded on a contract, and though no good purpose is answered by inventing a contract in order to deduce social obligations from it, everyone who receives the protection of society owes a return for the benefit, and the fact of living in society renders it indispensable that each should be bound to observe a certain line of conduct towards the rest'.[10] Nevertheless, where the individual's conduct is not prejudicial to the rest, 'there should be perfect freedom, legal and social, to do the action and stand the consequences'.[11] Mill recognized that such action would probably result in unpopularity and even penalties (especially the non-legal ones, such as ostracism), yet these are consequences of which the subject has no right to complain. The important factor is that the individual has his own sphere of free activity, what Mill calls, 'the department of human affairs, in which individuality has its proper field of action'. Such a field of action made possible self-development, as 'duty to oneself'. Mill's essay 'On Liberty' fostered the attitude of self-help in Victorian England.

On the cultural level, Herbert Spenser (1820-1903) en-

[9] J. S. Mill, *On Liberty*, Chap. IV (Title).
[10] *Ibid.*, Chap. IV, para. 3.
[11] *Idem.*

deavoured to champion individualism from another angle, namely, from a biological approach of evolution which justified (in his phrase) 'the survival of the fittest'. For Spenser, evolution moved from incoherent homogeneity to a larger differentiation of coherent heterogeneity which meant greater individuality and freedom. He viewed cultural development as a movement from kinship and custom-controlled societies, through militaristic and aristocratic dominated societies into industrially organized societies, which severally provided a wider opportunity for personal fulfilment. Prominence was also given to the claims of the individual in the economic sphere. Yet it is noteworthy that Spenser's conception of moral and social progress was part of an inevitable cosmic evolution which was consistent with a '*laissez-faire*' policy of a utilitarian-liberal kind which he approved. He did not regard evolution as synonymous with progress, but he did consider that man moved, both as an individual and as a social being, from a lower to a higher level—on grounds which are not always sufficiently clear. The ardent supporter of an individualist doctrine did, however, find comfort in a doctrine which appeared to give 'natural' justification to the fruits of competition and struggle as part of a fundamental process.

Spenser was, at the same time, desirous of expressing the unity of man in society. This he did by his use of 'the Social Organism',[12] in which he describes the political organization of society as a regulating system which corresponded to the cerebral system of an animal, whilst the industrial organization he described as a sustaining system which corresponds to the alimentary apparatus in the animal form. This use of the analogy of an organism to describe society has appealed to many thinkers. From the time of Plato to that of Oswald Spengler, writers have used this analogy to express the unity of men in society. It well expresses the sense of inter-dependence of men upon the endeavours and labours of one another. However, it has one great drawback, namely, it fails to give proper recognition to the autonomy and the initiative of the individual. The personality of the individual, though subjected and conditioned in many respects by his society, nevertheless has a distinctness which cannot be altogether absorbed within the mass. In fact, the contribution of the individual

[12] H. Spenser, 'The Social Organism', *Westminster Review*, Vol. XVIII (Jan. 1860) and *Principles of Sociology*, Vol. I, Pt. II, chaps. II-IX.

personality (in terms of leadership, negotiator or statesman) may well enable the whole community to be preserved, especially in times of crisis or danger.

To permit the fullest expression of individual ideals within society as a whole is no easy matter. Whilst it may be claimed that the cells exist for the sake of the body, yet it cannot be claimed that individuals exist for the sake of society. In fact, society's goals are attained by the fulfilment of the ideals of individuals within it, namely, such varied and specific goals as more knowledge, more pleasure, better living conditions and improved health. It is in individuals, together in society as persons, that social values are realized—in contrast to the analogy of the organism wherein the cells have significance because they are within the organism. It is therefore not without reason that the writers who have stressed the place of unity within the state have paved the way, not to the fulfilment of personal social values, but, to totalitarianism. In the case of Hegel, his teaching that 'the true is the whole' led to the rigid Prussian state. Although Hegel's influence spread personalism, yet he taught that the 'will of the state' is the true will of every individual who belongs to it. So an individual only acts morally when he acts in accord with his true will, namely, with the will of the state. Hegel distinguished between 'Civil Society', which is social organization created to enable different individuals to satisfy each other's wants, from 'the State', which is deemed to have a rational will to fulfil all the members. It is not made clear how the *rational will* may be ascertained, especially within a given situation. Such an intellectual re-inforcement for the significance of the State came to have ugly practical expression in National Socialism.

Jean Jacques Rousseau (1712-1778) shared the impatience of Georg Hegel (1770-1831) in regard to the differences created by the varied ideals of the individual wills. Rouseau differentiated between the general will on the one hand and the individual will, the majority will and the will of all on the other. The general will is a collective will—an organic combination of every member's will. 'The private will is inclined by its nature to partiality, and the general will to impartiality'.[21] Rousseau believed that

[21] J. J. Rousseau, *The Social Contract*, Bk. II, ch. I (Trans. *Social and Political Philosophy*, ed. J. Somerville & R. E. Santoni, p. 221).

Hebrew Thought and Later Theories of Society 205

'the general will is always right and tends always to the public advantage' in contrast to 'the will of all' which may be corrupted by private interests." 'It is therefore of the utmost importance for the obtaining the expression of the general will, that no partial society should be formed in the State.'¹⁵ Such partial societies were deemed to be factions which were divisive and injurious to the well-being of the whole. Rousseau endeavoured to place some limits on the Sovereign power in the interest of the individual. In particular, he recognized the necessity to distinguish the duties which were part of the responsibility of a citizen (i.e. the respective rights which were expected by the Sovereign from a citizen) and the 'natural rights which they enjoy in quality of men'. Then, he continues, 'it is granted that all which an individual alienates by the social compact is only that part of his power, and property, and his liberty, the use of which is important to the community; but we must also grant that the Sovereign is the only judge of what is important to the community'.¹⁶

The last sentence in this statement is the ominous one. Rousseau sought to give philosophic grounds to the doctrine of the equality of men in a society. 'The social compact establishes among citizens such an equality that they are all engaged under the same conditions, and should all enjoy the same rights.'¹⁷ Such a statement became the sheet-anchor of democracy. 'All should enjoy the same rights'. Discussion would still proceed on the issue of what constituted 'a citizen' but the rise of democracy had a sure champion in Jean Jacques Rousseau. Yet such was his concern to ensure the solidarity of the community that he held the 'sovereign power (to be) all absolute, all sacred and all inviolable' (though subject to general conventions). Such Sovereign power, as we have seen above, 'is the only judge of what is important to the community'. On this justification, Adolf Hitler could remove all democratic practice in the interests of the Sovereign and establish a totalitarian dictatorship. Herein lies the irony of Rousseau's position.

Rousseau recognized that the State has to have a large area of responsibility, however much one desires to secure that 'every man may fully dispose of what is left to him of his property and

¹⁴ Ibid., Bk. II, ch. III, pp. 223-4. ¹⁶ Ibid., p. 224.
¹⁵ Ibid., chap. IV, p. 225 ¹⁷ Ibid., p. 227.

his liberty'. Similarly, Hegel's argument that 'the right is the rational', which is only possible when men act in accord with universal reason in an organic state, gives an inclusive and all-embracing competence to the State. Both writers in fact share a Collective Doctrine of the State, which is attractive to those minds which fear the consequences of undue individualism. The Collective Doctrine takes a number of diverse forms. Even within the Hegelian school of 'idealist' collectivism there are a number of forms, whilst Hegel's position is very different from the 'materialist' or economic collectivism of the Marxian School. It cannot be denied that in the Hebrew view, there is a strong theocratic ownership which is different from both the positions of Hegel and of Marx. For Marx, the 'inevitable victory' in the class struggle lies with 'the proletarian movement—the self-conscious, independent movement of the immense majority, in the interests of the immense majority'.[18] The collectivist movement, as conceived by Marx, required that the proletariat in each country first of all settled scores with its own *bourgeoisie*. Then the national control which is held by the proletariat in one country is widened into a wider form of international control. Thus, an international form of collectivism can be established. Similarly, in the view of Friedrich Engels, 'division into classes has a certain historical justification' but 'will be swept away by the complete development of modern productive forces'.[19] But modern productive forces are wider than one nation, so some inter-national collective system to link together the activities of workers in all countries becomes a necessity. The alternative can only be the conflicting interests of different national groups, which will serve as an opportunity for the *bourgeoisie*. Presumably, the division into nations can be regarded as having 'a certain historical justification' but this division like others will also 'be swept away by the complete development of modern productive forces'.

The Collective view of society which is expressed so forcibly in these writers has to be balanced by a place for the *individual values* in any satisfactory approach to a philosophy of the State, which is here regarded as the embodiment of a national society

[18] K. Mark and F. Engels, *Manifesto of the Communist Party* (Trans. *Social and Political Philosophy* (as above), p. 355.
[19] F. Engels, *Socialism: Utopian and Scientific*, ibid., pp. 377-8.

Hebrew Thought and Later Theories of Society 207

in a constitutional form. Or to repeat in a different form, justice has to be done to the individual (which is the bearer and transmitter of human values) as well as the unity (corporateness) of the society, which sustains and promotes the human values of all. Herein lies the delicate balance which is sought in a true democracy, namely, that individual divergencies may exist within a corporate framework which is not shattered or rejected entirely by the divergencies. To require complete conformity by suppressing such differences will do violence to the inevitable human variants which is part of the stuff of human development. The more surely the common weal is recognized and accepted, the larger the measure of variance that may be permitted. It is only when the basic unity is seriously threatened that the guardians of that society have to limit the individual divergencies for the good of all. But a further word may be said concerning this basic unity, which is the bond within the continuing life of a community.

'The basic unity . . . is a consensus about values cherished in common, embodied in accepted usages and relationships, pursued through some inclusive organization'.[20] But the values which are sought in common are realized only in individual lives—in those who compose the whole. 'The collectivity as such never experiences these values. The collectivity is either an abstraction or a mechanism.'[21] Such an abstraction is seen in the Hegelian philosophers and in Adolf Hitler's adulation of the 'German race', as the spring of the values of mankind. As MacIver points out, 'such an abstraction is false—the will of the presumptive universal is always particular. It is the will of one or of some arrogating the title to be the will of the whole'.[22]

The struggle to uphold this basic unity lies behind the religious labours of the Jewish people. They had a clear conviction that their faith served as the basis of their 'consensus about values cherished in common'. Their law set forth the 'accepted usages and relationships' and also served, in large measure, as the 'inclusive organization' to set them apart as a community. But both ends were open for development. On the one hand, the prophetic figure acted to 'realize individual values'. As in the

[20] R. M. MacIver, *Webb of Government*, p. 415.
[21] Ibid., p. 417.   [22] Ibid.

case of Jeremiah, he might stand against the whole community and yet be vindicated; yet he held a common faith from which sprang values held in common. On the other hand, the 'inclusive organization' of the Jews was seen to be part (and only part) of the wider rule of God. All mankind formed a solidarity which had a unity by the common factor of creation. All creation was due to the will of God. But mankind's solidarity was seen even more clearly in men's solidarity in evil, which called for a Saving-Sovereign to fulfil the Creator's will.

Before we consider the New Testament view of Man in Society, as the response of a new kind to the older theocratic order, it is pertinent to refer to certain conditions which work together to make possible the goal of democracy. Some aspects of economic development were lacking in ancient times to make the rise of a democratic order possible, so that it is not surprising that the Jewish form of theocratic rule could not be considered democratic in the later Western sense of the term. Yet, it must be borne in mind that the egalitarian concept of society among the shepherd tribesmen bore close kinship to that of later democracy, in that a man was valued for his personal initiative and energy as a sign of merit. Only later did wealth and family affect this position, by creating an aristocracy. Wealth led to power struggles and the subjugation of weaker units, with slavery and class distinctions.[23] Even in the 'democracies' of Greece, there were large elements of the population which were excluded from power.

Three major conditions appear to characterize modern large-scale society. These are the increased diversity of economic interests in an industrial society; the rise of new power formations of hitherto subjugated classes and the widely differentiated groups of all kinds.[24] The first condition, namely, the diversity of economic interests has led to a large number of conflicts of power which have prevented the unity of front which appeared in earlier orders of society. (It must be admitted that earlier unified orders, e.g. in feudalism, were seldom so unified as their protagonists held. There was wide diversity.) But under modern conditions, the diversity is more fully recognized.

Of greater significance has been the rise of new power forma-

[23] cf. G. Landtmann, *The Origin of the Inequality of the Social Classes* (London, 1938), ch. 2.
[24] R. M. MacIver, *The Web of Government*, pp. 18-19.

Hebrew Thought and Later Theories of Society 209

tions, which have been due to the organization of groups and classes of hitherto subjugated status. Whilst the Middle Ages did have certain combinations of journeymen, where initiative and leadership made it possible, yet there were not organizations similar to the Trade Unions which could yield such power within the State. Merchant princes combined in the Hanseatic League but the lower orders in society had little opportunity to combine. It is not without reason that this century has been called, 'the century of the common man'.

To these two conditions, there has been added a third, namely, the proliferation of groups—not only economic but also religious, cultural, ethnic and others, in a bewildering variety, such as may be seen most clearly in American society. Even in the field of religion, some two hundred and fifty religious bodies are acknowledged in the Annual Year-book of the National Council of Churches. Such a diversity is abhorrent to the totalitarian desire for conformity and yet it appears to be the necessary path to prevent internecine and incessant futile strife. Competitive leadership and freedom of expression both appear to be required in the formation of the democratic process.

Furthermore, the democratic method calls for certain conditions within the social pattern—conditions which have a bearing on the doctrine of man as well as of society. These conditions include the need for the human material of politics to be of a sufficiently high order; that the range of political decision should not be extended too far; that there should be available a well-trained bureaucracy and that democratic self-control should accept the conditions.[25]

The human material which is required to govern in a democratic order must necessarily be of considerable ability and also of sufficient moral calibre. Traditional experience, professional codes of honour and a certain similarity of viewpoint serve to equip such men and women who have the continuing responsibility of governing a large state. But it is also necessary that there is confidence in the nature of man to undertake such tasks. If man is inherently self-seeking and is unable to rise above family, tribal or even national interests, then it is doubtful whether he is capable of ruling successfully or controlling

[25] J. A. Schumpeter, *Capitalism, Socialism & Democracy* (London, 1943), ch. XXIII, Section 2.

adequately the democratic process. If man, by nature, is able to transcend the natural order and even the social order, then there is hope that he can cope with the variety of demands which such a process places before him.

Whilst the quality of the men who govern is important, it is also important that the range and quality of matters which have to be tackled should be effective and not be extended too far. When a government has to struggle continually for its life, so that even a taxi-cab delay (with four Members of Parliament in the taxi) can cause the government to fall, then the whole programme of effective government has to be carefully watched. One large issue, such as a Housing Bill, may prove too large when the political machine is unable to bring sufficient pressure on public opinion. The recall of a form of punishment (e.g. the 'cat') may unseat the government. It is evident that those who are called upon to carry out such decisions must be seen to be effective in personal terms. When the government programmes are in the hands of those who are dealing in issues beyond their scope, then public opinion turns against them.

In modern industrial society, the democratic process needs to be able to use a well-trained bureaucracy, which has an established status and a firm tradition. It is necessary that this body has a strong sense of responsibility and of duty, which may limit the damage, which government by amateurs might otherwise inflict upon the public cause. When politicians are appointed as Ministers of State, in charge of Ministries such as those of Housing, Agriculture, etc., in which they have had little training or expert knowledge, it is then essential that they are able to call upon Permanent Secretaries in these Departments who can give them expert facts and figures.[*] The Permanent Secretaries have to be Civil Servants who are unaffected by the winds of politics yet who are at hand to provide the Minister, in charge of their Department for the time being, with all the intricacies of the particular field—sometimes at a moment's notice. In this aspect of the democratic process, the importance of the human material is again prominent. These Civil Servants need to be above petty sectional interests and devoted to the well-being of the whole polity, if they are to do their work effectively. It is not surprising that in some Departments of the British Civil

[*] J. A. R. Marriott, *English Political Institutions* (Oxford, 1924), p. 101.

Hebrew Thought and Later Theories of Society 211

Service (e.g. the Foreign Office and the Diplomatic Service), there has grown up a strong *'esprit de corps'* to offset any radical change which a political 'wind of change' might suddenly cause. The members of the bureaucracy need to be expert in the field of administration to be able to provide counsel as well as to be strong enough to instruct the politicians who head their ministries. Much may depend upon their corporate strength, especially in a time of crisis. The association of the expert and the amateur in the work of government calls for intellectual and moral qualities of no mean order. Co-operation and a sense of mutual dependence provide a way to the settlement of issues, which could create a deadlock in the democratic method.

Nevertheless, there remains one further element behind these other conditions—this is the pre-condition of democratic self-control. It is democratic self-control which is willing to recognize the necessity to obey the majority decision which is placed upon the statute book. This public 'common sense' acts as the proof against the 'crook and the crank'. Intellectual and moral qualities are required to work the electoral system effectively and provide responsible members to Parliament. This democratic self-control is expressed in a variety of different ways. The politician may often wish to oppose the policy of his party on a number of issues in Parliament but he has to avoid the practise of embarrassing his party too often (whether his party is the government or in opposition). There has to be a certain division of labour between the voters and the politician whom they appoint and also a considerable measure of tolerance in regard to differences of opinion, as in the case of the extreme wings of any party in relation to the other wings in their own party. The qualities which the democratic method demands arise out of a high doctrine of Man, his potentialities and his abilities. The ability of 'the common man' to accept responsibility in the democratic electoral process is based on a faith which is not only in man as man but also beyond man—in a doctrine of Creation, which provides ground for a belief in the individual and social endowments of Man. The democratic order is possible because Man is made as he is—due to the creative wisdom and purpose of God.

The theological grounds for a democratic order have not received much attention. In fact, there are not many studies on the nature and implications of democracy. Such a field is worthy of much further study if the democratic method is regarded as a primary means to establish a stable constitutional government."⁷⁷ There may be occasions, especially in time of war or of serious crisis, when a 'monopolistic leadership' rather than a competitive leadership may be justified for a period. But such monopolistic leadership has its place for only a limited period or 'for the present emergency', as even Rome found with her appointment of the *'magister populi'* or 'dictator' in the time of Sulla and G. Julius Caesar. When the emergency ends, then the 'thousand flowers' (the many opinions) will endeavour to bloom. It is the purpose of the democratic method to provide channels to permit such opinions, however diverse, to bloom, without undermining or overthrowing the general process of law and order.

The belief in the democratic order rests on a fundamental faith in the potentialities of Man, as he is endowed by God. This has its roots in the Old Testament prophetic message but it received a new emphasis and endorsement in New Testament teaching. It is not possible within the limits of this study to consider the whole of the New Testament material but certain aspects of that material will now be briefly considered as relevant to this theme, namely, the place of man within his society as seen by the New Testament writers.

⁷⁷ cf. A. D. Lindsay, *The Essentials of Democracy* (Philadelphia, 1929).

CHAPTER TEN

EPILOGUE

NEW TESTAMENT REFLECTIONS

1. *The Old Testament background to New Testament thought. The later inter-testamental period and Hellenization. Anthropology among the Greek-speaking Jews.*
2. *The Kingdom of God in the teaching of Jesus. The relation of the Church and the Kingdom. The place of man in the teaching of Jesus. Social obligations as seen in the parables.*
3. *Pauline psychology and view of man. Human solidarity in Adam. The solidarity of Israel within the purpose of God in the letters of Paul. Man and society in the redemptive will of God .*
4. *The concept of human worth. Individual development and social goals. Christian brotherhood and its implications. The significance of human fellowship with the divine.*

CHAPTER TEN

EPILOGUE

NEW TESTAMENT REFLECTIONS

THE early Christian Church inherited the tradition that honoured the Scriptures. The writer of 2 Timothy reminds his reader that 'from childhood you have been acquainted with the sacred writings which are able to instruct you for salvation through faith in Christ Jesus' (3. 15). At an earlier date, the Apostle Paul reminded the Church in Rome that the Jew did have the primary advantage because 'to begin with, the Jews are entrusted with the oracles of God' (Romans 3. 2). They had received the divine law. When Paul and Silas preached in Beroea, the Jews of Beroea were given greater credit than those of Thessalonica, because the former 'received the word with all eagerness, examining the scriptures daily to see if these things were so' (Acts 17. 11).

Moreover, it has been pointed out by Dr. C. H. Dodd that, in the preaching *(kerygma)* of the Church in Jerusalem at an early period, the Scriptures had an important place.[1] The ministry, death and resurrection of Jesus took place 'through the determinate counsel and fore-knowledge of God', so that the testimony of David, of Moses and other Old Testament figures are quoted, as pointing to the Christ. In the very first clause, which is claimed to be the word of Jesus, there is a reminder of the Old Testament background. 'Jesus came into Galilee preaching the gospel of God, and saying, "The time is fulfilled, and the kingdom of God is at hand"' (Mark 1. 14f.). To what 'time' does Jesus refer? He refers to the expectations of the Hebrew prophets which he believed had been fulfilled in his own coming. This was evident in the works he did, as he claimed ('But if

[1] C. H. Dodd, *The Apostolic Preaching and its Developments* (London, 1936), pp. 38-43.

Epilogue—New Testament Reflections

it is by the finger of God that I cast out demons, then the kingdom of God has come upon you': Luke 11. 20) and as he made clear to the disciples who came from John the Baptist. When these disciples asked, 'Are you he who is to come, or shall we look for another?' Jesus in that hour cured many of diseases and plagues . . . and on many that were blind he bestowed sight. And he answered these disciples, 'Go and tell John what you have seen and heard' (Luke 7. 18-22). The early Church similarly believed that his works proclaimed the source of his coming. He was 'Jesus of Nazareth, a man attested to you by God with mighty works and wonders and signs which God did through him in your midst' (Acts 2. 22). In the speech attributed to Peter and John, in the portico called Solomon's, this is made clear. 'But what God foretold by the mouth of all the prophets . . . he thus fulfilled' (Acts 3. 18). 'And all the prophets who have spoken, from Samuel and those who came afterwards, also proclaimed these days' (3. 24). Thus in accord with the Rabbinic tradition that the prophets looked forward to the 'days of the Messiah', so the apostles proclaimed that in Christ the Messianic day had come.

It is therefore necessary to bear in mind the continuing influence of the older doctrines as they were carried over into the teaching of the New Testament. Yet these doctrines were at the same time also affected by other currents of thought, since Hellenization had its influence on all literary and philosophical, apart from religious, ideas in the Middle East. Whatever may have been his intention as the scholar who sat at the feet of Aristotle, yet Alexander, in his conquests, certainly carried Greek thought and practice to the frontiers of India. The Jews in Palestine, from the time of Maccabaeus onwards, sought with all their power to resist the invasion of Greek thought especially in the field of their faith. They were willing to accept only books written in Hebrew or Aramaic into their canon. But the Jews who lived outside Palestine were more receptive in their attitude towards the new ideas. From the third century B.C. onwards, the Egyptian Jews show evidence of their interest in Greek ideas. These Jews used the Septuagint (LXX), the Greek version of the Old Testament Scriptures, which included the books of 'Apocrypha'. From this Greek version, the Old Testament Canon (including the Apocrypha) was received as the Christian Bible. Thus it remained until the time of the Reformation, when the Reformers reverted to the practice of the Palestinian Jews by excluding the Apocrypha. In the Reformation Churches, the Apocrypha remained, not as a basis of doctrine but only as an 'example of life and instruction of manners' (Thirty Nine Articles, No. VI).

It is therefore of consequence to consider the extent to which the Hellenistic ideas of the inter-testamental period affected the Jewish doctrine of Man. The Greek-speaking Jews handed on their Bible, through the apostles and the synagogues, to the infant Church, so their view of Man vitally affected Christian teaching, however much later reflection introduced new concepts and attitudes. It appears clear that the Greek-speaking Jews inherited the Hebrew idea that man is made of two elements—namely, 'soul' *(psyche)* and 'matter' *(hyle)*. Alongside of the term *psyche*, there is set by Ben Sirach the term *zoë* (life). *Psyche* and *zoë* have reference to the physical but there is also a connection with 'breath' *(pneuma)*. 'Matter' has only existence, which is the lot of 'dust' or flesh. The earlier Hebrew idea that a man's 'flesh' consists of a number of parts (namely, the hand, the heart, etc.), each of which has its own share of the 'life' that possesses a man, came to be replaced by the concept that everything made of 'flesh' together forms a unit, known as 'the body' *(soma)*.[2] The four principal terms used are *psyche, pneuma, kardia* and *nous*. The first three, which correspond to such English terms as 'soul', 'breath' and 'heart' respectively, are used to denote various aspects in the total experience of the one unit, though the whole range of human experience is ascribed to them all. As with the English term, *kardia* (heart), for example, in some instances loses its reference to the particular physical organ and takes on an emotional content to cover 'emotion', 'feeling', as in 'have a heart!' (Eng.). But in the use of the first two terms an important distinction came to be made. *Psyche* is ascribed to animals and men and 'has three chief meanings—it may mean "life"; it may stand for a personal or reflexive pronoun or mean "a man"; it may stand for the element in human nature that experiences".'[3] But *pneuma* (orig. 'wind') is used to denote an element which is shared by man and God. 'It is under *pneuma*

[2] C. Ryder Smith, *The Bible Doctrine of Man* (London, 1951), p. 96.
[3] Ibid., p. 71.

Epilogue—New Testament Reflections 217

that the thought of the Jews had its *differentia* among Hellenists." *Pneuma*, like *ruach*, is used of the 'spirit' of God as well as of the 'spirit' which is in man (Ps. 104. 30; 1 Es. 2. 2, 8). The fourth term, *nous* (mind) with its derivatives (some 19 in number),⁵ was a new term, for which there does not appear to be any true equivalent in Hebrew. An important derivative is *dianoia* ('understanding') which expresses the process of thought-activity which in earlier days the Hebrews had expressed in the use of the term '*leb*' (heart), which was deemed to be the seat of the emotions. It is probable that in the use of the term '*nous*' the Greek-speaking Jews were seeking a term to express the wholly immaterial aspect of human experience. The term is very prominent in Philo. This analysis of terms, which are used in the Septuagint, indicates that whilst different aspects of experience were recognized, yet the unitary nature of man was also borne in mind. There is little, if any, endeavour made (except perhaps by Philo), to differentiate such terms by their precise definition but rather man was regarded as a living being who exercised a number of functions as one being. Man as the unit is the important factor and the functions within that unit may be differentiated but not fundamentally separated.

These terms were carried over into the New Testament. The term '*soma*' (body) is used frequently in the Apocrypha and the New Testament in contrast to the rare Hebrew word for 'body'. *Soma* occurs 135 times in the Apocrypha and is specially frequent in the writings of Paul, occurring some 86 times.⁶ It refers to 'the whole body' and, in a later section, further consideration can be given to it. For the human body as a purely physical organ (but particularly prone to weakness through passion and infirmity), the term *sarx* (often translated 'flesh' is used). It occurs 142 times in the New Testament. For the rest, such Greek terms as *nous*, *kardia* and *pneuma* are used (sometimes synonymously) to describe human intellectual and emotional activities. However, the Aristotelian conception of man as composed of two disparate elements does not have appeared to have been endorsed by the Jews. Man remained unitary. The body *(soma)* per se is good as God made it. This view is pre-supposed in the New Testament and is in accord with the firm Hebrew belief that 'God saw every-

⁴ *Ibid.*, p. 96.   ⁵ *Ibid.*, p. 83, note 7.   ⁶ *Ibid.*, p. 161.

thing that he had made, and . . . it was very good' (Gen. 1, 31). The conception of man, which is found in inter-testamental times, has an important bearing on his place in the teaching of Jesus, which is not centred however on the nature of man but on the rule of God.

The significance of the rule of God (which is expressed in the Hebrew term *malkuth*—the active rule of God) in earlier times has been made clear. This needs to be borne in mind as the use of the phrase the 'Kingdom of God' has led to a number of misconceptions. In some circles, the idea of 'the Kingdom of God' has tended to be considered as an order of society, either according to God's pattern or as established by God. However, 'God's sovereignty in the hearts and lives of men expressed in the doing of His will describes in its fundamental aspects what Jesus meant by the Kingdom of God. The Kingdom is God's kingship, His kingly rule'.[1] The place of this conception is again brought out by Vincent Taylor when he writes: 'The thought of the rule of God persists all through the teaching of Jesus and it determines all his conceptions of his mission. Like the theme of a fugue it appears and re-appears and continues to the end. The Kingdom is basic.'[2] He calls it the 'Ariadne thread' which links together the Mission of the Twelve, the Fellowship meal in the wilderness, the confession near Caesarea Philippi, the last journey to Jerusalem, the Passion and the Cross. Such a rule as a basic conception reveals the close continuity of the Hebrew belief in this 'son of David'. The loyalty of Jesus to earlier teaching is here as elsewhere revealed.

Whilst the recurring theme is that of the divine kingship, so the relationship is primarily between sovereign and subject. It is the divine initiative which commands and the human responsibility to obey. The initative of the superior is taken for granted, though it is always recognized that such initiative is an act of grace. On the other hand, man has to show his loyalty as a subject by responding to the authority which alone belongs to God. This sovereign-subject relationship, however, is not simply an individual one between God and man as though he were alone. As has been seen, the individual came after the community, in

[1] V. Taylor, *The Life and Ministry of Jesus* (London, 1954), pp. 66-7.
[2] Ibid., p. 77.

Epilogue—New Testament Reflections

the sense that man was aware of his corporateness before he was aware of his individuality. It may be claimed that this principle is true for man in all early communities.

Therefore, as a corollary to the sovereign-subject relationship, there is the conception of the community, among whom this relationship is exercised. This conception of a community may take more than one form. It may refer to the idea of entering into a 'domain', a sphere within which the divine sovereignty is operative.[9] A number of passages in the Gospels appear to imply the idea of a community as the domain of God's kingly rule, such as the future *Basileia* (kingdom) in which men from all parts shall sit down together (Luke 13. 29); as the kingdom that is like a grain of mustard seed which becomes greater than all (Mark 4. 32)—together with those passages which refer to the fellowship of believers with one another (as well as with their Lord) in the coming Kingdom. 'As my Father appointed a kingdom for me, so do I appoint for you that you may sit and eat at my table in my kingdom' (Luke 22. 29-30). It has been pointed out, by R. Newton Flew, that the use of the verb 'to appoint' (*diatithemai*) has behind it the concept of a covenant-relationship. 'It is difficult to resist the conclusion that the conception of the New Covenant lies behind this word.'[10] But the covenant was always exercised within the chosen community, so covenant-relationship implied a community-relationship. However, it has always to be borne in mind that the Kingdom as a rule was both present in the person of Jesus as well as future in terms of completion. But no rule could be exercised without subjects who were themselves a community as 'the elect' or as 'the disciples', to whom he came to 'give the kingdom'.

If as some hold, the idea of a community or a domain in which the rule of God is exercised is in fact wanting, then how is this want to be met? Otto's *Kingdom of God and the Son of Man* endeavours to bring together the ideas of the Kingdom and of the Son of Man in that the Christ himself is the Elect of God, the channel through whom the divine rule is fulfilled. A closer approximation to Old Testament thought is evident in the 'communal' interpretation such as T. W. Manson gave in his *Teaching of Jesus* (1931). This interpretation seeks to bring together

[9] cf. R. N. Flew, *Jesus and His Church* (London, 1938), pp. 35-40.
[10] Ibid., p. 40.

both the *communal* and the *personal* aspects, so the 'Son of Man' refers both to the Elect Community as represented by Jesus as well as Jesus himself in his own person. A number of arguments have been set forth to substantiate this communal interpretation. The 'one like unto the son of man' (in Dan. 7. 13) has been shown to refer to 'the saints of the Most High', i.e. the term 'son of man' may be claimed to be a communal concept from the first. The pronoun 'I' in the Psalms may be communally interpreted, as it often refers to the people of Israel even though it may also refer to the personal misfortunes of the individual Psalmist. There is the oscillation between the communal and the individual which has been noted in connection with much Old Testament thought.[11] The same oscillation appears in the figure of the Servant of the Lord, in Deutero-Isaiah, in which the experiences of one or more individuals shades into the communal experience of the community of exiled Israel. Again, the concepts of the Kingdom of God and of the Son of Man are eschatological in origin. They each appear to imply the other, namely, that a rule of God implies those who are ruled and the elect implies the One who has called the elect. Furthermore, many of the Son of Man sayings such as Mark 8. 38; Luke 12. 8f. (=Matt. 10. 32) as well as Matt. 10. 23, Luke 12. 40; 17. 22, 24, 26f., 30 and perhaps Luke 17. 25 and Mark 8. 31, may be open to a communal interpretation. Similarly, certain parables may also be given such an interpretation, such as the Fig Tree in Summer (Mark 13. 28f.), the Thief at Night (Luke 12. 39 = Matt. 24. 42f.) and the Waiting Servants (Luke 12. 35-8). Finally, the Son of Man sayings which relate to the Parousia (His return in glory) are in most cases in the Lukan account connected with the Galilean ministry and the later stages of his ministry (e.g. Luke 12. 8f., 40; 17. 22-30; 18. 8b). If it is probable that Jesus used the term in the period in which he was in Galilee, it is also probable that he either differentiated the figure of the supernatural Son of Man from himself or he referred to the Elect Community as the Son of Man—in referring to a return in glory. If the latter is the case, then the early references to the Son of Man may have a communal interpretation in contrast to the later Son of Man sayings, in which there is reference to suffering and more personal predictions of the Passion.

[11] cf. pp. 33-37 above.

Epilogue—New Testament Reflections

Such evidence for a communal interpretation of the term 'Son of Man' has strong support from the Old Testament background of thought but it is not possible to establish conclusively such a view. Even if the name 'Son of Man' is regarded as solely a personal name for Jesus, it is well to bear in mind that there remains the important question whether there is a vital link between the idea of the Elect Community and the Kingdom of God. There are a number of sayings in the teaching of Jesus which refer to the 'little flock' (Luke 12. 32), to those who are to eat and drink in Christ's Kingdom (Luke 22. 30) and the gathering of the Elect from all points of the compass (Mark 13. 27). It appears to be implicit not only in such sayings but also in the calling of the disciples, who formed the beginning of a new community. Therefore, 'the value of the collective interpretation is that it names the community otherwise implied'.[12]

If such an interpretation may fairly be claimed, it has much bearing on the issue whether Jesus did in fact have in mind the idea of founding a body which became known as 'the Church'. His message was not to be left *in vacuo* but was consciously committed to a community, with whom he shared his intentions and purposes. There is no doubt that we possess only part of the teaching which he gave to that community but it leaves us in little doubt that this community was to serve as a means (if not *the* means) to set forth God's rule among all nations. He bade his disciples pray that God's rule might come (Matt. 6. 10), although, at the beginning of his ministry, Jesus proclaimed that the Kingdom is close at hand (Mark 1. 15) and is, in fact, present in the mighty works which were done by him (Luke 11. 20). The eschatological aspect of the Kingdom remains clearly in his thought, however, as in such sayings as, 'Truly, I tell you, there are some standing here who will not taste death before they see the Kingdom of God come with power' (Mark 9. 1) and, at the Last Supper, 'truly, I say to you, I shall not drink again of the fruit of the vine until that day when I drink it new in the Kingdom of God' (Mark 14. 25). Such sayings are stated within a communal context, amid his disciples, who were to form part of the covenant-community, which was sealed by the sacrificial offering of himself. As the ancient covenant between God and his people was preceded by the Passover, so 'Christ, our paschal lamb, has been

[12] V. Taylor, *The Life and Ministry of Jesus*, p. 75.

sacrificed' (1 Cor. 5. 7) as the new covenant-community is brought into being. The close relationship between the teaching and the work of Jesus, the proclamation of the rule of God and the establishing of the new community remains constant throughout. There is no suggestion that it was simply a case that Jesus called a number of disciples as separate individuals to himself. He called them to form a company with himself in the proclamation of the Kingdom but this company itself lived under the rule of God and was the spearhead in seeking to establish that rule. The Message, the Community and the Kingdom formed part of a common plan which were present in the Hebrew heritage, which Jesus held in high loyalty and carried on throughout his ministry. The allegiance of the individual belonged at the same time to the sovereign rule of God, to Jesus and to his company, the body which later became his Church. 'The individual allegiance to Jesus as Lord was no mere confidence in the salvation of the solitary soul, though it brought an expansion of the powers of the individual. It was adhesion to a message, and inclusion in a community . . . The Community, constituted by the Message, was God's instrument for the accomplishment of His final purpose.'[12] This close inter-weaving of Message and Community has a clear relevance to present-day discussions, which tend from time to time to separate the two, in order to exalt the significance of the Message. It has been the two together which has kept Christian allegiance over the centuries—an allegiance which has been centred in the person of Jesus Christ himself.

Nevertheless, whilst the communal interpretation takes a large place in the understanding of the teaching of Jesus, yet it is also true that the value of the individual man is given considerable place. The value of the individual was heightened in the teaching of Jesus by his shift of emphasis—from the older doctrine of the divine kingship to the less appreciated older doctrine of the divine fatherhood. Both conceptions of the divine kingship and of divine fatherhood are present in the Old Testament but it is the latter, which receives the greater attention by Jesus in relation to the individual man. Within the family relationship, which binds not only Jews together but all mankind, Jesus stresses the element of loyal obedience which is due to the Father-King of

[12] R. N. Flew, *Jesus and His Church*, pp. 205f.

all men. Because the filial relationship exists between man and God, then certain important results ensue. As man is in this relationship, he has a unique worth and significance in all creation, but with the corollaries that he has a duty as a son to the Father and as a brother to all the rest of the family. The unique value of the individual man in the eyes of God is seen in some of his sayings. When he was challenged over healing a sick man on the sabbath, Jesus did not hesitate to place human worth before cherished institutions: 'The sabbath was made for man and not man for the sabbath' (Mark 2. 27). When he compares the various parts of creation, he says, 'But even the hairs of your head are all numbered . . . you are of more value than many sparrows' (Matt. 10. 31) and elsewhere, 'Of how much more value is a man than a sheep!' (Matt. 12. 12). On this very account, a man's life (his spiritual potentialities) is of greater worth than the material possessions of the whole world (Mark 8. 36f.). In very picturesque language, he pointed out that a man's spiritual and moral concerns were of supreme importance, so that even a maimed body was preferable to a sinful whole one (Mark 9. 43-47). Mary was praised because she sought earnestly this supreme concern whilst her sister was bothered about many other matters (Luke 10. 38-42). It is therefore needful that if any man is to be 'as the Father' (Luke 6. 35), then he had to watch over those who were in need. 'It is not the will of my Father (some read your) who is in heaven that one of these little ones should perish' (Matt. 18. 14).

Thus, Jesus re-emphasized the old doctrine of Man as made in 'the image of God', revealing the height of self-transcendence in man's spiritual nature.[14] There follow the distinctive corollaries which Jesus also stressed, namely, man as the child of God and as the brother in the family. But the doctrine of man itself gave a value to every single human soul in a way that no other teaching has done.

The relationship of man to God as a filial one gives him an altogether different status from that of the rest of creation. 'Human existence, in contrast to every other form of existence, in responsive existence, that is, existence which must and can answer, and in so doing is free and yet bound.'[15] Elsewhere, Emil

---

[14] R. Niebuhr, *The Nature and Destiny of Man* (N. York, 1964), p. 12.
[15] E. Brunner, *Man in Revolt* (Philadelphia, 1947), p. 65.

Brunner wrote, 'The distinctive character of man, in contrast to the rest of creation, is based upon the fact that he is designed for freedom-in-God, for a personal existence which is distinct from God and yet dependent upon Him'.[16] In this state of man's weakness, dependence and finiteness, there may still be seen 'man as a unity of God-likeness and creatureliness in which he remains a creature even in the highest spiritual dimensions of his existence and may reveal elements of the image of God even in the lowliest aspects of his natural life'.[17] In this relationship, as envisaged in the teaching of Jesus, the ideal son is seen as the one who has a perfect trustful obedience on the Father's will. Such an obedience, in such an absolute form, may be described as one in which 'the *patria potestas* of the Roman father, which corresponds in some respects to Semitic kingship, is added to the looser legal relationship of father and child in the social life of Israel'.[18] Perhaps the most significant part of the relationship lies in the *personal* nature of it. It is because it is personal that the more distant elements in both the rights of the Roman *pater* and the Semitic king concepts have to be treated with care. Beyond the concepts, which arise out of a legalistic basis, there are the warm emotions aroused within the life of a family. 'As Berdyaev has suggested, the Gospel is "strange", not merely because it comes to us over a chasm of twenty centuries; it is "strange" because it is anti-legalistic. It is personal, whereas every culture's moral ideas—whether those of the first century or the twentieth century—tend to be collective and tyrannical. The relation to God it envisages is spontaneous, whereas all ethical law is abstract and compulsive.'[19] The nature of the Father's care is clearly taught by Jesus, in words quoted above, namely, that 'even the hairs of your head are all numbered' (Matt. 10. 30; Luke 12. 7). If reliance may be placed on a human father's care and provision, how much more we may depend upon the divine Father's provision (Matt. 7. 7-11). Not only daily bread and material needs fall within the same Father's care but also the crises of spiritual need which arise from time to time (Mark. 13. 11; Luke 12. 11f.).

[16] *The Divine Imperative* (Philadelphia, 1947), p. 62.
[17] R. Niebuhr, *Nature and Destiny of Man*, p. 12.
[18] H. W. Robinson, *Christian Doctrine of Man* (Edinburgh, 1911), p. 83.
[19] D. E. Roberts, *Psychotherapy and Christian View of Man* (N. York, 1950), p. 133f.

Epilogue—New Testament Reflections 225

The response of man to such faithful care on the Father's part is the attitude of faith, upon which Jesus insists so often (Mark 9. 23; Luke 17. 6). The denial of this attitude creates for man the problems with which he is faced. 'Man's freedom *for* God and *in* God is perverted to mean freedom *from* God.'[20] Herein lies the essential nature of evil for man—it arises out of his 'inevitable, though not necessary, unwillingness to acknowledge his dependence, to accept his finiteness and to admit his insecurity',[21] which results in accentuating for him his sense of insecurity. 'The fact of his origin is contradicted by the fact of his sin.'[22] But true freedom for man lies in loving trust which issues in duty. The kingly Father's love receives a response in the complete surrender to His will, as a merchant gives all for the unique jewel and the man who finds hidden treasure in a field. Such devotion finds expression in the words of the saying of Jesus: 'But seek first his kingdom and his righteousness, and all these things shall be yours as well' (Matt. 6. 33).

The insistence on the primary claim of the rule of God rings out clearly in the attitude of Jesus to the claims of family and friends, who would draw him away from his God-appointed task (Mark 3. 31-35), as well as his claims on others who place family claims before a wholehearted loyalty to him (Luke 9. 57-62). Perhaps no part of his teaching is such a 'hard saying' as the rejection of the claim of family ties as well as of one's own life for the sake of loyalty to the kingdom. The absoluteness of this claim is seen in the saying: 'Whoever of you does not renounce all that he has cannot be my disciple' (Luke 14. 33. cf. 14. 26-32). On the other hand, it has also to be noted that Jesus rebuked those who made use of a ritual obligation to avoid the responsibility of duty to one's parents (Mark 7. 9-13). In the Lord's Prayer, the petition for help in doing the will of God recognizes such loyalty as part of the life of heaven. In the fulfilment of this petition on earth, the two realms are drawn closer together. It is the divine rule which is the true characteristic of both.

From these two aspects of the teaching of Jesus, there follows the relationship between man and man. There has been a great emphasis placed on this social aspect of man's life. Even those

[20] J. S. Whale, *Christian Doctrine* (London, 1941), p. 63.
[21] R. Niebuhr, *Nature and Destiny of Man*.
[22] E. Brunner, *Xtn Understanding of Man*, p. 165.

who are most concerned to uphold man's individuality, like Kierkegaard, need to give some place to the inward core of humanity where men are at one. In the words of Kierkegaard, 'In the Creation and in the Fall, are "Adam"—that "Adam" is both the individual and the community ... At the deepest point of the existence of each individual, at the roots of his being, there too every other individual also has his roots; in Creation and in Sin we are, in an incomprehensible way, both individual and yet the whole of humanity'.[23] The same awareness of the social significance of man's life is found in the teaching of Dietrich Bonhoeffer (1906-1945). 'Bonhoeffer says that you must, and you actually can, think revelation only in social relations. All the great old dogmatic terms and loci—grace, justification, etc.—have a genuinely social sphere. They are social facts. Revelation exists in the fellowship of persons: "Christ existing as the community of men".'[24] In his book *Act and Being*, Bonhoeffer seeks to resolve the problem of 'act' versus 'being' in terms of the concepts of revelation and the church. The concept of revelation itself is understood within the community of persons—in contrast to a one-sided 'act' interpretation whether theocentric (as in Barth) or anthropomorphic (as in Bultmann) or a one-sided 'being' interpretation which threatens to bind God within his own freedom. It has also been a constant theme in the thought of Reinhold Niebuhr. 'The revelation of God to man is always a two-fold one: "a personal-individual revelation and a revelation in the context of social-historical experience".'[25] Such an emphasis is rooted in the teaching of Jesus.

The Fatherhood of God, like his sovereignty, is universal, so the brotherhood of man is universal. As the Father is depicted in his concern for the 'lost' son, so man's duty lies in brotherly affection for 'this your brother' (Luke 15. 32). In the teaching of Jesus, sonship appears to be realized through discipleship. 'One is your teacher, and you are all brethren ... you have one Father, who is in heaven' (Matt. 23. 8f.). Jesus regarded those who did the Father's will as his brethren (Mark 3. 33-35). The universal nature of men's brotherhood is reflected in the fact that the pattern for men was the universal love of the Father, who

[23] Quoted by E. Brunner, *The Divine Imperative*, p. 155.
[24] E. Bethge, 'The Challenge of Dietrich Bonhoeffer's Life and Theology', *Chicago Theological Seminary Register*, Vol. LI, No. 2 (Feb. 1961), p. 8.
[25] R. Niebuhr, *Nature and Destiny of Man*, p. 127.

'makes his sun rise on the evil and on the good, and sends rain on the just and on the unjust' so men's forgiveness for their enemies and persecutors should have a corresponding disinterested character (cf. Matt. 5. 44-48).

This combination of love to the Father with care for one's brother man appears as a refrain in many facets of the teaching of Jesus. He echoes the ethical emphasis of the prophets in declaring that 'the weightier matters of the law (are) justice, mercy and faith' (Matt. 23. 23: cf. Mic. 6. 8) and that God desires mercy rather than sacrifice (Matt. 12. 7; cf. Hos. 6. 6). This may be expressed in the simple acts, such as the cup of water which is given to the thirsty (Matt. 10. 42) and the meal to the poor, the maimed, the halt and the blind (Luke 14. 13). This is brought out very clearly in the parable of the Sheep and the Goats (Matt. 25. 31-46), in which care for those in need is regarded as service to the King Himself. In Luke's Gospel, the social relations of men have a large place, as may be seen from the many parables which are taken from the field of finance, namely, the Two Debtors, the Rich Fool, the Unjust Steward, the Rich Man and Lazarus and the Pounds, etc.[26] Wealth and poverty also appear prominently in this Gospel, so that the Beatitude claims 'Blessed are ye poor', whilst declaiming a woe on those who are rich (6. 20, 24). It may well be claimed that the strong eschatological interest of Jesus militated against a concern over 'social questions' as such, but there can be no doubt that his teaching has resulted in increasing measures of social amelioration wherever his message has been proclaimed. The new dignity given to women, the care of neglected children, the re-habilitation of the handicapped, the re-training of the prisoner and the general concern for the health of all—these concerns among others may fairly claim to have been awakened within a Christian nexus in which social relationships had an important place from the very beginning.

Yet across all this family intention of the Most High, there is the deep shadow of the broken relationship, expressed in the term 'sin'. Whilst there is no evidence of a consciousness of broken fellowship between the Son and the Father, as may be seen in such a saying as, 'All things have been delivered to me by my Father; and no one knows the Father except the Son and any one to whom the Son chooses to reveal him' (Matt. 11. 27;

---

[26] V. Taylor, *The Gospels* (London, 1956), p. 69.

Luke 10. 22), yet, at the same time, Jesus was vividly aware that this barrier existed for men. Even at their highest, as fathers who care for their children, Jesus recognizes that 'you . . . who are evil, know how to give good gifts to your children, how much more will the heavenly Father give . . ?' (Luke 11. 13). Throughout his teaching, there is the underlying need for repentence, the need for forgiveness, the realization that all men are in God's debt, that all men have fallen short of the glory of God. The message of Jesus goes beyond the duty of a Son or even that of a King, it underscores men's need for a Saviour. In this sense, there is the awareness that the Old Testament, with its covenant of law, has its weaknesses as an effective means to cope with the failure of man, through sin. It was wilful disobedience which had to be faced—the inner intention of rebellion which expressed itself by fruits of 'lawlessness' (cf. Matt. 7. 16; 12. 35). The power of inner motive and intention is clearly stated by Jesus (Matt. 15. 19-20), a recognition which received very potent support in the writings of Sigmund Freud on the influence of the sub-conscious mind. Fostered enmities and grudges have had to receive treatment by psychiatrists, as a branch of medical science, since the hidden dynamics of the mind are fruitful causes of organic disease. Such an emphasis necessarily leads back to individual responsibility. The community may legislate against theft and adultery and murder but the root of such ills lies in the evasive response, the lustful eye and the angry word which come forth from the heart of a man (Matt. 5. 21-37). Therefore, in his doctrine of sin, Jesus places clear responsibility on the individual for the use of all that he has received from the hand of God—including the power of speech and action as well as the inner thoughts of his heart.

The endorsement which Jesus gave to the Hebrew view of man finds elaboration in the writings of the Apostle Paul. It is clear that Paul reveals his Hebrew training, as a Hebrew of the Hebrews, however much he may have been aware of and made use of Hellenistic vocabulary which was in current use in his time. It may fairly be claimed that 'the advances he makes on the conceptions of the Old Testament are a natural Jewish development'.[27] This may be seen, perhaps, most clearly in his concep-

[27] H. W. Robinson, *The Christian Doctrine of Man*, p. 104.

Epilogue—New Testament Reflections 229

tion of the importance of ethnic Israel as an entity both over against humanity at large and distinct from the Church.

Some brief reference needs to be made to Paul's psychology, to which a brief reference has already been made.[28] By the close of the Old Testament period, four principal terms had come to be used in Jewish thought, namely, *leb* ('heart'), *nephesh*, *ruach* and *basar* ('flesh'), which had their Greek equivalents in *kardia*, *psyche*, *pneuma* and *sarx*. These four terms serve as a basis of Paul's conception of the human personality. But whilst the term *leb*, in earlier days, covered a wide field to describe the inner life,[29] the term *kardia* (which he uses 52 times) is supplemented by other Greek terms, *nous* and *suneidesis* ('mind' and 'conscience'), to denote particular groups of psychical phenomena. The term *psyche* (with its adjective *psychikos*) came, in Paul, to be specially connected with the life of the flesh in contrast with the term *pneuma* (with its adjective *pneumatikos*) which was associated with man's higher or 'spiritual' life. This contrast came to be emphasized still further by the use of antithetical terms for the 'inner' and the 'outer' man. For the physical life as a whole, the general term *soma* came to be used for 'body', for which there does not appear to be any exact Hebrew equivalent. To denote the aspect of human nature on its physical side, with particular awareness of its frailty and passion, the term *sarx* ('flesh') was used. Detailed references to the use of these terms may be found elsewhere[30] but a brief comment may be made on their use.

The term *kardia* is used for the inner life (1 Cor. 14. 25), for emotional states (Rom. 9. 2), for intellectual activities (Rom. 1 21) and as the seat of volition (Rom. 2. 5). His stress in the use of the term lies in its volitional aspect as compared with the intellectual one, for which the further terms *nous* and *suneidesis* have been brought into use. The term *nous* (used 21 times) denotes the intellectual faculty of the natural man (1 Cor. 14. 14) but is also applied to the 'mind' of God (Rom. 11. 34) and of Christ (1 Cor. 2. 16). In its moral aspect, *nous* may be immoral, vain, fleshly and defiled or, by Christian transformation, may be able to renew one's life (Rom. 12. 2). The term *suneidesis* is em-

[28] cf. p. 217 above. [29] cf. pp. 30-1 above.
[30] cf. H. W. Robinson, *Christian Doctrine of Man*, pp. 104-111; C. R. Smith, *Bible Doctrine of Man*, Part III, pp. 158, *et. seq.*

ployed to designate that ability to have moral judgement in oneself (Rom. 2. 15) as well as the recognition of a similar moral judgement in the consciousness of other people (2 Cor. 4. 2). The term appears to refer, not to denote the source of moral judgement but, to the judgement placed upon an action in terms of its moral quality. The moral law itself is considered to be 'the law of the *nous*' (Rom. 7. 23), which is 'written in the heart' (Rom. 2. 15).

The term *psyche* is in part significant by the limitation placed on its use by Paul, as it occurs only 13 times in his writings. Six of these occasions refer to 'life' without any psychological content, as in the case of Ephraphroditus who hazarded his 'life' (Phil. 2. 30). In only one case does the term appear in contra-position to 'spirit' *(pneuma)* and 'body' *(soma)*, namely, in 1. Thess. 5. 23 ('May the God of peace himself sanctify you wholly; and may your spirit and soul and body be kept sound and blameless at the coming of our Lord Jesus Christ.') In this instance, the term appears to be used to refer to man's emotional aspect in contrast to his intellectual aspect, which is represented by the use of the term '*spirit*', which covers also the volitional aspect of man's consciousness.

Of much greater importance is the term '*pneuma*' which is probably the most important term in Paul's psychological vocabulary. It occurs some 146 times and carries forward the earlier uses of the Hebrew term *ruach*, namely, as the impact of the Spirit of God upon the life of man. In particular, the Spirit of God is identified as the Spirit of Christ, so that the Apostle is able to write: 'God has sent the Spirit of his Son into our hearts, crying, 'Abba! Father!' (Gal. 4. 6). Paul seems to distinguish between the *pneuma*, which is the higher nature of a Christian man ('God is my witness, whom I serve with my spirit in the gospel of his Son' (Rom. 1. 9)) and a normal psychical element in human nature ('The Spirit himself bearing witness with our spirit that we are children of God' (Rom. 8. 16)). There is a close inter-mingling of the supernatural and the natural element in Paul's thought—a close connection which undoubtedly springs from the Hebrew fount from which he drank from his youth. But, in his Christian experience, the ancient doctrine of the Spirit of God has been identified with the activity of the Risen and Ascended Christ. The same power as of old is there: in

Jesus who was 'designated Son of God in power according to the Spirit of holiness by his resurrection from the dead' (Rom. 1. 4) and in us, 'so that by the power of the Holy Spirit you may abound in hope' (Rom. 15. 13). So identified are the activities of Christ and the Spirit of God that Paul writes, 'The Lord is the Spirit' (2 Cor. 3. 17). In fellowship with the risen Christ, the believer is now no longer defeated in seeking to keep the Law of God, he is now able to overcome the power of sin which is entrenched in the physical aspect of man's life *(sarx)*. The believer may 'be strengthened with might through his (God's) Spirit in the inner man' (Eph. 3. 16). The inner man now has freedom and fruit by God's Spirit.

Paul's doctrine of the Spirit has been claimed to be 'his most important and characteristic contribution to Christian anthropology'[21] and one is tempted to give it further consideration as an aspect of his treatment of the individual's faith. It is by the Spirit, that is active in the regeneration and sanctification of the believer, that a man can enter into God's fullness of salvation. But this activity is operative most effectively when the believer is united with Christ in faith and baptism. This union is the conscious and voluntary act of the believers who are drawn into this faith out of different races, classes and social backgrounds (Gal. 3. 28) to find a oneness in Christ.

However, a man has to face the fact that his actions are subject to the weaknesses of the 'flesh' *(sarx)*. Paul uses this term 91 times. It may refer to physical structure of kinship on the one hand or to fleshly weakness and ethical concepts on the other. In 35 cases there is apparently some ethical reference in that this element in human nature is regarded as at 'enmity with God'. In this element, there are the lusts of men which are evil (Rom. 13. 14) and opposed to the work of the Spirit (Rom. 8. 5). Because man is of flesh, sin has entered in and the work of Christ has become necessary.

Whilst there is debate in regard to the extent of Paul's own hand in the writing of his letters, or those attributed to him, so the use of all these terms (with the numbers given) has to be regarded as subject to revision in the light of further evidence. Nevertheless, the main outline of his psychology of man stands out clearly as a development of Jewish concepts, which sprang

[21] H. W. Robinson, *Christian Doctrine of Man*, p. 125.

from earlier Hebrew roots and grew under the pressures of national and social experience. It is to such social reference that we now have to turn.

Whilst the Pauline psychology of the individual may be claimed to have Jewish roots, it appears even more clearly that his conception of the solidarity of the group, including the conception of the corporate personality of the kin-group, arose out of the Old Testament. This solidarity of the group extended, at its widest, to the human race as a whole. Since creation came from the hand of God who is One, then there is unity with all mankind. This finds expression in the speech on Mars' Hill where Paul refers to the unity of mankind as the offspring of God (Acts 17. 28-29). 'He is not far from each one of us . . . being then God's offspring'. This solidarity arises out of a universal kinship which binds all men together, as may be seen from the same speech to the Gentile Athenians, to whom he says: 'And he (God) made from one every nation of men to live on all the face of the earth, having determined allotted periods and the boundaries of their habitation' (Acts 17. 26). It is evident from teaching elsewhere in the Pauline letters that the 'one' from whom all are descended is none other than Adam. In Adam, all men have a common kinship by descent from one man. It would appear that Paul accepted the historicity of Adam and then employed it as an argument for maintaining the solidarity of all mankind. It was from Adam that men inherited their mortality (1 Cor. 15. 47), their temporal *psyche* (1 Cor. 15. 44) as well as their *sarx*, the corrupt flesh which belonged to the Old Aeon. 'The "body" of Adam included all mankind.'[22] In this regard the whole of the human race may be seen to be the extension of the personality or soul of the ancestor, a conception which held so large a place in early thought. On the same account, all mankind is involved in the sin of Adam. All had sinned in the transgression of Adam. 'For as by a man came death, by a man has come also the resurrection of the dead. For as in Adam all die, so also in Christ shall all be made alive' (1 Cor. 15. 21-2). This theme is developed in Romans 5. 12-21, in which the disobedience of Adam is contrasted with the obedience of Christ. The Hebraic concepts of kinship and corporate personality are applied by Paul to the whole human race. Moreover, the corporate trans-

[22] W. D. Davies, *Paul and Rabbinic Judaism* (London, 1948), p. 57.

gression through Adam also finds expression in the idea of the Old Aeon, which is an integration of the ancient astral world and the spirit-world. As Adam's transgression violated the intention of the Creator, so all creation became subject to the elements (powers) of the Old Aeon. Release was only possible by the work of a New Man, completely obedient to the King-Creator, who could be the forbear of a New Humanity to usher in a New Age.[38] As all mankind is identified with one man, Adam, so the new humanity finds its expression in the man, Jesus Christ.

At the same time, Paul was careful to safeguard his loyalty to his own nation. He believed that the Jewish law embodied the revealed will of God for His creation (Rom. 2. 18). It served as a measure or gauge for the judgement of men (Rom. 2. 12; Gal. 3. 10). To the Jews had been entrusted the oracles of God (Rom. 3. 2), but, like the Gentiles, the Jews had fallen short of God's requirements (Rom. 3. 9). They were involved in corporate guilt and stood condemned before God. Thus in his view of mankind as well as in his conception of Israel, Paul carried over the concepts of solidarity which are so prominent in Hebrew thought. Man does not act solely as an individual, alone. He shares in the whole body, whether he be in a nation or in wider humanity. He enters into its privileges and benefits but he also shares in its sins and sorrows. He cannot contract out of this burden but must bear the consequences of it—whether he will or no. But just as there is hope for humanity because a New Man has come—the archetype of a New Humanity, so within humanity a new corporate entity, a New Israel, to bear the purposes of God, has appeared. A New Humanity has come into being because a Second Adam (1 Cor. 15. 45) has come. He is the New Man. (Col. 3. 9. 9-11) and in Him, there is a new creation (2 Cor. 5. 17). The corporate nature of this new creation is seen in the unity of corporate personality in Christ which goes beyond all recognized disunities of the old order. 'There is neither Jew nor Greek, there is neither slave nor free, there is neither male nor female; for you are all one in Christ Jesus' (Gal. 3. 28). But this does not mean that the older promises are nullified because Christ has gone beyond the Jewish Law. The Apostle continues: 'And if you are Christ's, then you are Abraham's offspring, heirs according to promise' (verse 29). As the type of Abraham expres-

[38] R. P. Shedd, *Man in Community*, pp. 112, et seq.

ses the loyal Israelite who believed God, so now the type of Christ fulfills the ancient promises. As the old Israel was proud to acknowledge that it was in the loins of Abraham and was of his seed, so the New Israel is the 'incorporation into a person', as the Body of Christ. The Christian believers are identified with Him. His righteousness is their righteousness (by faith) and His fellowship-community is 'in Christ'. 'The New Israel, according to the New Testament thought, is 'in Christ' as the Jews were in Abraham, or as mankind was in Adam. The Messiah is at once an individual person—Jesus of Nazareth—and He is more: He is, as the representative and (as it were) the constitutive Person of the New Israel, potentially inclusive.'[24] The corporate nature of the Church is expressed in a variety of figurative comparisons in the teaching of the Apostle. There is the image of the Church as a 'temple' of God. It appears as a corporate conception in 1 Cor. 3. 16-17 but in another passage, there is the oscillation between the individual and the community which has been noticed in the Old Testament. 'Do you not know that your (pl.) body (to *soma*—singular) is a temple of the Holy Spirit within you, which you have from God?' (1 Cor. 6. 19). Here the reference may be intended to mean that *soma* refers to the community (the Body of Christ) or to the individual bodies of believers or both. But the corporate aspect appears to be uppermost in his mind, as in, 'For we are the temple of the living God; as God said . . . I will be their God and they shall be my people' (2 Cor. 6. 16).

A further figure is that of the Olive Tree, which is rooted in the Christ and is an out-growth from the ancient stock of Israel (Rom. 11. 17-24). This figure is similar to the use of the metaphor of the Vine and the Branches by Jesus and seeks to convey the reality of organic connection between the Old Testament and the New. Similarly, the use of the metaphor of dough ('Cleanse out the old leaven that you may be fresh dough': 1 Cor. 5. 7) had deep roots in Israelite tradition. A little leaven of disloyalty might ferment the whole lump of social well-being. It was from such a foundation, that Paul went on to enjoin believers to be incorporated into Christ, by baptism and in the fellowship of the Eucharist ('Because there is one loaf, we who are many are one

[24] A. E. J. Rawlinson, 'Corpus Christi' in *Mysterium Christi*, ed. G. K. A. Bell and D. A. Diessmann (London, 1931), p. 235.

Epilogue—New Testament Reflections

body, for we all partake of the same loaf': 1 Cor. 10. 17). Thus, man and his society are knit together in a living relationship, in which the sin of an immoral member (1 Cor. 6. 19) or a marriage with an unbeliever (2 Cor. 6. 14-18) may violate the holiness of the corporate Temple. It is not enough to redeem the individual though the cleansing of that individual inevitably redounds to the advantage of the community. The corporate whole does not find its own redemption unless all the members of it have themselves entered into that redemption. The ancient concept of the community as a super-individual ('We the Tikopia') has to be transcended to give full account of the unique value and place of each individual member within it. It is in this setting that the New Testament conception of sanctification has its relevance and place. Whilst there is little doubt that sanctification is viewed as a corporate fulfilment, yet the sanctification of each member was recognized as the purpose of the redemptive will of of God. Therefore, Paul wrote his First Letter to the Corinthians, addressing it: 'To the Church of God which is at Corinth, to those sanctified in Christ Jesus, called to be saints together with all those who in every place call on the name of our Lord Jesus Christ, both their Lord and ours' (1 Cor. 1. 2). The individual believer and the community are called to be sanctified—set apart—to carry out God's purpose.

This brief consideration of certain aspects of New Testament teaching carries further the concepts which are set forth in the Old Testament. The polarization of the individual man and the community remain but both ends of the polarization have their importance. Neither can fully enter into its own heritage without due attention being given to the opposite polarity.

The place of individual worth receives a new significance in an age when standardization becomes increasingly accepted. The development of huge conurbations of people has made many people feel that they are lost in a vortex of humanity. Their work lacks significance because they, and their jobs, are merely cogs in a vast machine. The scientific mind, with a passion for orderly classification, has stressed the universal at the expense of the particular, the impersonal at the expense of the personal—with the result that the person feels pointless and rootless. The break-up of local groups and the passing of village life with the rise of mass communication brings the personal life into an inchoate mass of social life, in which the individual (unless very outstanding) does not seem to count.

The belief that the individual man is made in 'the image of God' provides an endless spring of new hope. Whatever a man may fail to be in the eyes of his fellows, he has significance and worth to the eternal God. His worth among his fellows has to be restored to the standard of his worth to God. All legal and social measures have this criterion. Discussions on moral issues, including gambling, divorce, criminology, A.I.D., birth control and road accidents, have to receive light from the lodestar of individual value. Trade union legislation and immigration restrictions, including housing and education, have to take into account the needs of individuals who are caught up in the mobility of the current situation. The place of the individual man or woman, *qua* individual (independent of race, colour, culture or creed), as of value to God, is of particular relevance in a world which is trying so desperately to work through ancient injustices between race and race and between class and class. The old religious barriers between caste and caste are heaving under the pressures of national feeling. New industrial structures are demanding skilled artisans independent of their family background and social prestige. The claims of the new rising social classes, based on economic power of international complexity, tend to by-pass the older landed estates which have dominated the economies of Continental countries for so many centuries. The different levels of industrial development makes conflict between nations inevitable unless some sense of wider responsibility is given to the whole process of human development. At the grass roots level, the criterion of the value of each unique individual, as a potential son or daughter of God, has to serve as a guide for personal relationships, legislation, politics and economics.

The moral philosopher, from the time of Plato and Aristotle, has, however, been aware that individual development is not divorced from social order or from social goals. The *omega* of individual recognition is not unbridled self-expression independent of the community in which the individual lives. Unbridled competition can merely lead back to the jungle, as the Marxist protagonists have not hesitated loudly to affirm. Each individual seeking only his own good, in terms of his private gain, may well find that he has overshot his own target. Thereby he loses the very prize which he seeks to win. This realization has lead to many international cartels, since competition can break as well as make when it reaches a certain pitch. It is then the individual development, within the discipline of social goals, which is the true *omega*[35] of man. Man is dependent upon man at every level of his being, so he cannot reach his goal without others.

It is at this point that the close identity of social and individual goals becomes so fundamental. The Israelites believed that the well-being of the individual was utterly dependent on the well-being of Israel as a whole. This could result in the subservience of the individual to the community to such an extent that the individual's existence was deemed to be merely for the sake of the whole. The end of this conception lies in totalitarianism. In National Socialism, it could be argued that it was in the interests of the State that girls should be partnered with good Aryan types for the sake of breeding the next generation of good Aryans—quite independent of any personal choice on the part of the individual. It may similarly be claimed that the same conception was present when the family decided who should mate with whom, as a Brahmin wife expressed to me, 'Of course, my family decided my husband for me. My family knows better.'

The New Testament goal of human development is beyond such handing over of responsibility to any group, however able that group may be. In the last resort, the individual has to take responsibility for his actions. His acceptance with God and with man has to depend, not upon his group relationship but, upon his reception of the existential challenge to his own life. It is for the individual believer to work out his own salvation with fear and trembling, though to do so it requires the fellowship of faith. When Paul bids the Christians in Philippi to work out their salvation, he addresses them in the plural—'my beloved' *(agapētoi)*, 'your salvation' *(tēn eautōn sōterian)*—to carry through this task (Phil. 2. 12). In the same passage, Paul shows his heritage in Hebrew thought, by reminding these Christians that the task of salvation is not only a communal endeavour as well as an individual one but also there is another partner, God.

---

[35] cf. P. Teilhard de Chardin, *The Phenomenon of Man* (London (Fontana), 1965), pp. 285-6, who used the term *'omega'* to indicate the point where the Universal and the Personal meet.

Just as of old, the individual Israelite was identified with Israel and Israel was identified with the purposes of Yahweh (even being an extention of Yahweh's personality), so the individual Christian is identified with those who are 'in Christ' with him, together with the God who is working through them all. Therefore, he writes: 'for God is at work in you, both to will and to work for his good pleasure' (verse 13). In a similar way, the writer of the Gospel of John refers to those who enter into the privilege of becoming children of God: 'to all who received him, who believed in his name, he gave power to become children of God; who were born, not of blood nor of the will of the flesh nor of the will of man, but of God' (Jn. 1. 12). The 'all' (*osoi*—'as many as' RV) expresses the individuality, the catholicity and the universality of the offer of Christ, but it also conveys the communal conception within the offer—'to them gave he the right to become children of God' (RV). Moreover, even this response is referred back to its initiator—'who were born . . . of God'. Individual, community and even the Deity Himself are brought into a living unity—which brings a fulfilment to them all. To call the relationship 'Christian brotherhood' is almost to bemean the intimacy which exists between believers because they find their oneness in their mutual unity in the divine relationship. Nevertheless, we have to use such modes of language and communication as we possess, therefore it is closest to human experience to express our relationship to God as 'Father' and to man as 'brother'. Yet no term can fully express the intimacy which binds all together.

On such a level of close relationship, such terms as class, race, culture and even sex, may be deemed to be intrusions upon a divine intention to bind all mankind into one. A man may be socially and economically a slave, yet in the divine intention that 'slave' has a potentiality and spiritual stature which is second to none, whether in the eyes of God or man. A man may be a prince in the eyes of man, yet he may fail to enter into the divine inheritance and so remain a pauper. As Jesus made clear, economically a man may be well-to-do but 'not rich towards God' (Luke 12. 21). A man may be wise in all varieties of human learning, yet remain foolish by a failure to discern the wisdom of God (1 Cor. 1. 19-21). So too the distinctions and deprivations which men impose on the opposite sex are a denial of the true stature of womanhood. To deny that God has given certain gifts to women—gifts which He appears to have given to men—is to fail to enter into the unity which God has emplanted in His whole purpose. Sex may imply a physical distinction for the purposes of procreation but does not indicate a spiritual contrast or distinction of spiritual function. Until all doors of intellectual, professional and social opportunity are open to women alike with men (whether within the Church or outside it)—so long the inner treasury of the Whole will be deprived of its assets.

The fullness of the Divine Intention may well be beyond our dreams and imaginings (1 Cor. 2. 9). Yet we may take courage to believe that we—as persons and as community—are called to be 'partakers of the divine nature', heirs of 'precious and very great promises', who have seen a foretaste of our inheritance in the person of the Christ, through whom we may come to share the true 'image of God'.

Index of Subjects

Aaron, 43, 103
Abar-nahara, 179
Abednego, 188
Abel, 192
Abiathar, 96ᶠᶠ
Abiezrites, 109
Abigail, 119
Abimelech, 46, 80
Abimelech (son of Gideon), 43, 85, 109, 112
Abner, 87
Abraham, 39ᶠ, 42-6, 48, 80, 95, 122, 120, 167, 192
Absalom, 75, 96, 104, 145
Achan, 34, 36, 88, 105
Adam, 232ᶠᶠ
Adonijah, 97
Adonizedek, 95
Adoption, 39
Agag, 88, 199
Ahab, 113, 117, 124, 139
Ahaz, 105, 138
Ahiquar, Proverbs of, 185
Allah, 195
Alexander, 163, 188, 215
Amelekite(s), 90, 138, 199
Ammonites, 36, 69, 87, 109, 139, 177ᶠ
Amnon, 42, 75
Amorites, 42, 76, 96
Amphictyony, 15, 68ᶠ, 84, 148, 165, 196
Amos, 120, 128ᶠᶠ, 192
Anat(h), 122, 124
Anathoth, 97, 115, 149, 163
Angelology, 159, 185ᶠᶠ, (93)
Anointing, 93
Anshan, 166
Antiochus IV (Epiphanes), 183, 187ᶠᶠ, 198
Apocalyptic writers, 159, 186-90
Apocrypha, 215, 217
Arabs, 78, 175, 177
Araunah, 95

Ariadne, thread of, 218
Ark, 84, 91ᶠ, 96ᶠᶠ, 137, 149
Armenia, 173
Artaxerxes I, 175, 177
Asherah, 122, 124
Assyria, 76, 130, 163, 195, 197
Astarte, 124, 161
Astyges, 166
Atonement, 74
Azariah, 97

Ba'al, 57, 123-28
Babylon, 14, 76, 148, 161, 164ᶠᶠ, 170, 173, 178, 180, 195, 197
Baptism, 181
Bathsheba, 97, 200
bayith, 50
Benaiah, 97
Benhadad, 120
Benjaminites, 75, 87
Beroea, 214
beten, 32
beth'abh, 50
Bethavon, 125ᶠ
Bethel, 50, 85
Bethlehem, 89, 109
Bethuel, 43, 46
Beth-anath, 124
Bilhah, 43, 48
Blessing, 35ᶠ, 46ᶠ, 87ᶠ, 145ᶠ
Blood, sacredness of, 52, 79ᶠ
Blood-feud, 14
Boaz, 66ᶠ
Boghazkoy texts, 45
Branch, the, 173
Bride-price, 60ᶠ
Buddha, 196
Bureaucracy, 209-11

Caesar, G. Julius, 212
Caesarea Philippi, 218
Cain, 192
Cambyses, 173
Canaan, 103, 108ᶠ, 144, 85

Index of Subjects

Capital punishment, 134
Chaldeans, 163
Chasidim, 169, 187, 189
chayyim, 24ᶠ
Chinese marriage, 47
Chiefs, 111
Church, 245, 272
Circumcision, 152, 163ᶠ, 181
City—importance of, 108ᶠᶠ; of refuge, 78ᶠ, 110; city-gate, 110ᶠ; city-elders, 110ᶠ
Collectivism, 206
Common law, 137
Clan-father, 51
Corporate personality, 33, 36
Covenant, 14ᶠ, 51, 71, 84, 91, 94, 100ᶠ, 117, 125, 128, 137ᶠ, 140ᶠ, 148ᶠ, 150, 160, 162, 165, 167ᶠ, 179, 181, 196, 219, 221ᶠ
Creator, 141-46, 166
Curse, 35
Cyrus, 166ᶠ, 170, 174

dabhar, 35
Dalai Lama, 196
Dan, 98
Daniel, 187ᶠᶠ
Darius, 173ᶠ
David, 15, 42, 46, 69, 72ᶠᶠ, 89-98, 100, 105, 109, 119, 121, 130, 137, 143, 160, 170, 200, 214
David, son of, 34, 101, 173ᶠ, 167
Dead Sea Scrolls, 187
Deborah, 103
Delilah, 72
Demiurge, 141
Democracy, 17, 207-12
Deuteronomic Code, 78, 116, 120, 136, 164, 198ᶠ
Dinah, 43
Diplomatic Service, 211
Divorce, 236
Doeg the Edomite, 96
Dothan, 50

Earth-Mother, 124
Edom, 175, 182
Egypt, 14, 29, 44, 49, 56, 84ᶠ, 130, 170
El, 123
Elam, 173
Elect, the, 46, 84, (95), (Election) 161, 167, 196, 219ᶠᶠ
Eliezer of Damascus, 44

Elijah, 28, 36, 124ᶠ, 139
Elisha, 119, 120, 124ᶠ
Elyon, 96
Ephraim, 127ᶠ
Ephraimites, 70
Esau, 46ᶠ, 87
Essenes, 187
Esther, 181ᶠ
Ethbaal, 119ᶠ, 194
Ethiopians, 129
Execration Texts (Egyptian), 49, 92
Exile, the, 160ᶠᶠ, 196ᶠ
Ezekiel, 95, 152ᶠ, 163, 165, 197
Ezra, 176, 178ᶠᶠ

Family, purposes of, 122
Fertility cults, 123ᶠᶠ
Fatalism, 152
Flesh, 32, 229
Foreign Service, 211
Freedom, 37

Gabriel, 186
Gad, 34
Gerizim, Mt., 182
Ghana, 12
Gibeah, 87, 126
Gibeonites, 74, 80, 87, 109
Gideon, 28, 43, 69ᶠᶠ, 85, 87, 89, 109
Gilboa, Mt., 74, 90
Gilead, 126
Gilgal, 89, 120, 125ᶠ
Goliath, 90
Greeks, 133, 143, 147, 153

Hadad, 123
Hagar, 43ᶠ, 120
Haggai, 172ᶠ
Hammurabi, 44, 67, 76, 101
Hamor, 27, 43, 109
Hanamel, 114
Hanseatic League, 209
Haremhab, 105
Hebron, 45, 91, 97
Hellenism, 17, 213, 215-218 (133)
herem (the ban), 88
Hezekiah, 196
Hitler, A., 205, 207
Hired workmen, 59ᶠ
Hittite law, 45, 77, 134
Holiness Code, 125

Index of Subjects

Honour of the family, 71ff, 76
Hosea, 125-28
Household-gods, vide teraphim
Hurrians (Horites), 44
hubris (pride), 142f, 145, 153
hyle (matter), 216

Immigration, 236
Incest, 48, 66
India, 215
Individualism, 200f, 204, 206
Individual responsibility, 37, 133ff, 144, 147, 149f, 153, 157, 222ff, 228, 236f
Individuation, 131ff
Inner devotion, 151
Inter-marriage, 175f, 179ff, 190
Isaac, 43, 45, 120
Isaiah, 29
Ishbosheth, 91
Ishmael, 45, 120
Ittoba'al, vide Ethbaal

Jabbok, 36
Jabesh-Gilead, 74, 87, 109
Jacob, 21, 28, 36, 39, 43, 45-52, 87, 112
Jaxartes, 166
Jebusites, 92f, 96 (et vide Mt. Zion)
Jehoiachin, 165
Jehoiakim, 163
Jehoshaphat, 105
Jehu, 113, 124
Jephthah, 36, 69, 87, 104, 120
Jeremiah, 114f, 125, 149-52, 163, 197
Jerusalem, 50, 92, 95, 97, 99 (et vide Mt. Zion), 105, 129, 140, 149f, 160ff, 165, 170, 174, 177f, 185, 196
Jethro, 103
Jezebel, 117, 120, 139, 194
Jezreel, 117,
Joab, 69, 97
Job, 111f, 120, 143, 161f
John (Baptist), 215
Jonah, 148
Jonathan, 74, 89
Joseph, 28, 36, 46, 93, 95
Joshua, 88, 95
Josiah, 78, 131, 149, 196
Jotham, 85f
Joy, 146
Judges, 69-72, 84, 87

Justice, 15, 71, 74ff, 100-6, 136, 157 161ff
Jubilee, year of, 114-17, 119, 121, 199

kardia (heart), 216, 229
Keilah, 109
King and Yahweh, 92ff
King, divine, 95f, 99, 218
Kingship, 14, 17, 37, 46
Krt, Legend of, 102f

Laban, 43, 47ff
Lamech, 72
Leah, 43, 45, 48, 115
leb (heart), 30f, 229
Levi, 43
Levitical priests, 98, 117, 175, 178
Levirate marriage, 36, 62-66, 110
Lot, 48
Lydia, 166

Maccabaean War, 189, 198, 215
Machpelah, Cave of, 45
malkuth, 218
Man and Nature, 143f
Manasseh, 106, 138
Marduk, 102
Marriage, as religious symbol, 122, 125,136
Matriarchal family, 42f
Media, 166, 173
Medo-Persian Empire, 188
Melchizedek, 95f, 110
Mentality, pre-logical, 20
Mephibosheth, 74, 117f
Meribba'al, 74
Meshach, 188
Michal, 91f, 145
Michael (angel), 186
Middle Ages, 209
Middle Bronze Age, 39
mishpaha, 43, 50
Mithras, 141
Mizpeh, 104
Moab, 22, 32, 139
Mohammed, 194f
mohar, vide bride-price
Monotheism, 161, 166, 168, 182
Moses, 36, 43, 84, 103, 214
Mother's brother, 39, 47
Moral issues, contemporary, 236

Naaman, 125
Nabal, 119

Index of Subjects

Naboth, 117ᶠ
Nabonidus, 166
Nabopolassar, 161
Nahash, 87
Name, a man's, 36
Names, Divine, 184ᶠ
Naomi, 65
Nashwi, 49
Nathan, 92, 97, 193, 200
National Socialism, 200, 237
Nature, 13, 143ᶠ, 155, 201
Near-kinsman (go'el), 63, 75, 78, 114, 118, 121
Nebuchadnezzar, 160ᶠ, 165ᶠ, 170, 187ᶠ.
Negeb, 50
Nehemiah, 175ᶠᶠ
nephesh, 24, 27, 31ᶠ, 229
neshamah, 25, 27
Nineveh, 148
Noah, 143
Nob, city of, 96, 109
nous, 216ᶠ, 229ᶠ
Nuzi texts, 44ᶠᶠ, 49

Oath, 80ᶠ
Officials, city, 110ᶠᶠ; royal, 113ᶠ
Ophrah, 109
Othniel, 69

Paddan-aram, 47
Parousia, 220ᶠ
Parthia, 166
Participation, law of, 20
Passover, 196
Paul, 213, 217, 228-35
Pentateuch, 180, 198
Permitted marriage, 39, 48
Permitted relationships, 66ᶠ
Persia, 173, 177ᶠ, 195, 198
Peter, 215
Pharisees, 169
Philistines, 72, 85ᶠ, 91, 129, 177, 182
Phoenician texts, 102
pneuma, 216, 229ᶠᶠ
Polygamy, 12
Preferential marriage, 39, 47
Pride, vide hubris
Priestly Code, 116, 120ᶠ, 164, 180
Property, 114-19
Prophets, 16, 86, 118, 123, 140, 146, 148, 160ᶠ, 162, 165, 193-6, 199, 214, 227
Psalms, Royal, 94

psyche, 216ᶠ, 230ᶠ, 232
Psychology, primitive, 19-24
Puhi-shenni, 49

rachemim, 32
Rachel, 46, 48ᶠ, 115
Raphael (angel), 186
Ras Shamra, 102, 124
Rationalism, 153ᶠ
Reason, Age of, 154
Rebekah, 45ᶠᶠ
Redeemer, 144ᶠᶠ, 168, 208
Reformation, 216
Remnant, 173-6, 180
Renaissance, 153
Retaliation, law of, 76-9
Revolution, French, 153
Righteousness, 94, 100ᶠ, 160, 184, 197
Rights, Natural, 16, 201
Rizpah, 74ᶠ
Road accidents, 236
Rome, 198, 212
ruach, 24, 28ᶠᶠ, 217, 229-31
Ruth, 148

Sabbath, 152, 163, 178ᶠ
sadiqa (marriage), 42
Sacrifice, 181
Samaria, 120, 170ᶠ, 174, 177ᶠ, 182
Samson, 43, 69, 72, 89
Samuel, 86-9, 139ᶠ, 199, 215
Sanballat, 177ᶠ
Sarah, 42, 45ᶠ
sarx, 217, 229, 231ᶠ
Saul, 34, 69, 72, 74, 86-92, 95ᶠ, 105, 109, 138ᶠ
Second Isaiah, 166-9, 197, 220
Seleucids, 183, 188
Septuagint, 215, 217
Sex regulations, 52, 57, 60-7, 146ᶠ
Shadrach, 188
Shaman, 21
Sheba, Queen of, 28
Shechem, 27, 43, 50, 109, 112
Shema, 136
Shepherd tradition, 51ᶠ, 192ᶠ
Sheshbazzar, 170ᶠ
Shimei, 72ᶠ
Shiloh, 96
Shumen, woman of, 119
Silas, 214
Simeon, 43
Sin, 227ᶠ

Index of Subjects

Slave-mother, 44ᶠ, 120
Slave-races, 147
Slavery, 56ᶠᶠ, 115ᶠ, 119
Social measures, 227, 236
Sojourners (*gerim*), 146-9, 168, 232ᶠ, 236ᶠ
Solomon, 28, 32, 85, 93, 97ᶠ, 104, 112, 193
soma, 217, 229ᶠ, 234
Son of Man, 219ᶠᶠ
Sororal polygamy, 48
Soul-stuff, 24
Succoth, 111
Suffering Servant, 168ᶠ, 220
Sulla, 212
Sultans, 195
suneidesis, 229ᶠ
Symbolism, prophetic, 35ᶠ, 125, 150
Synagogue, 152, 181
Syria(ns), 129, 198

Tabernacles, Feast of, 99
Tamar, 63, 66
Tamar (daug. of David), 42, 75
Tattenai, 174
Tekoa, wise woman of, 104, 121
Temple, 98, 172ᶠᶠ, 180, 189
teraphim (household-gods), 49, 51
Thebez, 109
Theocracy, 165, 195ᶠ, 198ᶠᶠ, 208
Thessalonica, 214
Thummim, 84, 104
Tibet, 196
Tikopia, 33, 235
tobh, 22
Tobiah, 177ᶠ
Torah, 104, 180ᶠ, 198

Totality of experience, 22ᶠ, 33
Trade Unions, 209, 236
Tribal life, 12, 42-53, 70ᶠ, 84ᶠ
Tyre, 194

Umim, 84, 104ᶠ, 110
Unam Sanctam, 195
Unchastity, 110, 61ᶠ
Universalism, 148ᶠ, 166ᶠ 170, 208
Uriel (angel), 186
Uppsala School, 40

Valour, men of, 110

Washington, D.C., 95
Women's standards and society, 123
Word, a man's, 35
Wilkes, John, 203
Wullu, 49

Yehimilk, 101

Zadok, 96ᶠᶠ, 193
Zadokite priesthood, 98, 165
Zalmunna, 71
Zarathustra, 194
Zebah, 71
Zebul, 112
Zelophehad, daughters of, 121
Zerubbabel, 170, 173, 197
Ziba, 117ᶠ
Zilpah, 43, 48
Zimri, 76
Zion, 15, 92ᶠ, 95ᶠ, 98ᶠ, 108, 124, 152, 160, 167, 173, 196ᶠ
Ziph, 109
zōe (life), 216

Index of Authors

Albright, W. F., 42, 50, 105
Alt, A., 51, 68
Anderson, G. W., 79
Aristotle, 199, 215, 236

Bacon, F., 155
Baillie, J., 17
Barth, K., 226
Baudissin, G., 102
Berdyaev, N., 153
Bethge, E., 226
Bevan, E. R., 200
Bonhoeffer, D., 226
Boniface VIII, 195
Bright, J., 41, 69, 85, 160, 164, 185
Brunner, E., 133, 223-6
Bultmann, R., 226

Calvin, J., 48, 156
Chardin, P. Teilhard de, 237
Charles, R., 184
Crawley, E., 21

Davies, W. D., 232
Dawson, C., 193
Demant, V., 154
Democritus, 133, 155
Descartes, R., 156
De Vaux, R., 14
Dodd, C. H., 214

Eichrodt, W., 37, 68, 133, 136^f, 142, 145, 147, 153
Eissfeldt, O., 102
Eliot, T. S., 156
Emmet, D., 35
Engels, F., 206
Epstein, L. M., 63
Evans-Pritchard, E. E., 12

Feuerbach, L., 155
Firth, R., 12, 33
Flew, R. N., 219, 222
Forde, C. D., 47^f

Fox, J. R., 48
Frankfort, H., 13, 21
Freud, S., 155, 228
Frost, S. B., 186

Gordon, C. H., 41, 103
Gore, C., 155
Graf, K. H., 78
Grayston, K., 78

Hegel, G., 17, 204, 206
Herodotus, 198
Hobbes, T., 201^f
Hoebel, E. A., 67
Hsu, F. L. K., 47
Hume, D., 155
Huxley, J., 155

James, E. O., 20
Johnson, A. R., 24, 27^f, 34, 92^f, 99^f
Josephus, F., 119

Kennett, R. H., 78
Kierkegaard, S., 156^f, 226

Landtmann, G., 208
Lazard, J., 47
Leucippus, 155
Lindsay, A. D., 212
Locke, J., 16, 174, 201^f
Lods, A., 43
Lucretius, 155

MacIver, R., 122, 207^f
Mair, L., 20
Malinowski, B. G., 12, 67
Manson, T. W., 219
Marriott, J., 210
Marx, K., 206
Menander of Ephesus, 119
Mencius, 61
Milik, J. T., 187n
Mill, J. S., 202
Morganstern, J., 65

Index of Authors

Niebuhr, R., 156f, 223-6
North, C. R., 40, 169

Otto, R., 219

Patai, M., 99
Pedersen, J., 22, 30, 33ff, 46, 50, 60, 72, 78, 104, 113, 121, 162
Plato, 198, 203, 236
Pope, A., 154,
Pritchard, J., 44f, 49, 101f, 185

Quistorp, H., 156

Rad, G. von. 48
Radcliffe-Brown, A. R., 47f
Rawlinson, A. E. J., 234
Roberts, D. E., 224
Robertson, E., 78
Robinson, H. W., 25, 43, 224, 228f, 231

Rousseau, J. J., 17, 204f
Rowley, H. H., 41, 43, 62ff

Schapera, 1, 12
Schumpeter, J., 209
Shedd, R. P., 168, 181, 233
Smith, C. R., 25, 33, 216f, 229
Smith, W. R., 42
Snaith, N. H., 99
Spencer, H., 201ff
Spengler, O., 203

Taylor, V., 218, 221, 227
Terrien, S., 162

Welch, A. C., 78
Wellhausen, J., 40, 78
Wette, W. M. L. de, 78
Whale, J. S., 225

Index of Biblical and Extra-Biblical References

A. OLD TESTAMENT

Genesis
1...141
1^2...29
1^{11}...24
$1^{20, 24}$...24
1^{26}...37
1^{27}...57, 142, 147
1^{28}...144
1^{31}...218
2...142f
2^{2f}...164
2^7...24f
2^{15}...144
2^{18}...57, 146
2^{19}...24
2^{21-22}...57
2^{24}...42
3^5...28
4^{10}...52
4^{23f}...52, 72
6^{1-8}...187
8^{7f}...22
9^2...37
9^4...79
9^6...79
9^9...143
9^{16}...147
10...147
12...41
12^{1-3}...168
$12^{16, 24}$...45
14^7...103
14^{14}...57
14^{18ff}...95
15...51
15^1...35
15^{1-4}...44
15^2...57
15^3...120
15^4...57
15^6...51
15^7...111, 126
16^{1-4}...44
16^4...43
16^6...44
17...57
17^{11}...164
$17^{12, 27}$...57
18^{18}...168
19^{30-38}...48
20^5...46
20^{12}...42
20^{16}...80
21^4...45
21^{10}...120
21^{10f}...45
22^{16-18}...45
22^{17}...46
22^{20}...35
23...45
24...57
24^2...111
$24^{4, 28}$...46
24^{26}...120
24^{50}...43
24^{66}...35
24^{67}...46
25^{5f}...120
25^9...45
25^{26}...46
25^{29-34}...46
25^{33}...46
$26^{4, 24}$...46
26^{12}...45
26^{15}...24
26^{29}...46
27^{12}...47
27^{35}...35, 47
27^{46}...47
28^3...47
28^4...48
28^{6ff}...47
28^{8f}...48
28^{13}...50
29^{20}...48
$29^{23, 30}$...43, 48
30^{1f}...61
30^4...43
30^{37-42}...23
31^{14}...49
31^{16}...115
31^{19}...49
31^{30-35}...49
31^{34}...49
31^{40}...52
$31^{42, 53}$...50f
31^{50}...49
32^{29}...36
34...41, 109
34^3...27
35^{29}...45
37^5...46
38...63
44^5...36
44^{16}...36
45^{27}...28
46^{27}...26
49^{5-7}...41
49^{24}...51
49^{31}...45
50...41
50^{12}...45

Exodus
4^{8f}...36
4^{19}...26
6^{20}...43
15^{18f}...95
17^9...36
18^{2-6}...43
18^{12-23}...103
18^{13-27}...70

Index of Biblical and Extra-Biblical References 249

Exodus—contd.
18^{18}...81
19^{6}...95
20-23...37, 134
20^{10}...60
21^{2}...58
21^{7}...135
21^{7f}...58
21^{7-11}...135
21^{12-14}...71, 78
21^{12-17}...134
21^{15}...71
21^{17}...71
21^{20f}...58, 135
21^{21}...135
21^{22-25}...76
21^{26f}...58
21^{27}...135
21^{29}...134
21^{30}...80
21^{36}...134
22^{1}...134
22^{1-4}...71
22^{2}...58
22^{5}...134
22^{6}...134
22^{16f}...62
22^{18-20}...135
22^{20}...71
22^{21}...60
23^{6}...60
23^{19}...144
28^{2}...29
31^{12-17}...164
34^{15}...125
35^{21}...30

Leviticus
3^{9-11}...31
8^{16}...31
11^{43}...26
14^{9}...32
17^{7}...125
17^{10-12}...79
17^{11}...27
17^{14}...27, 52
17-26...164
18^{6-18}...48
18^{9}...43
18^{16}...65
18^{22}...144
19^{10}...60
19^{18}...136

19^{19}...144
19^{28}...27
19^{29}...62
19^{23f}...60
19^{34}...136
20^{5}...125
20^{11-21}...67
$20^{12, 14}$...66
20^{15}...144
20^{21}...65
21^{9}...62
22^{10}...57, 60
22^{10-12}...57
23^{22}...60
23^{40}...146
24^{20}...76
24^{22}...182
25^{6}...60
25^{25-28}...114
25^{28}...116
25^{29f}...116
25^{31-34}...117
25^{39ff}...58
25^{40}...60
26^{43}...27
27^{17ff}...116

Numbers
2^{34}...50
5^{11-31}...81
6^{6}...27
10^{10}...146
16^{22}...29
21^{4}...26
23^{11f}...35
23^{21}...95
27^{1-11}...65
27^{8-10}...121
27^{8-11}...76
35^{9-29}...79
35^{31f}...79
36^{9}...121

Deuteronomy
1^{16}...60
4^{35}...141
4^{41-43}...78
6^{4-6}...136
7^{9}...186
8^{14}...31

9^{5}...31
10^{20}...60
11^{25-28}...145
12^{7}...146
12^{23}...27
13^{11}...32
14^{26}...146
14^{29}...60, 137
15^{1-3}...115
15^{7}...31
15^{12f}...116
15^{12-18}...58
16^{18-20}...103
17^{8-13}...103
17^{9}...98
17^{16-20}...139
17^{18}...100, 200
17^{18}...98
17^{20}...100
18^{7}...98
19^{1-9}...110
19^{5}...78
19^{12}...110
19^{21}...26, 76
20^{10}...25
21^{7}...80
21^{15f}...120
21^{19-20}...110
22^{9f}...144
22^{13-21}...110
22^{17-21}...62
22^{23-27}...61
22^{28f}...61
23^{11f}...62
24^{14}...60
24^{17-19}...60
24^{20}...60
25^{5f}...63
25^{5-10}...62
25^{6}...36
25^{7-9}...110
25^{7-10}...64
26^{5}...50
27^{14-26}...137
32^{28}...23
33^{5}...95
$33^{8, 10}$...104
34^{9}...29

Joshua
7...105
$7^{16, 25}$...88
8^{24f}...34

Joshua—contd.
10^{1-27}...95
16^{10}...59
17^{13}...59
20...79
20^4...110

Judges
$1^{28,\,29}$...59
$1^{33,\,35}$...59
3^{10}...69, 85
4^5...103
5^{25}...122
6^{25}...123
7^{24ff}...70
8...109
8^3...28, 70
8^{4-21}...71
8^{5f}...111
8^8...111
8^{14f}...111
8^{16}...111
8^{28}...85, 95
9^{1-5}...43
9^2...111
9^{7-15}...86
9^{20}...112
9^{50}...109
11^3...120
11^{11}...104
11^{12}...36
11^{30f}...87
12^1...70
14^6...69
15^1...43
15^8...72
15^{20}...28
17^2...80
17^6...104
17^{7-9}...59
18^{19}...57
18^{30}...98
19^{16}...59
19-21...75
21^{25}...104

Ruth
4^{1-2}...64
4^4...111
4^9...65
4^{11}...111

I Samuel
1^{6f}...61
2^{25}...81
4^3...111
8^4...111
8^7...95
8^{14}...113
9^{1-10}...86
9^{12}...109
9^{16}...86
9^{22}...96
9^{25}...109
11...109
11^{1-7}...87
12^{12}...95
13^{11}...88
13^{15f}...88
13^{19-22}...85
14^9...96
14^{24}...87
15...138
15^{22}...139
15^{22-23}...88
15^{28}...109
16^{1-13}...89
16^7...146
16^{11}...46
16^{13}...93
17...89
17^{24}...22
18^5...90
20^6...109
22^{6-7}...87
22^{9-23}...96
22^{19}...109
23...109
24^6...90
25^{18}...119
26^{10f}...90
26^{22f}...90

II Samuel
1^{18}...90
2^4...93
2^{10}...91
3^4...97
3^{17}...111
5^3...91, 93, 111
5^6...26
6^5...91
$6^{14,\,18}$...91
6^{21}...92
7^{10}...92

8^6...92
12^{13}...137
12^{17}...111
12^{28}...69
13...75
13^{28}...42
14^{1-20}...104
14^7...121
14^9...75
$14^{17,\,20}$...93
15^6...104
16^4...118
16^{5-8}...72
17^{10}...31
18^{15}...36
19^{11}...96
19^{22}...72
19^{29}...118
20^{25}...96
21...109
21^{1-14}...105
21^4...80
21^9...34, 75
23^{1-7}...94
23^5...100
24^4...31
24^{10-25}...34
24^{26ff}...95
24^{17}...105
25^{24-29}...96

I Kings
1^7...97
1^{24}...97
1^{30}...93
1^{50}...78
2^{5-9}...73
$2^{15,\,27}$...97
2^{35}...97
2^{39-46}...73
3^6...98
3^{16-28}...105
4^2...97
4^{7-19}...112
8^{15}...80
8^{aff}...168
8^{61}...31
9^4...31
9^{22}...59
10^5...28
11^{28}...59
16^{11}...76
17^{17}...25

Index of Biblical and Extra-Biblical References

I Kings—contd.
18^4...139
18^{19}...124
18^{46}...139
19^{10}...26
19^{18}...139
19^{40}...199
21...113
$21^{3, 7}$...117
21^8...112
$21^{10, 13}$...93
22^{28}...113

II Kings
2^9...28
4^1...58
4^{1-37}...119
4^{29}...36
4^{38}...120
5^{12}...57
5^{17}...125
6^{25}...120
9^{15}...27
10...113
10^1...112
10^{21}...124
23^1...112
23^6...114
23^8...113
25^{27-30}...165

II Chronicles
19^{8-11}...105

Ezra
1^{2f}...167
1^{2-4}...170
4^{7-23}...175
4^{8ff}...170
4^{12}...174
5^{14}...170
6^2...170
6^{3-5}...170
6^{13-18}...173
6^{19}...170
10^{1-6}...179

Nehemiah
2^{19}...177
4^{7-12}...177

5^{1-5}...175
$5^{4, 14f}$...175
5^{14}...177f
$6^{1, 6}$...177
6^{10-14}...177
$8-9$...178
9^{38}...179
10^1...177f
10^{29}...179
10^{30-39}...179
10^{31}...121
12^{27-43}...177
13^{4-9}...178
13^{10f}...175
13^{15-22}...175

Job
1^{19}...28
6^{21}...26
18^{27}...36
21^{41}...30
26^{13}...30
28^{12-28}...143
29...162
29^{7-11}...111
30^{25}...26
31^{22}...59
32^8...29
$38-41$...141, 143
38^{4-5}...143
38^7...146
42^3...143
42^{15}...120

Psalms
5^{12}...146
6^4...26
8...141
8^{2-6}...142
8^6...37
9^{1f}...183
11^5...26
14^7...146
16^6...33
16^{10}...26
17^{13}...26
18^4...95
19...141f
21^8...30
22^{14}...31f
22^{24f}...95
24^4...31

$25^{9, 22}$...140
25^{14}...140
29...99, 141f
29^{1-9}...99
30^3...26
35^9...26
35^{28}...30
36^{11}...30
42^3...26
44^{23f}...171
45^4...30
47...183
48^7...28
51^1...32
51^{10-12}...30
63^1...32f
66^{14}...30
71^8...32
72^4...94
74^1...31
74^{9f}...161
79^{20}...32
84^3...31, 33
87...183
89...94
89^{20f}...94
90^{14}...146
93...183
95...99
$96^{3, 10}$...149
$96-99$...183
97...149
99...149
101^4...31
103...95
104...141f
104^{27-30}...144
104^{29}...25
104^{30}...217
104^{35}...144
105^5...144
107^{25}...28
110...95
119^{68}...182
132...94
132^{1-10}...94
132^{11-18}...94
135...142
135^{15-21}...183
137...165
139^7...29
139^{20}...32
$143^{4, 7}$...28
143^{10}...29

Psalms—contd.
145^{21}...33
147...142
147^{19-20}...182
148...141

Proverbs
8^{20-31}...185
8^{12-31}...143, 146
9...185
10^8...31
12^{10}...32
12^{28}...23
14^{10}...152
16^9...31
18^8...32
20^8...30
22^4...145
22^{18}...32
23^2...27
30^{22}...44
31^{27}...123

Ecclesiastes
2^{26}...146
3^{11}...184
8^{16f}...184
8^{17}...143

Song of Songs
3^{1-4}...26

Isaiah
3^{16}...123
3^{24}...123
5^8...118
$6^{1,5}$...30
6^{10}...31
$7^{2,18}$...105
8^2...42
8^{10}...23
9^2...29
11^2...29
13^1...165
13^{18}...32
14^{22}...165
16^{11}...32
19^{14}...29
19^{16-25}...183
20^{2f}...35
20^3...125
28^6...29
28^{29}...23
29^{10}...29
30^{28}...25
31^2...29
32^6...31
40^{1-11}...167
40^{3-5}...167
40^5...33
40^{12-26}...166
40^{29f}...166
40-55...166
41^{2-4}...166
41^{8-10}...166
41^{21-24}...166
42^{1-4}...168
42^{24f}...167
43^{8-12}...166
43^9...168
43^{16-21}...167
44^{1-5}...167
44^6...166
44^{12-20}...166
44^{24}...167
45^1...166
45^7...167
46^{5-7}...166
48^{9-11}...167
48^{17-19}...167
48^{22}...145
49^{1-6}...168
49^3...169
49^8...167
49^{9-11}...167
49^{14ff}...167
50^1...167
50^{4-9}...168
51^{1-16}...167
51^9...30
$51^{9-11,17}$...167
52^{13}...167
52^{13ff}...168f
53^{12}...168f
54^{1-3}...167
54^{9f}...167
55^{12f}...167
56^{1-8}...163, 171f, 182
56-66...171
57^{3-10}...172
57^{15}...30, 172
58^{1-12}...171
58^{13f}...163
59^{1-11}...171
60^{1-22}...171
61...171
61^3...28
63^{1ff}...165
63^{15}...32
63^{19}...161
64^{12}...165
$65^{1-7,11}$...172
65^{17-25}...171
66^{3f}...172
66^{7-14}...171
66^{18f}...149
66^{18-21}...182
66^{21}...174

Jeremiah
1^2...16
2^{2f}...52
2^7...144
2^{13}...150
2^{14}...57
2^{17}...150
2^{19}...150
2^{24}...28
3^{1f}...144
$4^{3,14}$...150
4^{19}...32
4^{31}...26
6^{16-20}...150
7^{22}...150
$11^{6,21}$...150
12^1...162
14^{19}...27
15^4...106
15^9...27
16^2...150
17^5...32
17^{19-27}...163
20^9...150
22^{13ff}...163
23^{5f}...173
25^{15ff}...150
26^{11ff}...113
26^{16}...113
26^{23}...114
27^2...125
31^{29f}...151
31^{31-34}...151
32...163
32^8...115
36^{20}...113
44^{15-19}...161

Index of Biblical and Extra-Biblical References

Lamentations
2^9...161
2^{14}...160
5^7...161

Ezekiel
2^2...29
$3^{12, 14}$...29
4^{12-13}...164
4^{14}...26
5^2...140
8^1...29
11^5...29
16^8...96
17^{20}...28
18^4...152
18^{19f}...152
18^{25}...161
20^{13}...164
22^{26}...164
33^{10}...152, 161
33^{11}...152f
33^{24}...171
34^{23f}...165
36^{25}...31
37...165
37^{11}...152
37^{24-28}...165
40-48...164f
40^{46}...98
43^{18}...165
43^{19}...98
44^{10}...98
44^{15}...98
44^{23}...164
45^8...116
46^{16-18}...116
48^{29}...165

Daniel
2^{31-35}...187
2^{44}...188
3^{16-18}...188,198
$4^{13, 17}$...186
4^{23}...186
7...188
7^8...188
7^{9-14}...189
7^{13}...220
7^{21}...189
$7^{22, 25}$...189
7^{27}...189

8^{9-13}...189
8^{16}...186
8^{23-5}...189
9^{27}...189
10^{13}...186
11^{36}...189
11^{40-5}...189
$12^{2, 11}$...189

Hosea
1^1...16
$1^{4, 6}$...42
1^9...42
2^{1ff}...126
2^8...126
2^{14-20}...128
3^1...126
$4^{2, 3}$...127
4^{4-14}...126
4^{4-14}...126
4^{13}...29
4^{15}...125f
5^4...126
5^6...125f
5^7...126
5^{10}...118
5^{15}...128
6^6...227
7^9...126
$8^{1, 4-6}$...126
$8^{8, 13}$...127
8^{13}...125
9^1...126
9^2...127
9^{4f}...125
9^{10}...128
9^{11}...127
$10^{1, 5-6}$...126
10^8...128
10^9...126
11^2...126
11^3...128
12^9...128
12^{11}...127
12^{13}...126
12^{14}...128
13^2...126

Amos
1^3...129
$2^{3, 5}$...129
2^{6-8}...129

$2^{11, 14}$...129
$3^{2, 14f}$...129
$4^{1, 4f}$...129
4^{6-11}...129
4^{13}...130
5^{4-6}...129
5^8...130
5^{11}...119
$5^{16, 18ff}$...129
5^{19}...22
5^{21f}...129
6^2...129
6^{4-6}...119
6^8...129
7^9...129
8^4...119
9^4...30
9^7...129, 168
9^{11}...130

Obadiah
1^{14}...175
1^{15ff}...149
1^{18}...175

Jonah
1^4...28
4^{11}...148

Micah
2^{1f}...118
6^8...227

Nahum
3^1...148

Habakkuk
1^{2-4}...163
1^{5-11}...163
1^{13}...163

Zephaniah
1^1...16

Haggai
$1^{1, 14}$...170, 173
1^4...171

Index of Biblical and Extra-Biblical References

Haggai—contd.
1^{9-11}...171
1^{12}...173
2^{10-14}...171f
2^{15-17}...171
2^{20-3}...173

Zechariah
1^{7-17}...173
1^{8-17}...185
1^{13}...171
1^{16}...173

2^{6-13}...173
2^{11}...172, 182
3^{8}...173
4^{b}...173
4^{a}...173
4^{10}...186
6^{15}...173
$8^{2, 6}$...173
8^{19}...171
8^{12}...173
8^{22f}...172
9^{11}...149
11^{6}...149

12^{10}...30
14^{9}...99
14^{16}...99

Malachi
1^{2-5}...175
1^{6-14}...175
1^{11}...182
2^{11f}...175
2^{13-17}...175
$3^{5, 7-20}$...175
3^{19-15}...175

B. APOCRYPHA

I. Esdras
$2^{3, 8}$...217

Tobit
3^{17}...186
5^{4}...186
12^{15}...186
13^{9f}...183
13^{11}...183
14^{6f}...183

Wisdom of Solomon
7^{26-7}...185
9^{9-13}...185
18^{15f}...185

Ecclesiasticus
1^{1-10}...185
3^{21-4}...184
15^{11-20}...184
17^{17}...182
18^{1-14}...184

24^{1-24}...185
35^{12-20}...184
39^{12-21}...184
39^{22-7}...184
42^{28-21}...184
50^{25f}...182

Epistle of Jeremy
v. 5...183

I Maccabees
1^{11}...182

C. PSEUDEPIGRAPHA

I Enoch
9^{1f}...186
10^{21f}...183
20...186
42^{1f}...185
60^{1f}...186

Jubilees
7^{20}...80
8^{19}...182

12^{25f}...182
21^{3-5}...183
21^{10f}...80
22^{26}...182
30^{7-20}...181

The Testaments of the Twelve Patriarchs

Testament of Benjamin
10^{10}...183

Testament of Levi
4^{4}...183

Testament of Naphtali
8^{3}...183

D. NEW TESTAMENT

Matthew
5^{21-7}...228
5^{44-5}...227
6^{10}...221
6^{22}...225
7^{7-11}...224

7^{16}...228
10^{28}...220
10^{30}...224
10^{31}...223
10^{32}...220
10^{42}...227

11^{27}...227
12^{7}...227
12^{12}...223
12^{36}...228
15^{18f}...228
18^{14}...223

Index of Biblical and Extra-Biblical References

Matthew—contd.
23^{8f}...226
23^{23}...227
24^{42f}...220
25^{31-46}...227

Mark
1^{14f}...214
1^{15}...221
2^{27}...223
3^{21-5}...225
3^{33-5}...226
4^{22}...219
7^{9-13}...225
8^{31}...220
8^{36f}...223
8^{38}...220
9^{1}...221
9^{23}...225
9^{42-7}...223
12^{18ff}...65
13^{11}...224
13^{27}...221
13^{28f}...220
14^{25}...221

Luke
$6^{20,\,24}$...227
6^{36}...223
7^{18-22}...215
9^{57-62}...225
10^{22}...228
10^{38-42}...223
11^{13}...228
11^{20}...215, 221
12^{7}...224
12^{8f}...220
12^{11f}...224
12^{21}...238
12^{22}...221
12^{24-8}...220
12^{39}...220
12^{40}...220
13^{29}...219
14^{13}...227
14^{26-32}...225
14^{28}...225
15^{8f}...226
17^{6}...225
$17^{22,\,24}$...220
17^{25ff}...220

17^{30}...220
18^{7}b...220
22^{29f}...219
22^{30}...221

John
1^{1-4}...185
1^{13}...238
1^{14}...185

Acts
2^{22}...215
3^{13}...215
3^{24}...215
17^{11}...214
17^{26}...232
17^{28f}...232

Romans
1^{4}...231
1^{9}...230
1^{21}...229
2^{5}...229
2^{13}...233
2^{15}...230
2^{18}...233
3^{2}...214, 233
3^{5}...233
4^{11}...45
5^{12-21}...232
7^{25}...230
8^{5}...231
8^{16}...230
9^{5}...229
11^{17-24}...234
11^{24}...229
12^{2}...229
13^{14}...231
15^{13}...231

I Corinthians
1^{2}...235
1^{19-21}...238
2^{9}...239
2^{16}...229
3^{16f}...234
5^{7}...222, 234
6^{19}...234f
10^{27}...235

14^{14}...229
14^{25}...229
15^{21f}...232
15^{44}...232
15^{45}...233
15^{47}...232

II Corinthians
3^{17}...231
4^{2}...230
5^{17}...233
6^{14-18}...235
6^{16}...234

Galatians
2^{1-9}...181
3^{10}...233
3^{28}...231, 233
3^{29}...233
4^{6}...230

Ephesians
3^{16}...231

Philippians
2^{12}...237
2^{13}...238
2^{30}...230

Colossians
3^{9-11}...233

I Thessalonians
5^{23}...230

II Timothy
3^{15}...214
3^{16f}...10

Hebrews
4^{12f}...185

I John
1^{1}...185